Clifford Mark McCormick
Palace and Temple

Beihefte zur Zeitschrift für die alttestamentliche Wissenschaft

Herausgegeben von
Otto Kaiser

Band 313

Walter de Gruyter · Berlin · New York

2002

Clifford Mark McCormick

Palace and Temple

A Study of Architectural and Verbal Icons

Walter de Gruyter · Berlin · New York
2002

∞ Printed on acid-free paper which falls within the guidelines of the ANSI
to ensure permanence and durability.

Die Deutsche Bibliothek — CIP-Einheitsaufnahme

MaccCormick, Clifford Mark:
Palace and temple : a study of architectural and verbal icons / Clifford
Mark McCormick. — Berlin ; New York : de Gruyter, 2002
  (Beihefte zur Zeitschrift für die alttestamentliche Wissenschaft ;
Bd. 313)
  Zugl.: Diss.
  ISBN 3-11-017277-1

Printed in Germany
Cover design: Christopher Schneider, Berlin

For Faye, who planted the seed
For Paige, who nurtured it
For Gwenafaye, who will enjoy its fruit

Preface

This study, as in all studies of this type, is the product of long conversations, intensive readings, and mentorial proddings to see clearly the implications of taking a particular stand in the discussion of ancient cultures. My own interest in the palace of Sennacherib at Nineveh had long been keen when I first approached John Van Seters with the topic. It was he who first suggested that I take a look at I Kings 6-8 and the description of Solomon's temple in Jerusalem that is found there. It was indeed a fortuitous suggestion. For his guidance through the process of dissertation writing, but more for his willingness to mentor me through the intellectual development that is graduate study, I will always be grateful to John. His skill as a scholar is well recognized, his intellectual engagement as a mentor benefited me immeasurably.

There are others on my dissertation committee, without whose willingness to guide me through the research, the work would have been impossible. Jack Sasson's keen mind in matters editorial and intellectual never ceased to amaze me. His comments kept me from many unfortunate errors of logic and rhetoric, and his refusal to settle for second-rate treatment of Akkadian sources may spare me the scorn of Assyriologists. However, as much as the good one sees in the Akkadian translations found herein is attributable to Jack's mastery, the errors are attributable to my fledgling attempts to work with the intriguing and beautiful language of ancient Assyria.

Joanne Waghorne's encouragement and ready interest in iconographic issues was one of the early voices that sent me toward the palace and the temple with an eye toward what they might communicate to us. Norris Johnson and Tom Tweed, though having different ideas about the function of architectural space, were helpful in the ways that they constantly pointed me away from the errors that come from seeking the quick answer in the process of architectural and spatial interpretation. For the generous gift of their time and their guidance, I am grateful to all of them. The weaknesses that remain in this study are my own.

Finally, there are members of my family to whom many thanks are due. My mother, Faye Tucker McCormick, was a woman who valued knowledge and education. My thirst for understanding came from her and the more I study, the more I learn, the more I realize the gift she gave me when she planted this hunger within me.

My wife, Paige Reece McCormick, is a woman of expansive knowledge and acute insight. Editorially, she is a genius with a talent for clean crisp language. She read everything before it went to the committee and she questioned and proposed and removed with such proficiency that, without their knowledge, she made their job much easier. The strengths and clarity in this study are a tribute to her ability to question me to the heart of my argument and then say, once more, "Now, why do you not say that in here?" For her determined reading and re-reading, for her willingness to devote an incredible amount of time to bringing clarity to a project she herself believed in, and for her constant encouragement to keep going, she has my perpetual gratitude. For her reminders that one should get out into the woods, take a walk and relax occasionally, and for a myriad of other reasons that are renewed every day, she has my undying love and devotion.

My daughter, Gwenafaye Adanma McCormick, is, in short, the greatest joy of my life. She came to us in the Fall of 1997, and the first years of her life were filled with catching her father at the computer in the early morning hours and working hard to distract his attention away from those words and that keyboard. She was generally successful, and I am certainly the happier for it. She continues to grow into a smart little girl with an eager eye that misses little, a sharp mind that is always questioning and loves stories, and a ready invitation to play. I do my best to accept those invitations when they come, and I hope that our times of reading and play will give her an appreciation for the benefits of learning and relaxation.

Because I have learned so profoundly from them, I dedicate this study to my mother, my wife, and my daughter.

C. Mark McCormick   Tuscaloosa, Alabama
                                                     Fall 2001

Table of Contents

Introduction

This book is a study of the archaeological and textual evidence from two cultures, that of the Neo-Assyrian empire in the eighth and seventh centuries B.C.E., and that of the Judahite culture of the sixth and fifth centuries B.C.E. The application of built environment analysis to these cultures reveals their royal and religious ideology and the methods used in the ancient world to promote these sometimes conflicting, sometimes confirming realms of thought and behavior.

Sennacherib reigned over the Neo-Assyrian empire between 704 and 681 B.C.E. He had political and military interaction with Hezekiah, the king of Judah, around 701 and was assassinated by one or two of his sons in 681. Building upon recent portrayals of Sennacherib as a builder and architectural innovator, this study suggests that specific architectural elements reflect the new religious and political agenda he was incorporating into the Assyrian social order when opponents to these ideas brought his reign and his life to an abrupt end.

The evidence for these conclusions comes in two forms. First, there is the architectural evidence left behind in the destruction of Nineveh and Assur by the Babylonians in the last quarter of the seventh century B.C.E. and discovered by A. H. Layard in the middle of the nineteenth century C.E. Second, there is the textual evidence created by the administration of Sennacherib, which describes and interprets his building program. More than a mere description of the construction process, the texts also clearly indicate the desired effect of the structure of the palace. While there is little that is new in the evidentiary base for this study, the innovation I offer here is the application of built environment analytical categories to this base, providing a theoretical framework that supports a new interpretation of Sennacherib's political and religious intentions.

The evidence for the temple in Jerusalem is limited to the biblical description of the structure. Without physical evidence for the spatial arrangement and decorative program, the application of built environment analysis is necessarily a literary discussion of the structure of the text, with no attempt to reconstruct the visible appearance of the building. Issues of historicity and accuracy have long been important when biblical scholars approach Solomon's temple and these issues are addressed in this study, but they are not its focus. It is my contention that these discussions do little to advance an understanding of the biblical description of the temple as a text because they relegate the text to a secondary position behind an essential referent to which it points, i.e., an actual temple.

Focusing on the text itself moves the discussion away from issues of Solomonic or Davidic intent to offer a centralized place in a central capital in hopes of unifying a disparate people. My concern is the ideology of the Deuteronomistic historian and how the description of the built space of the temple functions within that ideology. The application of built environment analysis highlights the text's function as a verbal icon of Deuteronomistic ideology. It is a construction of the historian that supports Deuteronomistic theological positions, the spatial arrangement of the temple is structured by the ideology of the historian rather than a concern for an accurate presentation of the appearance of the temple.

Chapter one sets forth the method and theory behind the application of built environment analytical categories to the Neo-Assyrian palace and the Jerusalemite temple. After providing the history of the development of this new method, I explain how the evidence available for the palace and the temple respond to the requirements of built environment studies, providing a new way of interpreting the biblical text and palace.

Chapter two explicates the evidence for the palace of Sennacherib, focusing first on the texts that describe the palace construction and then the building itself. This study draws attention to two areas of the palace, Courtyard VI, a large open area surrounded by bas-reliefs depicting the quarrying and the transportation of winged bull colossi into the palace, and Room XXXVI, commonly referred to as the Lachish Room, located at the end of a unique entryway arrangement that incorporates the winged bull colossi. Using these two areas of the palace, I conclude that Sennacherib set himself in a unique position among Assyrian kings.

Chapter three presents the evidence for Solomon's temple in Jerusalem. It provides background for the issues of historicity, which have recently been the primary concern of archaeological discussions regarding tenth century evidence in Jerusalem and the so-called Solomonic gateways at Megiddo, Gezer and Hazor. Given that the biblical text is our only evidence for Solomon's temple, the discussion turns to textual approaches typical of biblical scholars. A close reading of the temple description highlights the difficulties with taking the text at face value. The chapter concludes with a reading of the text as a verbal icon for the historian's ideology, using built environment analysis to interpret the icon.

Chapter four brings the palace and the temple back together as examples of the role of architectural and verbal icons in religious and political reform. It provides an expanded look at Sennacherib's building program and his political and religious policies with regard to Babylon. It seems clear from the evidence that Sennacherib was beginning a new religious and political day in Assyria, which may not have been as well received as he anticipated. In any case, the building program he promoted and the controversion of his Babylonian policy by his son provide fodder for possible motivations behind Sennacherib's assassination. While it has previously been suggested that Sennacherib's Babylonian policy is at the root of his assassination, what has never been elucidated prior to this study is how his Babylonian policy was part of his larger political and religious reform. I contend that Sennacherib not only continued his father's consolidation of Babylonian religious forms into Assyrian forms, but also identified the king directly with the god Assur in a way no earlier king had. This claim to divine status is supported architecturally and textually in the evidence provided and constitutes a new stage in the discussion of Sennacherib's royal ideology and possible causes for his assassination.

The verbal icon of Solomon's temple promotes a new way of envisioning divine presence with the text at the center of a theological debate and religious reform movement played out between the Dtr and Priestly groups. Each represents differing visions of the proper religious relationships between people and deity. This debate provides a context for the composition of the text. Through supplementation, one group reworks the composition of another, without wiping out the earlier work. The innovation that remains is the first temple tour text, and the shift toward textuality as a vehicle for political and religious reform. This is a victory for the Dtr reform insofar as the iconic model of textuality changes the way the post-exilic theologians presented their ideology. The verbal icon, and its power to present religious ideology in such a manner that it is released from spatial limitations, becomes the primary mode of religious and theological debate. The end result of the Priestly counter-reform is the reintroduction of spatial limits on religious behavior, along with the mediating role of the priesthood in that place. The Dtr verbal icon subverts the idea that one must go the place by indicating that YHWH is not there. The function of the place as the central sanctuary is modified by the proposal of the verbal icon in the text. The counter-reform destroys this concept by its confirmation that the place and the role of the priests do matter, but they do it through reworking the verbal icon.

The verbal icon of Solomon's temple in I Kings 6-8 is only one part of a much larger verbal icon. The Deuteronomistic History itself may be read as just such an icon created to provide a people with an image by which they might identify themselves. It is a powerful act to write a text, but even more powerful is that first moment when all the divinity that is imagined to reside in the temple is displaced from a particular space and replaced by a text. This innovation, begun by the historian, promotes textuality as the primary vehicle of divine manifestation. The place is no longer the referent. The text itself, the verbal icon, becomes the mode of interaction with the metaphysical. It is an act of brilliance to interpret an ancient text, a brilliance that is only surpassed by the innovative collapsing of divine presence and textuality.

The underlying issue for this study is the use of architecture and textuality in support of theological and political ideologies. In each case, an ideology that challenges the status quo is manifested through iconic presentation in differing media. In each case there is a response that comes as a counter-reform. For Sennacherib there are dramatic consequences. For the historian, however, the counter-reform does not demolish his creation, but rather adjusts its challenge by supplementing the existing text with its own ideology.

Chapter 1

Method of Architectural and Textual Study
for the Palace and Temple

Palaces and temples are distinctive among the monumental structures created by civilizations of antiquity. The palace, at face value, was the dwelling of the king and royal family and the temple was the dwelling of the god. Ancient written records, however, indicate that these structures functioned as more than dwellings. Much of the administrative business of the realm was carried out within the palace, while temples were often vast economic centers, as well as the centers where people expressed their dedication to the god.

The palace of Sennacherib in Nineveh and the temple of Solomon in Jerusalem are two examples of such structures in the ancient world. Assyriology, the study of ancient Assyria, is a discipline largely dominated by textualists and philologians since the days of the discovery of the library of Assurbanipal, the last great Assyrian king. The decorative art of the palace, placed in the museums of the west, received little scholarly attention until taken up again by art historians in the twentieth century. Recent interest in the artistic use of bas-relief to line the palace walls has led to the understanding that these reliefs were more than mere decoration; indeed, they told a story. The palace of Sennacherib has received considerable attention recently from the perspective of art history. No one, however, has yet consistently applied the theories and methods of built environment studies to this ancient palace. This study addresses this lack.

As for the study of the temple of Solomon in Jerusalem, there are multiple approaches. Though there is no archaeological evidence for the temple, scholars have reconstructed its appearance using biblical descriptions, studying the text for information on the religious history of ancient Israel and offering interpretive explanations of its architectural and decorative forms. What has not been done is an interpretation of the relevant biblical text without reference to the actual existence of the structure. This study addresses this gap by

approaching the text itself as a verbal icon that is the product of a
society much later than the building it purports to describe. This
approach has serious ramifications for the standard method and
assumptions of biblical studies.

When proposing a comparison such as this, it is an obvious
question to consider why not compare like with like; why not study
an Assyrian temple in comparison with Solomon's temple? The
reasons are twofold: first, we do not have an Assyrian temple so well
documented and excavated as Sennacherib's palace at Nineveh;
second, the comparison made in this study focuses on the function of
the palace or temple and not on the modern terms for them.[1] The
palace in the Assyrian state was more reflective of the king's societal
intent than was the temple, but the temple in the exilic author's work
reveals more social information than does Solomon's palace. Indeed,
though the temple and the palace in Jerusalem are described as part
of the same royal building project and the palace apparently took
more time to construct than the temple (seven years for the temple
vs. thirteen years for the palace, I Kings 6:28-7:1) much more detail
is provided in the description of the palace than in the description of
the temple.

Bringing together the palace of Sennacherib and the temple of
Solomon in this way highlights a larger issue to be addressed later:
both structures contain cultural and social information that was
passed from one segment of society to another. They are both iconic
presentations of social structure and identity, which are created by
the elite of the society and influence social behavior through the
delineation of status and power. As such they are two examples of
the same human communicative phenomenon: Sennacherib's palace
is evidence of the way the physical built environment embodies
social structure and maintains the status/power relationships

---

1   In fact, in the ancient world there was no vocabulary distinction between
the name for the building itself. Akkadian *ekallu*, comes from the
Sumerian é.gal, which means "big house." These are translated "palace"
or "temple" depending on whether they are appended to a divine name or
to a royal name. By the same token, the Akkadian *bītu*, "house," was used
for both the palace and the temple. We also have the sam relationship in
Hebrew vocabulary where we find the use of בית and היכל for "house"
and "palace/temple".

necessary for such a structure. This function of the built environment is so pervasive that even the literary creation of a purported built environment, as in the case of Solomon's temple, was used to create such relations and thereby establish identity.

The approach of this study is developed from methods of built environment studies, which have seriously modified the study of architecture by moving it away from its genetic connection with art history. The source materials for Sennacherib's palace respond well to the requirements of built environment studies. Enough evidence survives for a recreation of the appearance of the palace and an interpretation of its function and meaning in Neo-Assyrian rhetoric.

In the same manner, the approach of this study to the temple of Solomon is, in part, derived from built environment studies. The distinction must be made, however, that Solomon's temple is not an actual structure. The temple is a literary description after the fact, a description that may bear no resemblance at all to an actual structure. Before offering an interpretation of this literary representation, the text must be explained as a verbal icon for the temple. While this presents a considerable challenge in a field that possesses an accepted method and interpretive assumptions as entrenched as those of biblical studies, this new approach exhibits the text's ability to present an image which influences social structure and identity in the present through an iconic appeal to the past.

The first section of this chapter discusses the relationship of architecture and built environment studies. The second section outlines the evidence for Sennacherib's palace and describes the history of approaches to Assyrian palaces before introducing a new approach to Sennacherib's palace at Nineveh. The third section describes the literary evidence for Solomon's temple and the history of approaches by biblical scholars to the temple. A new approach to the temple will propose the application of the method of built environment studies to the literary description of the temple and discuss the significance of viewing the text as an icon. The conclusion will draw parallels between the physical structure of Sennacherib's palace and the literary structure of Solomon's temple in Jerusalem as an icon.

Architecture and the Built Environment

The innovations of the built environment studies must be seen against the background of architectural studies. In the early part of this century, P. Frankl identified purposive intention as one of his four categories for architectural analysis.[2] He added this new category to the already standard categories of spatial form, corporeal form and visual form. For Frankl, architectural monuments were "molded theatres of human activity."[3] One could understand the meaning of a building only by understanding the relationship between the building and the human activity within it. The life of the structure continued only as long as there was human social activity occurring within it. Yet, "a trace of this vanished life remains behind in a building to the extent that the purpose is incarnated in the form of the space."[4] For Frankl, building programs were part of cultural history. The intention that was the foundation of a building program of a given culture was the "practical and material certainty of purpose that determines the building program and hence the spatial form."[5]

Frankl attempted to move architectural study beyond its connection with art form to include human intention and activity in the understanding of a building. S. Giedion is a modern example of the failure of Frankl's method to take hold.[6] For Giedion, architecture is geometry in the round and buildings are made of the juxtaposition of plane, axis and symmetry.[7] His work is an example of a diachronic approach in which the geometrical forms that

---

2 P. Frankl, Principles of Architectural History; The Four Phases of Architectural Style, 1420-1900, translated and edited by James F. O'Gorman (Cambridge, MA: MIT Press, 1968). Originally published as Die Entwicklungsphasen der neueren Baukunst (Stuttgart: Verlag B. G. Teubner, 1914).

3 Frankl, 159.

4 Frankl, 160.

5 Frankl, 161.

6 S. Giedion, Space, Time and Architecture, Bolingen Series XXXV (Princeton: Princeton University Press, 1964).

7 See his discussion, 445-495.

constitute an architectural creation are traced through time from their earliest appearance to their adoption by later builders. In his opinion, the transmission of one form from culture to culture is evidence of the transmission of cultural traits inherent in the form. The form possesses a meaning that is constant, regardless of the society that produces it. Understanding the meaning of the form is equated to understanding something about that culture. Interestingly, the builders need not be aware of the incorporation of cultural information in the architectural form. He writes,

> However much a period may try to disguise itself, its real nature will still show through in its architecture, whether this uses original forms of expression or attempts to copy bygone epochs.[8]

Giedion's notion that cultural information is readily available to scholars from different cultures is a survival of the idealism of the nineteenth century that held high confidence in universal human development. What he does not take into account is the distinct probability that, even if architecture is geometry, geometrical forms can have entirely different meanings in different cultures.

The omissions and assumptions of Giedion are addressed by built environment studies, which developed from psychological and cultural anthropological approaches to architectural forms. These studies once again concentrate on the relationship between the built structure and the cultural categories that influence it. This return to the significance of this relationship is, in part, the influence of studies of material culture and the recognition that the material objects created by a culture take a particular form based on the concern for utility as well as specific cultural categories.[9] In addition, built environment studies are influenced by environmental psychology and

---

8　　Giedion, 19.
9　　On material culture studies see the essays in T. J. Schlereth, ed., Material Culture: A Research Guide (Lawrence, KS: University of Kansas Press, 1985) and S. Lubar and W. D. Kingery, eds., History from Things: Essays on Material Culture (Washington and London: The Smithsonian Institution Press,1993).

the study of the relationship between the physical elements of the
built environment and the human social activity occurring within it.[10]

   Amos Rapoport's study entitled The Meaning of the Built
Environment; A Nonverbal Communication Approach, is a
theoretical explanation of the influence the physical constitution of
an environment has upon the human activity within it. He explains
the built environment on two levels: perceptually and
associationally. Perceptual description notes the physical items and
elements perceived by the user, while associational description is
concerned with the different associations the user makes with the
physical elements.[11] The social behavior of a person within a
particular built environment is a function of the relationship between
what that person perceives in that environment and the associations
that person makes with that perception. The built environment offers
"cues" for expected social behavior and the individual's actions are
responses to those cues. For instance, individual and corporate
behavior in a cathedral is entirely different from that in a shopping
mall. The difference in behavior is the response to the different cues
received from these distinct built environments. Rapoport writes,

> The critical point is that the effects are *social* but the cues on the
> basis of which the social situations are judged are *environmental-*
> -the size of the room, its location, its furnishings, the clothing and
> other characteristics of the experimenter (which are, of course,
> part of the environment). They all communicate identity, status,
> and the like and through this they establish a context and define
> a situation. The subjects read the cues, identify the situation and
> the context, and act accordingly. . .*it is the social situation that
> influences people's behavior, but it is the physical environment
> that provides the cues.*[12]

   And again,

---

10   See H. M. Proshansky, et. al. eds., Environmental Psychology: People
      and Their Physical Settings, 2nd edition (New York: Holt, Rinehart and
      Winston, 1976).

11   A. Rapoport, The Meaning of the Built Environment; A Nonverbal
      Communication Approach (London: Sage Publications, 1982), 19ff.

12   Rapoport, 56 (italics his).

The environment thus communicates, through a whole set of cues, the most appropriate choices to be made: The cues are meant to elicit appropriate emotions, interpretations, behaviors, and transactions by setting up the appropriate situations and contexts. The environment can thus be said to act as a mnemonic reminding people of the behavior expected of them, the linkages and separations in space and time--who does what, where, when, and with whom.[13]

Rapoport delineates three perceptual categories of architectural elements that work together to provide the environmental meaning for a particular structure. The first of these is the fixed-feature elements, architectural elements that either do not change or change only rarely and slowly, such as the forms of walls, ceilings, and floors. The second category, semi-fixed elements, are those which exhibit much more change and innovation in a shorter period of time. Among these are types of furniture, decorative elements such as wall hangings and paintings, garden and landscape layouts, differing levels of elevations between the structure and the surrounding area or within the structure itself, and the accessibility of the structure. The third category is the nonfixed-feature elements. These are related to the human occupants or inhabitants of the settings, their shifting spatial relations, their body positions and postures, hand and arm gestures, and even facial expressions, along with other nonverbal behaviors.[14]

In addition to these three elements, Rapoport discusses the use of three further categories directly related to the physicality of the architectural form itself: height, color, and redundancy.[15] Any of these elements may be used in the built environment to provide clues to the meaning of a given spatial segment. Height, color, and redundancy are visual elements which communicate status and/or power because of the associations made between these elements and the concepts of status and power. These three decorative elements bear particular social cues as they are used in specific contexts. The availability of color, or the lack of its availability, in a particular

---

13   Rapoport, 80-81.
14   Rapoport, 96.
15   Rapoport, 117.

society would provide this decorative element with special significance in that social group. When these elements are examined in specific settings they are important cues for the meaning and significance of specific built environments[16]

These associations are culturally bound and are not universal. The individuals within the cultural unit learn how to relate the perceptual and associational aspects of the environment through the process of enculturation, that is, they are taught these associations as they are reared within the society. In Rapoport's opinion, the outsider can also learn these cues and associations through acculturation. This is the process in which an individual foreign to the source culture learns the cultural nuances and categories that influence the formation of its built forms.[17]

R. E. Blanton's work in the domestic environments of Southeast Asia, Egypt and Mesoamerica is an example of Rapoport's categories applied to actual structures.[18] Blanton elicits cultural information from the built environment and shows that the theory set forth by Rapoport is applicable across cultural boundaries. He incorporates a study of the physical environment with the social activity he witnessed in those environments. Blanton says that domestic settings communicate social structure either canonically or indexically. Canonical communication is the way the house and its form set the parameters for behavior and the structure of relationships among its inhabitants. This arrangement is influenced by the established cultural-familial pattern of interaction with multi generational inhabitants and a hierarchy of power from older to younger. The form of the dwelling facilitates and promotes the very behavior that influenced its form. Indexical communication is external communication to those outside the house and focuses on social identity. Here the inhabitants may use various levels of

---

16   These latter three elements are, in fact, a subgroup within the semi-fixed
     features of a given structure, since it includes decorative elements. These
     merely specify more clearly *what* Rapoport understands to be key
     communicative elements within the decoration of a structure.

17   Rapoport, 65-66.

18   R. E. Blanton, Houses and Households: A Comparative Study (New York
     and London: Plenum, 1994).

decorative elaboration to communicate the wealth and status of their household in relation to other households.

While Blanton does not use Rapoport's terminology, his canonical communication of these structures is a function of the fixed-feature, semifixed-feature and the nonfixed feature elements proposed by Rapoport. For instance, the arrangement of the walls, and thus the boundaried units, limit access to the deepest areas of the houses to the privileged older generations, while the younger generations are made to remain in the outer chambers. Walls are fixed feature elements which either do not change or change only very slowly over long periods of time. The decorative elements, as well as different levels of elevation within the structures are clear signals within that culture of the privileged status of the elders over the younger members of the household.[19] These are all part of Rapoport's semi-fixed features. Finally, Blanton's attention to the spatial proxemics and positions and postures of the inhabitants are clearly what Rapoport designated as non-fixed features of the built environment in the form of human behavior within the physical structure.

Indexical communication is a function of the semi-fixed feature elements of external decorative processes in combination, specifically, with the elements of height, color and redundancy. Elaborate colorful and redundant forms on the external walls of the houses are indicative of high social status and the wealth that go with it, while the height of the house, in terms of raised floor level or high roof, is an indicator of longstanding familial importance within the community.[20] The house performs an important social function that is the product of, and promotes the continuance of, a particular social and familial order.

> Typically, symbolic communication through the medium of a dwelling involves the creation of a built environment that manifests social divisions based on gender, generation, and rank, linked to cosmological schemes that express categorical oppositions like order/disorder, elite/nonelite, and purity/danger.[21]

---

19   Blanton, 102
20   Blanton, 117
21   Blanton, 10.

The goal of canonical communication is the continuity of the particular household within the social structure. Successive generations, as they are reared in the society, are enculturated to the familial structure which privileges the earlier generations. The lessons they are taught are supported by the physical structure of their environment, which is likewise promoted as based upon the cosmic order.

> I hypothesize that through its material expression of cosmological principles . . . linking rank and power to gender and generation, the canonical communication of the house serves to sanctify the social conventions of the household continuity strategy . . . This argument implies that such conventions may seem arbitrary and counter to the interests of junior members, thus requiring sanctification as part of this kind of social reproductive strategy, to assure compliance to its demanding requirements.[22]

In his application of Rapoport's theory, Blanton expanded the influence of the built environment with his claim that it influences social behavior not only in the context of that environment, but throughout all levels of the society. He demonstrates that the built environment is an important element that defines and maintains the social structure on individual, familial, corporate and public levels.

The principles in the works of Rapoport and Blanton require knowledge of the society as a whole in addition to the material form of the built environment. Consequently, Thomas A. Markus' study, Buildings and Power: Freedom and Control in Modern Buildings Types,[23] also influenced by the work of Rapoport, exhibits an approach to the meaning of a structure that incorporates Rapoport's two elements of building and users. In addition, Markus includes a third element: the texts, which he identifies as evidence for the purposeful intent that Frankl had called for in architectural analysis. Markus argues that these three "domains" are necessary elements for any attempt to interpret the meaning of a structure. Though studies that focus on the built environment yield much information on the

---

22   Blanton, 102-103.
23   T. A. Markus, Buildings and Power: Freedom and Control in Modern Building Types (London and New York: Routledge, 1993).

structure, the form of the structure alone is simply not enough for a full understanding of the meaning of the building.

Like Rapoport, Markus believes social behavior within the structure is important, but he includes all available information on a building. The texts concerned with its planning and construction offer information on purposeful intent of the planners and builders. Texts concerning the understandings of the viewer and user of the structure offer an interpretation of the building based upon its actual role within the human society.

The textual "domain" offered by Markus is significant because the focus is no longer primarily on the structure and its form but on the planning and the social activity that occurred within it. The difference between the approaches of Markus and of Rapoport and Blanton is one of emphasis rather than substance. Both methods consider the structure as well as the social activity within it as evidence for meaning. The distinction between them lies in how much evidentiary weight should be placed upon the structure itself and how much should be placed on the social activity and the documentation surrounding the structure. Rapoport refers, somewhat vaguely, to the need for the interpreter to become acculturated to the society within which the structure was created. Markus more specifically outlines and illustrates the use of actual documentation as fundamentally important for an interpretation. In either case, more evidence is required beyond the physical form of the structure.

The type of evidence that Markus requires, however, is much less open to interpretation than that required by Rapoport and Blanton. Documents that report on the planning and construction of a building are more likely to spell out precisely what the goals of the planners were when they planned the building, as well as how certain architectural features were included in order to focus the attention and activity within the structure in a particular manner. Moreover, texts which report information concerning the public reception and use of the structure once it is completed offer clear evidence of the significance and meaning of that structure within a particular segment of the society for which it was created.

Rapoport's primary focus is upon structural components which communicate specific information concerning the meaning and use of the structure. These components have a cultural basis which must be understood before the interpreter is able to achieve a viable interpretation of the structure. Working without documentation forces the interpreter to rely upon his/her own sensitivity and creativity to offer an explanation that approaches the cultural and social significance of the structure.

The application of built environment categories to the physical reconstruction of the palace of Sennacherib at Nineveh provides a fresh approach to the substantial evidence for this structure. The diachronic study of architecture as the development and use of geometric forms, as characterized by Giedion, has proved inadequate for an understanding of such structures and their relationship to the cultures that produced them. The theoretical work of A. Rapoport set forth a method of approach to the built structure that highlights the relationship between the structure and the cultural activity that occurs within it. This work influenced the approaches of both Blanton and Markus. Blanton shows that built environments influence cultural activity beyond the individual structure in his study of domestic settings and their relationship to social structure. Markus is the clearest example of Frankl's influence on built environment studies. His three domains, buildings, users and texts, which build on Rapoport's analysis of fixed, semi-fixed and non-fixed features of the built environment, incorporates Frankl's ideas regarding purposive intent of the builders as an important category for understanding a building. The application of built environment method offers a significant opportunity to understand the importance of the palace in Neo-Assyrian culture more clearly.

Sennacherib's Palace in Nineveh

There is extensive evidence available for a reconstruction of the ground floor of Sennacherib's palace, thanks to the records maintained by Sir A. H. Layard, published in his Nineveh and Its Remains.[24] While archaeological excavation was still in its infancy

---

24   A. H. Layard, Nineveh and Its Remains, 2 volumes (London: John Murray, 1849).

in the middle of the nineteenth century when he discovered the palace, Layard nevertheless kept meticulous records of the excavated floor plan and the bas-reliefs that lined the walls, making it possible to recreate the arrangement of the walls and open spaces (boundaries and accesses), and the arrangement of the reliefs on the walls. Unfortunately, because the palace was destroyed in 612 B.C.E. with the capture and destruction of Nineveh by Medes and Babylonians, there is no information on the appearance of the upper levels.[25]

Rapoport's architectural elements of fixed, semi-fixed, and non-fixed features, as well as those of height, color and redundancy can be applied to the portion of the palace that can be reconstructed. Fixed feature elements can be identified with the layout of the walls and doorways; that is, the style of arranging the spatial units in the palace. These floor plans were fairly stable over about two hundred years in Assyrian palace architecture, but a study of Sennacherib's palace reveals an interesting innovation significant for his definition of Assyrian kingship. Height, color and redundancy in the palace offer concrete examples of Rapoport's semi-fixed features, making clear that it was a built environment in which relationships based on status and power were controlling factors in the planning.

Height is a key element in the courtyard areas, which were apparently open to the sky. The courtyards provided access to different suites of the palace. The walls were lined with reliefs and the doorways on each of the four walls were, in most cases, flanked by the *aladlammû* guardians. Height is an important element in any discussion of these winged bull colossi. These figures are always much taller than average human height and provide support for arched doorways. There are three pairs of these colossi, however, which exhibit the use of height in an innovative way. The three doorways which lead to Room XXXVI are progressively shorter as one moves away from Courtyard XIX. This use of height provided a visual effect found nowhere else in the excavated palaces of Assyria.

---

25 Reconstructions of palace facades above the ground level, such as that offered by James Fergusson, The Palaces of Nineveh and Persepolis Restored (London: John Murray, 1851) are not based on any archaeological evidence.

Color is also an integral element in Assyrian palace decoration. Traces of color have been found on enough of the reliefs to show they were once painted.[26] In addition to the color used on the reliefs, there is evidence of painted murals in other ancient palaces which justify the assumption that Sennacherib included such frescoes in his own palace in Nineveh.[27] The use of color in Layard's reconstruction of Assurnasirpal II's (883-859 B.C.E.) throne room at Nimrud (ancient Kalhu) is conceptually informative. While Layard's presentation of the layout of the room and the arrangements of the reliefs is fanciful, his use of color and design patterns is based on evidence found elsewhere in the palace and not merely upon his imagination. This reconstruction thus provides a reasonable idea of the use of color in Assyrian palaces.[28]

Redundancy is a hallmark of Assyrian decorative style, found in all areas of the palace. On the floors, particularly the flooring of the thresholds, carpet patterns are engraved into the stone flooring. The border of this design is a recurring pattern of palmettes and cones. Secondly, identical excerpts from royal annals are repeated on the bull colossi, almost as a decorative form. Decorative motifs are repeated continuously around single rooms. Numerous reliefs depicting the king victorious in battle appear throughout the palace. The effect of these instances of redundancy give the impression of greater volume by emphasizing the length and breadth of a space.

---

26   See Layard's discussion of painted reliefs and sculptures in Nineveh and Its Remains, vol. 2: 238-243.

27   For evidence of painted murals in ancient palaces see André Parrot, Mission Archéologique de Mari 2: Le Palais: Peintures et Murales, Bibliothèque Archéologique et Historique 69 (Paris: Institut d'Archéologie de Beyrouth, 1958). For Assyrian palaces see Layard, Monuments of Nineveh (London: John Murray, 1849), plates 86-87 for examples of painted upper chambers from the Northwest palace at Nimrud. These plates are reproduced in J. M. Russell, From Nineveh to New York: The Strange Story of the Assyrian Reliefs in the Metropolitan Museum and the Hidden Masterpiece at Canford School (New Haven and London: Yale University Press, 1997), 49: figures 28 and 29. See also the palace of Tiglath-pileser III at Til Barsip in F. Thureau-Dangin and M. Dunand, Til Barsib (Paris, 1936), 45ff.

28   Layard, Nineveh and Its Remains, plate 2, reproduced in Russell, Nineveh to New York, 105: figure 81.

The positioning of the three pairs of bull colossi leading from Courtyard XIX to Room XXXVI mentioned above is an example of redundancy which made the distance into the focal chamber appear greater than it actually was.

Finally, non-fixed features of Sennacherib's palace consist of the human social behavior that occurred within it. Since there is no way of interviewing palace inhabitants, the wall reliefs must substitute. Many of these reliefs depict the king in various activities. In Courtyard VI the reliefs show the work of quarrying, sculpting and transporting the winged bull colossi. They contribute information on the process of building the palace. They portray people in captivity and the attitudes of their captors. The posture, body language and proximity of the people to the king exhibit categories of status with the king as the primary point of reference. Here the reliefs function on two levels. They are part of the semi-fixed features of palace architecture because they function as decorative elements that line the walls of particular palace areas and provide evidence for the developing artistic and decorative programs of Assyrian palaces. They are also witnesses for activities of the king within and without the palace. They show the demeanor of the king and those around him. They are both evidence for the appearance of the built environment and "documentary" evidence for the non-fixed features of the built environment, presenting images of posture, motions and general protocol for activity in the presence of the king.

The Texts

The textual information concerning built environments in the ancient world must be pieced together from different sources. In the ancient world, the creation of monumental structures, such as palaces and temples, was the prerogative of kings. Rather than risk their accomplishments to the memory of successors and later administrators, ancient kings followed a standard practice of recording their deeds. These records have been discovered in the form of foundation deposits and royal annals. The foundation deposits are clay tablets or cones inscribed with information regarding the planning and construction of the structure. They record the king responsible for the construction and often praise his accomplishment as more elaborate than any conceived by earlier kings. Assyrian kings in particular regularly included injunctions for those who might discover their foundation inscriptions when performing renovations upon the same structure.

Building inscriptions in the form of entries into the royal annals also survive, as well as dedicatory inscriptions probably on public display at the entrances of the structure. In many cases these inscriptions were formulaic and offered little in the way of detailed information regarding the planning and construction of the building. There are some, however, which do offer more detail. In either case, the primary goal of building inscriptions was the identification of particular achievements of the king as part of a general presentation of his rule as favored by the gods, and thus unequaled by his predecessors.

For Sennacherib's palace in Nineveh there were standard inscriptions on the *aladlammû*, the human headed winged bulls that flanked the major thresholds of the palace. These offer little more than annalistic information regarding the yearly campaigns of the king into different regions of his realm. The more comprehensive annals of Sennacherib, however, provide more detail concerning the planning and construction of the southwest palace.[29] He intended for the palace to impress and inspire awe in all who saw it. The palace was larger than any previous palace on the site and precious and exotic materials were used in its construction.

The evidence for the palace of Sennacherib at Nineveh can be divided into the three categories that Markus identified as necessary for understanding the meaning of a structure: the building, the texts and the users.[30] While the palace responds most clearly to the categories of building and texts, the witness of the users must be reconstructed using the palace reliefs as evidence for social activity within the palace. All of this material, however, comes from the administrative level of Assyrian society, from the top down. Without recourse to the point of view of the "average Assyrian" there is a

29   D. D. Luckenbill, The Annals of Sennacherib, Oriental Institute
      Publications II (Chicago: University of Chicago Press, 1924).
30   Buildings and Power, 9-13.

lack of other testimony to the significance of the palace in Assyrian society, which is necessary in any study of modern architecture and built environments. The interpretation of the palace must be from the point of view of the king and his administration and the significance they attributed to it.

History of Approaches

Studies of the architecture of the ancient Near East often take a diachronic approach to Mesopotamian architecture by tracing monumental forms through time by distinguishing elements such as size and decoration.[31] These works build upon the labor of scholars who reconstruct the appearance and arrangement of reliefs found in particular palaces.[32] For instance, Frankfort traces the development of art and architectural forms in the ancient Near East, establishing their earliest appearance in the Proto-Literate Period and showing their adoption by the various empires through the Persian Period. At each stage of his discussion, Frankfort offers a judgement on the

---

31   Examples of this approach are H. Frankfort, The Art and Architecture of the Ancient Near East, 5th edition (New Haven and London: Yale University Press, 1996, First edition 1951) and E. Heinrich, Die Paläste im alten Mesopotamien, Denkmaler Antiker Architectur 15 (Berlin: Deutsches Archäologisches Institut, 1984).

32   Treatments of individual palaces include A. Parrot, Mission Archéologique de Mari (II)I Le Palais: architecture (Paris: Institut d'Archéologie de Beyrouth, 1958); R. D. Barnett and M. Faulkner, The Sculptures of Tiglath Pileser III (London: British Museum, 1962); W. Nagel, Die neuassyrischen Reliefstile unter Sanherib und Assurbanaplu (Hessling, 1967); J. E. Reade, Assyrian Architectural Decoration: Techniques and Subject Matter, Baghdader Mitteilungen 10 (1979): 17-49; idem, The Architectural Context for Assyrian Sculpture, Baghdader Mitteilungen 11(1980): 75-87; J. Meuszynski, Die Rekonstruktion der Reliefdarstellungen und ihrer Anordnung im Nordwest palast von Kalhu (Mainz am Rhein: Verlag Philipp von Zabern, 1981); S. M. Paley and R. P. Sobolewski, The Reconstruction of the Relief Representations and their Positions in the Northwest Palace at Kalhu, II (Mainz am Rhein: Verlag Philipp von Zabern, 1987); M. I. Marcus, Geography as an Organizing Principle in the Imperial Art of Shalmaneser III, Iraq 49 (1987): 77-90.

artistic quality of the decorative reliefs and paintings discovered in Mesopotamian palaces and credits the Assyrians with the most profound advances in decorative art. He provides a type of evolution of art and architectural forms and shows how each subsequent ruler built upon previous rulers' accomplishments.

While Frankfort offers some discussion of the narrative style of Assyrian reliefs, Irene Winter moves the discussion of the reliefs in Assyrian palaces from their significance as decorative art to their significance as narrative presentations of the recreational and political activities of the king.[33] In 1993 Winter described the Assyrian palace as an element of royal rhetoric in which the king characterizes his reign through the decorative program.[34] Through the various presentations of the king in the role of warrior, victor, religious officiant and hunter, Winter shows how the royal administration defines the reign of the king as secure and favored by the gods. This rhetorical role of the palace is so strong, in Winter's opinion, that she identifies the physical structure as an embodiment of the Assyrian state.[35]

Two years earlier John M. Russell studied a single palace by focusing on Sennacherib's palace at Nineveh. He identified a rhetorical program that was in part based upon traditional forms, yet incorporated innovative elements and forms expressive of the king's individual reign.[36] Russell concludes that the palace of Sennacherib in Nineveh is a message from the king to his subjects and to foreign dignitaries that he was able to maintain control at the periphery of his realm, allowing him to beautify and develop the center of the realm

---

33   Irene Winter, Royal Rhetoric and the Development of Historical Narrative in Neo-Assyrian Reliefs, Studies in Visual Communication 7,2 (1981): 2-38; idem, Art as Evidence for Interaction: Relations between the Assyrian Empire and North Syria, in Mesopotamien und seine Nachbarn: politische und kulturelle Wechselbeziehungen im Alten Vorderasien, ed. H. Kühne, H.-J. Nissen and J. Renger, Berliner Beiträge zum Vorderen Orient, Band I, Teil I (Berlin: D. Reimer, 1982): 355-382.

34   "Seat of Kingship"/ "A Wonder to Behold": The Palace as Construct in the Ancient Near East, Ars Orientalis 23 (1993): 27-55.

35   Winter, "Seat of Kingship," 38.

36   Sennacherib's Palace without Rival at Nineveh (Chicago: University of Chicago Press, 1991).

for the pleasure and astonishment of all peoples.[37] This is, according to Assyrian rhetorical style, attributed to the favor of the gods that rests upon Sennacherib.

This approach of Winter and Russell is significant in that it is a move from concentration upon the physical form of the palace toward an understanding of its function as the elucidation of a singular message. While Winter's primary concern is with the reliefs, Russell discerns the message of the palace through a study of the reliefs and the inscriptions and their juxtaposition throughout the palace. Russell argues that the inscriptions serve to specify the events depicted in the reliefs.

The identification of the rhetorical function of Assyrian palaces based upon reliefs and inscriptions is important for the understanding of royal ideology in the ancient world. Approaches like that of Winter, which focus on the reliefs as narrative, or Russell, which understands the entire palace as a message, do not address the obvious fact that a palace is not a text. While, for modern rhetorical purposes, one may resort to analogies of written language for an interpretive angle on the material, it should not be forgotten that the material evidence was/is a building.

The reliance upon the textual metaphor as an interpretive device is, in part, based upon the human dependency on verbal language to convey meaning as well as to form thought. It is also a function of the presumption in semiology, the study of signs, that any communicative system is analogically equivalent to spoken language, which may itself be attributable to the fact that semiology developed from linguistics.[38] This analogy is significant not so much in its indication that material culture, in this case the palace reliefs, is like a text but rather in indicating that the two are like each other. The analogy goes both ways. Both are distinctive communicative devices; they do not communicate in the same way. While a text

---

37   Russell, Sennacherib's Palace, 260-262.
38   Particularly from the distinction Saussure made between *langue* and *parole*, in which meaning resides in the relationship among signs (in this case, words) and not in the sign itself. A good example of a semiotic study of symbols which uses the textual/linguistic metaphor as a rhetorical device is Christopher Tilley, Material Culture and Text: The Art of Ambiguity (London and New York: Routledge, 1991).

communicates through its phraseology and syntax, a building, as the arena within which human social relations are enacted, communicates through its decoration and spatial arrangement, which embody the social structures of power and status. The rhetoric of one cannot solely interpret the other, as in the approaches of Russell and Winter.

As Blanton and Markus have shown, social relations are embodied in the structure in the way spatial units are delineated one from another and the way they are accessed. Moreover, the decorative elements of a given spatial unit offer cues to the expected emotional response and behavior within the particular bounded units. This approach to the built environment, which contemplates the spatial arrangement of the various segments of the palace, maintains the distinctive expression of the structure as a built environment and corrects the limitations of a purely textual approach to such a built structure.

G. Turner offers such a study in his identification of the function of specific suites in several Assyrian palaces.[39] After identifying what he considers common floor plan patterns in the areas adjacent to throne rooms, Turner describes the function of these suites as reception areas with bathrooms and waiting rooms where individuals and groups gathered to await their opportunity for an audience with the king. His primary evidence for the function of these rooms is their placement and arrangement, as well as the wall reliefs found in certain more private areas.[40]

Granting his delineation of spatial units, Turner's proposal looks somewhat convincing. Closer scrutiny, however, reveals discrepancies which have yet to be accounted for. A formal study should be controlled by the form and not by preconceived notions of meaning and/or function. Turner approaches his subject with the identification as reception suites already in mind, which makes it easier to group forms together which do not otherwise match. The segment from the palace of Assurnasirpal II is, in fact, nothing like the suite he isolates from Sennacherib's palace when the entire area

39   G. Turner, State Apartments of Later Assyrian Palaces, Iraq 32(1970): 170-213.
40   Turner, 131.

that comprises both suites is included. The Sennacherib suite does not center around a throne room, as the others do, unless Room XXXVI is precisely that.[41] Consequently, Turner's study does not allow spatial arrangement to identify function.

D. J. W. Meijer contests interpretations of function and meaning, like Turner's, based on the floor plan of a structure.[42] The form is not necessarily indicative of function, which means that different forms could be used for the same function and that the same form could be used for different functions. Much more must be known about a structure and site before such an interpretation can be made.[43] Turner uses fixed feature elements, the arrangement of the walls and doorways, and semi-fixed feature elements, the reliefs in the washroom areas, to describe a possible function for these rooms. His interpretation is necessarily influenced by his designation of these suites as associated with throne rooms in the palaces. One would expect that the throne room suites would incorporate areas where people could wait and prepare to see the king.[44] There is not enough evidence to support Turner's interpretation and simply arguing that such an area would have been logical and necessary does not prove the interpretation.

The studies surveyed so far approach the palaces of the ancient Near East mainly from the perspective of art history. Frankfort's diachronic analysis presents a brief overview of the development of decorative reliefs and their use in Mesopotamian palaces. Winter and Russell focus this approach to deal with the narrative capabilities

---

41   Room XXXVI, the Lachish Room, has received much discussion because of the wall reliefs which depict the battle for Lachish and Sennacherib receiving the spoils of victory. So far no one has understood this room as a throne room and its size would indeed seem to preclude such a designation.

42   D. W. J. Meijer, Ground plans and Archaeologists: On Similarities and Comparisons, in To the Euphrates and Beyond: Archaeological Studies in Honor of Maurits N. Van Loon, ed. O. M. C. Haex, H. H. Curvers and P. M. M. Akkermans (Rotterdam: A. A. Balkema, 1989), 221-236.

43   Meijer, 223. Note the similarity of this approach to that of Markus discussed above.

44   Turner, 192-193 considers the wash areas, with their associated protective figure reliefs to be chambers where individuals made themselves ritually pure before confronting the king.

of the Assyrian bas-reliefs.   Russell's synchronic study of
Sennacherib's palace explains how one king incorporated his royal
self-identification into the walls of his palace. Though these studies
are informative on an art historical level and identify the palace as an
element of Neo-Assyrian royal ideology, they lack the ability to
understand the palace as a built environment that is the context for
social activity. Because of this, they are unable to provide an
assessment of the ancient structure's meaning as a monumental
building.

Turner's study of reception suites in Neo-Assyrian palaces
purports to identify the function of these suites based on a spatial
analysis of their form. Yet he presents suites as conforming to
particular types which do not appear to be formally related. One can
only assume that the function he had in mind for these suites is his
"control" for such a grouping. This weakens the study as a formal
study based on spatial arrangement. The form and structure of the
spatial units must be the control in such a study.

The theories of Rapoport, carried forward by Blanton and Markus,
have yet to be applied to an ancient built environment. The benefit
of approaching the ancient palace using the methods of built
environment studies is that the building is not forced into a textual
metaphor to explain its ability to communicate cultural information.
This maintains its status as an ancient built environment and
illustrates how the Assyrian royal administration influenced social
structure and cultural forms through the way they shaped the
environment in which social relations were enacted. In this way
Sennacherib's architectural innovations are allowed to communicate
the social reforms that characterize his reign.

A New Approach to Sennacherib's Palace at Nineveh

This approach begins with the documentation from Sennacherib's
reign in Nineveh. The records specifically mention palace planning
and construction, providing a clear image of Sennacherib's own
views and ideas about what he intends to accomplish by constructing
a new palace. Recognizing the possibility that many people were
involved in the composition and structure of the royal documents, it

seems likely that the king had the final word on what was included and what was not.[45] The documents are written in first person and tell of the king's active involvement in the palace building. The wall reliefs often present an image of the king overseeing the work of his captured labor force. Thus, whether this is ideological or factual, the witness of the ancient records, both written and pictorial, is uniform in presenting the king as having a significant role in the planning and overseeing the construction of his palace.

Because much of the evidence is textual or consists of relief images, the tendency in scholarship has been to concentrate on that textuality and to reduce the palace and its meaning to a text which exists not in its own right but to direct attention elsewhere, to its referent. The referent has alternately been understood as the reign of the king or the Assyrian state. While this is an entirely natural approach given human reliance on language and texts to present and communicate concepts, the present study concentrates on spatial arrangement, boundary and access, and the decorative program of the palace. The application of built environment categories outlined above will highlight the palace's ability to communicate cultural cues and information, without depending upon a textual metaphor as an interpretive key. This approach will be applied to the arrangement of the spatial units of a particular suite in the palace together with the entryway and the associated reliefs. It recovers the architectural embodiment of Sennacherib's notions about the meaning and significance of his kingship over the Neo-Assyrian Empire, showing that modern theories of built environment can be faithfully applied to ancient structures.

The spatial arrangement of this particular suite provides a map, as it were, of the social relationships envisioned by the king and his administration. Using Rapoport's and Blanton's categories of access to deep spaces as indicative of high status, it is evident that the arrangement of boundaries and access (fixed features), in particular the triple threshold entryway to Room XXXVI, was a domain within

---

45   See the comments of H. Tadmor, Propaganda, Literature, Historiography: Cracking the Code of Assyrian Royal Inscriptions, in Assyria 1995, ed. S. Parpola and R. M. Whiting (Helsinki: The Neo-Assyrian Text Corpus Project, 1997), 328.

which these social categories were cued. The reliefs are semi-fixed feature elements which contribute to cuing social behavior within this domain. Color, height and redundancy contribute to the communicative ability of the reliefs and spatial arrangement. These are the categories which replace the textual metaphor in the interpretive discussion of this suite of rooms.

Solomon's Temple in Jerusalem

This study of Solomon's temple in Jerusalem is considerably different from that of Sennacherib's palace because there are no physical remains of the temple. All ideas concerning the ground plan and arrangement of the rooms and domains within the temple complex are derived from textual descriptions in the Hebrew Bible. The discussion concerning the precise nature of the material continues to move away from confidence in its antiquity or its own concern for historical accuracy. The archaeological evidence once cited as solid proof of Solomon's building programs has increasingly come under fire and scholars have begun to speak of the "myth of Solomon."[46] The existence of Solomon and the attribution of gateways and the Jerusalem temple to early building programs in his reign have become such points of contention that even the finding of the Aramaic inscription at Tel Dan, which appears to mention the "House of David," has not been able to bolster scholarly confidence in the history as told in the biblical material.[47]

---

46   G. J. Wightman, The Myth of Solomon, BASOR 277-78 (1990): 5-22. The
       most recent discussions of the issues surrounding the question of Solomon
       can be found in G. N. Knoppers, The Vanishing Solomon: The
       Disappearance of the United Monarchy from Recent Histories of Ancient
       Israel, JBL 116/1 (1997): 19-44; and in the essays collected in L. K.
       Handy, ed., The Age of Solomon: Scholarship at the Turn of the
       Millennium (Leiden: Brill, 1997).
47   A. Biran and J. Naveh, An Aramaic Stele Fragment from Tel Dan, IEJ
       43(1993): 81-98. Knoppers, Vanishing Solomon, 36-40 provides an
       exhaustive trail of the published scholarly discussion concerning how one
       should understand this inscription.

Evidence

The primary evidence for Solomon's temple is the biblical text I Kings 5-8. The context of this four chapter narrative concerning the temple is the beginning of Solomon's reign after his succession to the throne of David. The narrative recounts Solomon's decision to build the temple, includes a description of the construction process along with the negotiations for materials with Hiram, King of Tyre, and provides a description of the physical appearance of the structure. It ends with Solomon's dedicatory prayer outlining the purpose and function of the temple in the religious life of ancient Israel. The establishment of the temple provides the religious center that unifies the peoples of Israel and Judah in David's capital city.

Further material describing the temple may be found in II Chronicles 2-5. Scholars have recognized the dependency of the material in Chronicles upon that found in the books of Kings.[48] This dependence does not lessen the significance of the Chronicles material for understanding the meaning of the temple in the ancient world. On the contrary, it illuminates the developing conceptions of the temple in post-exilic Judean society. The differences in the two accounts sheds light on the Chronicler's subsequent concerns and the willingness to modify the earlier description in accordance with those concerns. The descriptions of sanctuaries in Exodus 25-35 and Ezekiel 40-48, while not concerned with Solomon's temple, provide information on the tabernacle and Ezekiel's vision of the temple. These must be analyzed since they serve as source material for the Chronicler's image of the temple.

History of Approaches

Previous approaches of biblical scholars to Solomon's temple are characterized by their utilization of various methods that do not

---

48   S. L. McKenzie, The Chronicler's Use of the Deuteronomistic History, Harvard Semitic Monographs 33 (Atlanta: Scholars Press, 1985); S. Japhet, I & II Chronicles: A Commentary, Old Testament Library (Louisville: Westminster/John Knox Press, 1993).

clarify the meaning of the text. Among these one can find an assumption of historicity that influences the basic conceptions scholars have about the narrative. This assumption leads to the creation of source evidence to provide a foundation for the supposed historical knowledge contained in the narrative. A compromised code of archaeological evidence, which provides archaeological support for the structure without the necessary excavation and interpretation of physical remains, offers further support for the assumptions held by scholars. Finally, an interpretive method based upon a myth-ritual pattern creates evidence by associating the religious thought and forms of ancient Israel with those of her neighbors. These approaches have developed in the field of biblical studies in the twentieth century and form its response to the difficulties of maintaining its claim as a historical discipline. Questions of the historicity of the biblical material were virtually ignored, or at least not considered, until the nineteenth century developments in German historical study that tried to establish what events actually occurred, and in what sequence.

Biblical study had to take one of two roads. It either had to seek extrabiblical evidence for the events narrated in the Bible, providing independent testimony to the accuracy of the biblical account of history, or to take the route of literary study of the biblical material, which seeks to understand the literary development and/or composition of the material without attempting to prove its historicity. The first of these led to the use of archaeological evidence for history as told in the biblical narrative. If one could establish physical evidence for biblical history then biblical studies would be confirmed as a "hard" historical discipline. The second path led to form criticism, which was less concerned with proving the biblical narrative as historical and approached the material with the generally accepted assumption in its antiquity. This allowed form critics to assume that the narratives contained ancient information about religious practice and belief, whether or not the events recounted ever happened just as they were narrated. This freedom granted literary critics an exemption from hard evidence while also giving them the ability to incorporate methods and assumptions from literary study of non-biblical materials as a control over how scholars could use the biblical narrative.

The first characteristic, the assumption of historicity, is found in the many studies which attempt a visual reconstruction of Solomon's temple based on descriptions found in the biblical material. These studies, which reach back to the eighteenth century, have been gathered together in the comprehensive study of T. Busink.[49] They all agree on the fact that no one biblical passage is complete enough to provide all the information necessary to achieve a full reconstruction. This necessitates the combination of the different descriptions to realize a complete image of the structure, even though it means combining materials from different settings and time periods.

Other approaches which also assume the historicity of the material come from the German religionsgeschichtliche Schule.[50] These history of religions approaches to the temple attempt to understand the biblical descriptions in terms of what they reveal of religious life and practice in ancient Israel. Schmid and Rupprecht assume that the material in I Kings presents an accurate account of Solomon's building the temple on a site purchased by David from a Jebusite individual. They suggest the site was a pre-existing Jebusite shrine dedicated to El-Elyon and that Solomon chose this site in an attempt to unify the Israelites and Jebusites of Jerusalem through an association of Yahweh and El-Elyon.[51] The meaning of the temple texts rests in the historical information of religious formation gleaned from the material.

The second characteristic, the creation of source evidence, is found in literary critical approaches to the biblical material, which typically have been concerned with establishing source materials upon which the biblical material is based. James Montgomery proposes that material in the books of Kings is based on royal and

---

49   Der Tempel von Jerusalem von Salomo bis Herodes: eine archäologisch-historische Studie unter Berücksichtigung des Westsemitischen Tempelbau, 2 Bände (Leiden: E. J. Brill, 1970 and 1980).

50   H. Schmid, Der Tempelbau Salomos in religionsgeschichtlicher Sicht, in Archäologie und altes Testament: Festschrift für Kurt Galling, hg. A. Kuschke and E. Kutsch (Tübingen: Mohr Siebeck, 1970), 241-250; K. Rupprecht, Der Tempel von Jerusalem: Gründung Salomos oder jebusitisches Erbe? BZAW 144 (Berlin: Walter de Gruyter, 1977).

51   See Schmid, 249-250 and Rupprecht, 100-105.

temple archival documents.[52] He emphasizes the detailed nature of the temple description as evidence for the existence of temple archives which would have contained detailed, and therefore accurate, architectural and decorative records. Montgomery's circular reasoning is evident when he argues that the description of the temple is accurate and historical because it is based on these archival materials. His "proof" for these archives is the detail in the biblical material. M. Noth follows a similar path in his discussion of the temple description. In Noth's opinion, the accuracy and detail of the description indicates that it came from actual architects' and builder's notes. These, he believes, had been incorporated into a record of Solomon's reign which was subsequently incorporated in the book of I Kings.[53]

This creation of source materials, followed by several later commentators, appears to provide a genealogy of the historical record of the building of the temple.[54] Yet there is no evidence for the source materials they describe as necessary for such detail. The assumption of earlier documents based on literary form is not substantial evidence that such documents were ever consulted, much less that they existed. Moreover, the citation of these so-called archival materials is not evidence for the existence of the structure.

A more recent attempt to establish source materials for the biblical accounts is the work of A. Hurowitz.[55] His study takes him

---

52 J. A. Montgomery, Archival Data in the Book of Kings, JBL 53 (1934): 51-52; The Book of Kings, International Critical Commentary (Edinburgh: T. & T. Clark, 1951), 30-38.

53 Martin Noth, Könige 1 BKAT 9/1 (Neukirchen-Vluyn: Neukirchener Verlag, 1968), 104-106.

54 See J. Gray I & II Kings, Old Testament Library (Philadelphia: Westminster, 1970), 157-158, and Simon DeVries, I Kings, Word Biblical Commentary (Waco, Tex.: Word Books, 1985), 90-93. Gray holds that the source for the material is annalistic texts, while DeVries proposes architectural records, based on the distinctive usage of the Hebrew words באמה/אמה, and a Book of the Acts of Solomon.

55 Avigdor Hurowitz, I Have Built you an Exalted House: Temple Building in the Bible in Light of Mesopotamian and Northwest Semitic Writings, JSOTS 115 (Sheffield: Sheffield Academic Press, 1992). See also an earlier study using the same approach, A. S. Kapelrud, Temple Building: A Task for Gods and Kings, Orientalia (ns) 32 (1963): 56-62.

to the royal building inscriptions of Mesopotamia and the Levant. Citing formal similarities between these documents and the biblical account in I Kings 5:15-9:25, Hurowitz claims that the material is of similar genre. He identifies the description of Solomon's temple building as analogous to, and possibly dependent on, Assyrian building inscriptions. He thus provides a historical connection for the genre and identifies the source of the building account as a royal inscription in the time of Solomon. Though Hurowitz collects important information regarding the form of building reports in Assyria and Babylon, as well as the Levant, it is not clear that the acceptance of genre similarity insures the historicity of a written account. In fact, the building account of the temple does not match well with Assyrian building inscriptions, which more often deal with palaces than temples and usually include curses and blessings in their conclusion.[56] While Hurowitz' study is helpful in the identification of the genre, it is not able to offer an interpretation of the significance and meaning of the temple description.

Hurowitz' approach is one more attempt to invoke source materials for the biblical description. He states at the outset that he is not concerned with the accuracy of the description or with reconstructing the appearance of the temple,[57] yet he reaches the same conclusion as Montgomery, though through a different method. For all the contributions his study makes to biblical studies, his dating of the temple description to the Assyrian period is problematic for several reasons, not the least of which is the Assyrian preoccupation with structures other than temples. The composition may fit better in the Neo-Babylonian period, when there is much more attention given to royal construction projects focused on temples, but the question remains open.

The third characteristic, a compromised code of archaeological evidence, is found in symbolic interpretations of the description of the temple and its furnishings as representative of religious motifs from Israel's past. This symbolic approach to the temple accepts the biblical description as factual and offers an interpretation of the

---

56   See the comments of Seton Lloyd in S. Lloyd and H. W. Müller, Ancient
      Architecture (New York: Electa/Rizzoli, 1986), 38.
57   Hurowitz, 23-24.

significance of the furnishings and temple appearance in light of
other materials in biblical literature. Questions of whether there ever
was a temple built by Solomon or whether it looked anything like the
description in I Kings are never entertained. Moreover, a lack of
physical evidence is not considered a problem. An example of the
confidence of this approach in the literary description is found in
Carol Meyers' mid-1970s study of the tabernacle,

> The description of some appurtenance in the
> tabernacle texts must be considered as belonging to
> the same order of evidence as the published plate of
> some such object in an excavation report. We
> should not be concerned if the verbal description
> found in the biblical account does not always
> provide us with an accurate mental image or an
> exact image or object; for the possession of such an
> image or object would tell us no more than does the
> possession of an actual artifact.[58]

This statement is evidence of Meyers' inability to relinquish the
archaeologist's desire for physical objects while relegating the one
physical object she has, the text, to the position of secondary
evidence. In her work, the primary referent is still the object and not
the text. Understanding the text as merely evidence for the object
supports visual reconstructions based upon biblical descriptions.
Meyers opens the gate for such visual reconstructions by arguing that
physical evidence for the object is unnecessary. Nothing could be
further from accurate when discussing the material culture of a
society. This line of thinking must be modified to understand that the
text itself is the primary concern and not the object(s) it describes.

Meyers modifies this approach somewhat in her discussion of
Solomon's temple in the Anchor Bible Dictionary.[59] She states there:

---

58   Carol Meyers, The Tabernacle Menorah: A Synthetic Study of a Symbol
     from the Biblical Cult, ASOR Dissertation Series No. 2, ed. D. N.
     Freedman (Missoula, MT: Scholars Press, 1976), 2.
59   Anchor Bible Dictionary, Volume VI (New York: Doubleday, 1992), 354-
     369.

> Whether or not the text preserves an accurate picture
> of the Temple, the idea of an extraordinary and
> precious sacred structure located on Mt. Zion in
> Jerusalem is emphatically presented in the Kings
> account.[60]

Yet she does not treat the description as an "idea" but discusses the temple as an actual structure whose description is a "veritable blueprint in words."[61] Even though there is no physical evidence for the temple of Solomon, Meyers discusses the structure and its accoutrements as though she possesses excavated remains which could be studied and understood from the perspective of art history and religious iconography.

Meyers' approach exhibits a reliance upon the object even when there is no physical evidence for it. While physical evidence for an object is unnecessary in a visual reconstruction of an admittedly literary construct, this is not Meyers' intention. The importance of archaeological discovery is the provision of physical evidence for past cultures. The statement that a literary description of an object is as valid as the discovery of the object is simply preposterous. What is significant, however, is the role and importance the object has in the text. This does not make the texts evidence for the temple. On the contrary, the texts must remain the primary material and the temple a single element in the larger story.

Elizabeth Bloch-Smith offers a similar interpretive approach to the descriptions of the temple.[62] Stating that her purpose is to use archaeological and biblical evidence "to reconstruct the Temple and its symbolism,"[63] Bloch-Smith offers an interpretation of the furnishings and architectural features of the temple in light of West Semitic and biblical literature. Strongly influenced by the patternism

---

60   Ibid., 359.
61   Ibid., 352.
62   "Who is the King of Glory?" Solomon's Temple and its Symbolism, in Scripture and other Artifacts: Essays on the Bible and Archaeology in Honor of Philip J. King, ed. M. D. Coogan, J. C. Exum and L. E. Stager (Louisville, KY: Westminster John Knox, 1994), 18-31.
63   Bloch-Smith, 18.

of the myth-ritual school represented by Frank Moore Cross,[64] she understands the entire courtyard area as symbolic of Yahweh's victory and enthronement in a pattern pieced together from Ugaritic literature. Her use of Ugaritic materials, the Pentateuchal narrative and material from the Psalms to identify the biblical pattern of creation through victory over chaotic nature on the analogy of the Baal-Yam episode, or the less well known Adad-Tâmtu episode,[65] requires further scrutiny.

The use of literary materials from Ugarit to shed light on the biblical narrative is a method pioneered by F. M. Cross in order to explain ancient Israelite religious concepts and practice. The pattern consists of the divine warrior marching forth to battle and then returning victorious to his holy mountain and is developed through a comparison of the Exodus story in biblical material and the Baal cycle from Ugarit. There are several elements in this comparison that are problematic. While it does appear that Baal battles Yam in KTU 1.2, there is no indication that this victory has anything to do with creation.[66] Furthermore, the creation story of Genesis includes nothing that leads to a conclusion that there was any sort of cosmic struggle involved in the creation. The primary criticism that the Ugaritic materials do not present themselves in any clear sequence so that one may state certainly that this pattern was ever part of that cycle of materials is the most salient for this theory.[67] The use of biblical material to confirm such a pattern is merely circular and proves nothing with regard to the recovery of an ancient mythic pattern which was historicized by the Hebrews.[68]

---

64   Frank Moore Cross, Canaanite Myth and Hebrew Epic: Essays in the History of the Religion of Israel (Cambridge, MA: Harvard University Press, 1973), 147-177.

65   See J.-M. Durand, M.A.R.I. 7, 41-61.

66   See M. S. Smith, The Ugaritic Baal Cycle, Volume I: Introduction with Text, Translation and Commentary of KTU 1.1-1.2, Supplement to Vetus Testamentum 55 (Leiden: E. J. Brill, 1994), 319-324.

67   For the current state of the question see M. S. Smith, The Ugaritic Baal Cycle, 2-20.

68   For a fuller presentation of this critique and others see J. Van Seters, The Life of Moses; The Yahwist as Historian in Exodus-Numbers (Louisville, KY: Westminster John Knox Press, 1994), 257-259.

The above approaches fall into the traditional biblical methods which assume the historicity of the description of Solomon's temple, create source evidence for the narrative as it now reads, compromise physical archaeological evidence, or rely on a myth-ritual patternism. In addition to these, one might also include approaches that use the descriptions found in Josephus or in the Mishnaic tractate Middoth as later literary witnesses to the temple or those that take a purely archaeological approach to the temple. Reliance on later literary materials that attempt to establish continuity between the first and second temples does not provide any clarity on the significance of the description of the first temple in I Kings 6-7. Modern historical studies can no longer assume historicity of any material without corroborating evidence for the described events. The creation of source evidence, and the resulting pedigree that has become such an assumption of commentators on the material in the books of Kings is simply not sound historical methodology in any field of research. The issue at the crux of the use of archaeological evidence to elucidate the biblical narrative is the precise identification of what type of literature one understands the biblical narrative to be.

Archaeological evidence, when retrieved in controlled excavations, can provide physical testimony to cultures and events from the distant past. Even this evidence must be interpreted in conjunction with other forms of evidence in order to establish a complete image of the ancient society and culture. To date there has been no scientific excavation of the area that comprised the temple platform, which means that there are no physical remains of the temple attributed to Solomon. This lack of physical evidence for the temple is overcome in the field of archaeology by the assumption that the biblical narrative is an accurate presentation of the appearance of Solomon's temple. This assumption results in the appearance of the floor plan of Solomon's temple in illustrations that present a comparative view of different excavated temples in Late Bronze and Early Iron Age Israel.[69] This incorporation of the

---

69   This type of assumption of accuracy for the biblical narrative can be found in W. G. Dever, Monumental Architecture in Ancient Israel in the Period of the United Monarchy, in Studies in the Period of David and Solomon and other Essays, ed. T. Ishida (Winona Lake, IN: Eisenbrauns, 1982), 269-306; idem, Archaeology and the "Age of Solomon": A Case Study in

reconstructions based on the biblical description, without the support of excavated evidence, constitutes the current rhetorical victory of archaeology. The form of Solomon's temple is treated as an archaeological fact, even though there is no archaeological evidence for the Jerusalem temple. The appearance of excavated temples from other regions in the Iron Age cannot be taken as support for the accuracy of the biblical description without seriously compromising archaeology's position as a scientific approach to the ancient society. Furthermore, there is no evidence for any of the accoutrements described as part of the courtyard or the internal furnishings of the temple itself. In the face of such a dearth it is surprising to find trained archaeologists composing such detailed analyses of the temple and its furnishings as that described above based solely on the literary description. This difficult issue will receive more attention in the discussion of archaeology and Solomon's temple in chapter three below.

A New Approach to Solomon's Temple in Jerusalem

The discussion of previous approaches to the temple description in I Kings faulted each on issues concerning evidence. What has traditionally been accepted in biblical studies as evidence for the accuracy of the narrative is in fact no evidence at all. Without extant evidence for source materials for the description, or extant physical evidence for the appearance, much less the existence of the temple, the only useful evidence is internal literary comparison with other biblical materials or external literary comparison with the same genre in other cultures. Both of these types of evidence were set forth by J. Van Seters in his 1983 study of the rise of Israelite

---

Archaeology and Historiography, in The Age of Solomon, 217-251; and A. Mazar, Temples of the Middle and Late Bronze Ages and the Iron Age, The Architecture of Ancient Israel from the Prehistoric to the Persian Periods, ed. A. Kempinski and R. Reich (Jerusalem: Israel Exploration Society, 1992), 161-187, particularly 163: figure 14.

historiography,[70] as well as his more recent studies of the Chronicler's history.[71]

Internal comparison entails intertextual study of materials in the Hebrew Bible in order to establish what type of relationship exists between them.[72] External evidence consists of comparison of Israelite historiography with other forms of history writing in antiquity and examination of the relationships that emerge. Van Seters' work shows that even though the nations surrounding Israel possessed history writing in the form of annals, chronicles, king lists and the like, none developed the type of national history found in biblical material. The closest parallel he finds for biblical historiography is among the classical writers.[73] This establishes a genre relationship between biblical and classical historiography. This study approaches the temple description found in the Deuteronomistic history based on these assertions about the material.

This approach also relies upon the groundwork laid by Michael Dick in his 1984 study of prophetic material.[74] Dick discusses his theory of a shift from orality to written composition and compares this phenomenon in the prophetic material to a similar shift which occurred at about the same time in classical compositions. He dates this change to the late seventh century B.C.E. for the biblical prophets and identifies it as the result of an "approaching catastrophe which would foreseeably interrupt the social matrix necessary for oral transmission."[75]

His work is important for two reasons. First, he provides a general dating for the shift that converges with a tumultuous period in Israel's history. Dick's dating of this change in prophetic

---

70   J. Van Seters, In Search of History: Historiography in the Ancient World and the Origins of Biblical History (New Haven and London: Yale University Press, 1983).

71   J. Van Seters, The Chronicler's Account of Solomon's Temple-Building: A Continuity Theme, in The Chronicler as Historian, JSOTS 238 (Sheffield: Sheffield Academic Press, 1997), 283-300.

72   On this see more below.

73   In Search of History, 8-54, note particularly his discussion on pages 51-54.

74   M. Dick, Prophetic *poiesis* and the Verbal Icon, CBQ 46 (1984): 226-246.

75   Dick, 230.

compositional practice to the late seventh century B. C. E. dovetails nicely with the generally accepted dating of the beginning of Deuteronomistic composition during the reign of Josiah. Secondly, Dick establishes a connection between Hebrew writers and Greek writers by quoting classical materials which identify the author as a ποιητής (craftsman) and the created document as an ἐικών (icon).[76] Like Van Seters' work, Dick's discussion can be divided into internal and external evidence. The internal evidence consists of his study of the change in prophetic role from the speaking prophets to the writing prophets, while the external evidence consists of his discussion of the shift from orality to writing in classical materials.

The third component of this approach is the application of the types of evidence proposed by Van Seters and Dick. This approach is supported by two recent studies of temple descriptions found in biblical material. Both studies approach their respective texts as the product of literary craftsmanship. The first of these, by J. Z. Smith, interprets the temple vision of Ezekiel as a map of status and power in ancient society.[77] This approach to the text considers the document as an image of the social structure of post exilic Israel, or at least of one conception of ideal social structure which the prophet promotes through the spatial arrangement of his description. Smith's treatment of Ezekiel's vision does not attempt a reconstruction of the appearance of the structure but rather an interpretation of the *meaning* of the document as an icon. The form of the icon is influenced by the author's notions of status and power structure in post-exilic Israelite society and his skillful creation of a textual image of that structure.

The second study is J. Van Seters' recent investigation of the Chronicler's account of Solomon's temple building.[78] Van Seters demonstrates that the Chronicler freely reworked his Vorlage (the I Kings account) in order to incorporate his own perspective into the temple description. The result is a temple that has key elements not

---

76   Dick, 236. He refers to the Greek poet Simonides of Ceos. His discussion in pages 236-240 cites Hebrew expressions that confirm the same notion in ancient Israel.

77   J. Z. Smith, To Take Place (Chicago: University of Chicago Press, 1992), 47-73.

78   Van Seters, The Chronicler's Account, see above, note 71.

found in the I Kings description, but which the Chronicler has supplied from the tabernacle description in Exodus.[79] As Van Seters has shown in his study of the temple description, and P. Ackroyd earlier exhibited in his study of the temple vessels,[80] the Chronicler's work is an example of the creative reformulation of received materials which provides a cultic continuity with Israel's distant past. The Chronicler is viewed as an author who created an image of Israel's past shaped by his own perspective, bringing the Deuteronomistic history in line with the Priestly material.

The current study will represent the third element in the application of evidence to the temple descriptions. It will treat the description of Solomon's temple in I Kings 6-8 as a verbal icon created by the Deuteronomistic historian. The description is one element in a longer national history constructed by the historian. The national history provides a national identity for a people in exile. Van Seters has already highlighted the innovative nature of the development of a national narrative history like that found in the Deuteronomistic History. This study will show that the historian's innovative literary approach is even more profound. The Deuteronomistic Historian embedded a verbal icon within his national history in the form of the description of the temple built by Solomon. The icon embodies the historian's own ideology regarding proper religious practice and relationship between humanity and the deity. There is no value in recreating the appearance of the structure as a historical presentation of the temple since it is the creation of the historian, and in many respects is influenced by the architectural forms he and the rest of the nation met in exile. These forms are used by the historian to present what was a truly innovative concept of divine presence and to fuel a religious reform that sought to reshape Israel's basic notions about YHWH.

This study will show how the temple description incorporates royal and divine emblems known in the ancient near east without any apparent conflict with the so-called aniconic tradition of Israel. Furthermore, the dedicatory prayer of I Kings 8, a composition of the

---

79   Van Seters, The Chronicler's Account, 292-293.
80   P. R. Ackroyd, The Temple Vessels: A Continuity Theme, VTSup 23
      (Leiden: E. J. Brill, 1972), 166-181.

historian that is attributed to Solomon, gives the temple a central role as the national sanctuary, even though this type of centralized worship was quite probably an innovation that developed much later in the nation's history (see II Kings 23:23). Even while identifying the temple as a central sanctuary, the historian offers a novel explanation of its function in that central role.

This approach to the temple moves away from traditional attempts at reconstructing physical evidence for such a building. By approaching the text through literary criticism and the application of built environment analysis, it will become evident that the Deuteronomistic historian crafted a literary icon that is not directly related to an actual Solomonic structure for its form or decoration. Like the work of Ezekiel and the Chronicler, this temple description is a literary image created for the exilic community.

Conclusion

The palace built by Sennacherib in Nineveh at the beginning of his reign was the product of a traditional royal act. Each Assyrian king began his reign by building a palace in which to live and carry out imperial business. Through the work of art historians, appreciation of Assyrian culture has moved from mere textuality toward recognition of their mastery of the use of images and decorative programs to communicate nonverbally. It is clear from the studies of Frankfort, Winter and Russell that Assyrian palaces were an element of royal rhetoric in which the administrations defined the reign of particular kings using texts and relief images. This in itself is a significant development toward the understanding of Assyrian culture and society.

There is, however, an adherence to the textual metaphor as an interpretive key to the palace which fails to recognize the distinctions to be made between architecture and textuality. The contribution of the current study emphasizes that the palace is yet a built environment, and as such it possesses elements that are quite distinct from a text. Architectural theories and methods developed by Rapoport and others to study the built environment and its role in social structure and activity provide an interpretive method that is not bound to the textual metaphor. By concentrating on the issues surrounding the fixed, semi-fixed and non-fixed architectural features and their significance as outlined above, the existence of the palace as a significant built environment in the ancient world remains the primary focus. The architectural innovations of Sennacherib can then be seen as evidence of ideological innovations that characterize his reign.

In regard to the temple of Solomon in Jerusalem, this study is based upon the literary development of biblical material as well as upon historiography in the ancient world, both areas of study which have matured in the last twenty years. It challenges the standard methods of biblical studies *per se* insofar as it is able to establish the literary description of the temple as an icon created during the exile of the sixth century B.C.E. The temple description is an element in the formation of a religious reform in exilic Israel. Earlier sources for the document cannot be retrieved after so long a loss. Reconstructive essays which attempt to explain the developmental process through which information contained in royal or temple records was consulted in order to provide an accurate description of the temple are not historical evidence for ancient record keeping and accuracy. Without more evidence for source materials, these attempts do not further knowledge of the appearance or existence of the ancient structure, much less increase confidence in the material as historically accurate documentation of the structure. Yet the temple became a focal point of national identity for the Israelites; a national identity shaped through the literary presentation of their national history. The temple description is a verbal icon for which there is no physical evidence: the text *is* the icon.

Juxtaposing the palace of Sennacherib, for which there is substantial physical evidence, and the temple of Solomon, for which there is no physical evidence, highlights the broader question of this study. I regard the physical built environment and the literary built environment as two facets of the same human phenomenon. As Markus, Blanton, and Rapoport have indicated, the built environment influences social behavior and has an effect on the structure of social interaction. Sennacherib's palace is the embodiment of status and power distinctions within Assyrian society.

The description of Solomon's building activity and the temple which resulted from that activity is a literary embodiment of the status and power of Solomon as an early great king in Israel in the days of the United Monarchy. It functions within the national narrative composed by the historian as a verbal icon of the proper religious conceptions regarding the presence of the deity among the people of Israel. As such it must take its place within the context of the theological debates that developed in the aftermath of the destruction of Jerusalem. It is no longer useful as a historical source for the appearance of Solomon's temple, but rather an icon for religious contemplation regarding the presence of YHWH.

Chapter 2

Sennacherib's Palace in Nineveh

Therein I had them build a palace of ivory, ebony, boxwood, *musukannu-*wood, cedar, cypress, and spruce, the "Palace without Rival," for my royal abode.

-Annals of Sennacherib

The palace is a monument to power, to wealth, to taste, to ability, to a refined way of living. As a whole, it is a monument to its owner's glory, his self-acquired glory.

-Paul Frankl, *Principles of Architectural History*

The palace of Sennacherib was excavated by A. H. Layard in the middle of the nineteenth century. In the intervening years the palace has remained a center of attention for western scholars. Sennacherib's palace is an extensively excavated Neo-Assyrian structure that provides evidence that Sennacherib was the most innovative builder among the Neo-Assyrian kings. As indicated in the preceding chapter, the most recent approaches to the palace come from art historians interested in how the bas-reliefs that adorned the walls and doorways of the palace were part of the royal rhetoric that defined the significance of the king's reign. Irene Winter explains Mesopotamian palaces as rhetorical devices for royal propaganda.[1] John Malcolm Russell follows her general methodology but focuses specifically on the palace of Sennacherib in Nineveh, showing how the reliefs and the wall inscriptions in the palace identify this king as one who controlled the periphery of his realm while beautifying the center.[2]

---

1   I. J. Winter, Royal Rhetoric and the Development of Historical Narrative in Neo-Assyrian Reliefs, Studies in Visual Communication 7, 2 (1981): 2-38.

2   John Malcolm Russell, Sennacherib's Palace without Rival at Nineveh (Chicago: University of Chicago Press, 1991).

This chapter approaches the palace using the methods developed by built environment studies with two goals in mind. The first is to demonstrate that the theories of built environment analysis, developed in studies of Renaissance and modern building types, are applicable to ancient structures for which there is sufficient evidence. The second goal is to propose a new understanding of the significance of Sennacherib's palace that reinforces to his unique position among Neo-Assyrian kings. Built environment analysis recognizes the use of spatial arrangement and decorative elements to communicate information to the users of a particular domain. The application of this method of study to the palace reveals a new level of communication in Sennacherib's construction project and demonstrates how the king's innovative architectural forms are indicative of his innovative notions of his status in Assyrian society.

Thomas Markus' discussion of the study of building types offers the most structured method for approach to built environments.[3] He explains that the interpreter needs information beyond the physical appearance of the building. Through studying the texts associated with the planning of the structure, as well as the plans, Markus demonstrates that the textual information contains useful evidence of the intent of the planners, and thus for the significance of the structure. Secondly, Markus studies the building itself, its layout and decorative elements, explaining that spatial arrangement of structures is significant for understanding which persons had access to what areas. The ways that segments of society are allowed or denied entry into specific areas are indicative of social structure and are physical maps of power and status within society. The third element in Markus' method is the users of the structure. Where possible, the users and their impressions and thoughts concerning the structure and its meaning were evidence for the perception of the building within the society that was using it.

This study approaches Sennacherib's palace first through the documents which mention and describe its construction. These provide evidence for royal intent behind palace construction as well

---

3   Thomas Markus, Buildings and Power; Freedom and Control in the Origins of Modern Building Types (London and New York: Routledge, 1993).

as describe the construction itself. To keep the task manageable, only representative texts from Sennacherib's reign are chosen.[4] Documents from early in the construction of the palace, as well as midway and at the conclusion of construction, provide an image of the development of the project. The later documents contain statements of the king's assessment of his accomplishment once the palace was completed. The evidence from the texts tells more about the meaning of the palace as an element in the royal rhetoric of Sennacherib's reign than about its appearance. These documents demonstrate how the description of construction is used as a literary device to identify the status of the king and to elucidate his power as the ruler of the Neo-Assyrian Empire.

The second category of evidence is the building itself. Although a vast number of excavated areas are available, two sections of the palace will be specifically addressed. This will limit the study to information that is manageable within the scope of this work, while also highlighting specific unique elements of Sennacherib's palace. The first area is Courtyard VI. This large open area within the palace is a connecting area between suites of rooms. The walls were lined with wall reliefs that depict the manufacture of one of the most significant elements found in Sennacherib's palace, the human headed winged bull (^{d}aladlammû). A study of this area shows how Sennacherib uses the spatial arrangement of the courtyard and the reliefs that line its walls to create a domain within the palace that extolls his skill as a builder.

The second area is the suite of rooms that focused on Room XXXVI. Room XXXVI is the so-called Lachish Room, due to the reliefs that lined its walls which depict the battle for Lachish. This room stands at the center of a very interesting spatial arrangement not found anywhere else in Neo-Assyrian palaces. Moreover, the relief program of the room itself exhibits an interesting demand on the viewer, which has yet to be elucidated, even though the room itself has received the attentions of many scholars in the past. The unique nature of this room is fully appreciated only when the built environment method is applied.

---

4   See the text discussion below, p.48ff., for a description of the specific
     documents consulted in this study.

The palace of Sennacherib at Nineveh provides an excellent case with which to test the proficiency of built environment theories on an ancient structure. Excavations since the middle of the eighteenth century provide ample physical evidence for the appearance and arrangement of the palace walls. These same excavations furnish the documentation that exists concerning the royal administration's planning, construction, and assessment of the completed task. The one element lacking is the testimony of the users of the palace. There is no evidence at all for the types of people who would have seen many of the architectural forms to be discussed. Russell offers a speculative discussion about who might have been invited into these chambers.[5] He presents possible viewers in the ranks of royal family, the palace staff, and foreign dignitaries or representatives of conquered peoples. Without royal documentation that lists palace visitors, or other personal or official reflections upon what these people thought about the palace and its king, it is impossible to reconstruct the significance of the palace for other levels of Assyrian society. In this chapter the discussion is limited to what the evidence will support. It will be necessary to limit the statements concerning the meaning and significance of the palace to the royal documents cited above. While this is a one-sided view, it is nonetheless the view that exists of the Neo-Assyrian empire, regardless of what specific issues one studies. All extant documentation comes from the administrative levels of society and is evidence only for the official views of the administration.

The Texts

The textual evidence for Sennacherib's palace is found in the royal annals that recount the yearly military campaigns of the king to expand the boundaries of his realm or to solidify his control over restless hinterlands. Yearly editions were composed describing the past year's conquests and concluded with an account of construction projects carried out by the king and funded by the spoils of his

---

5   Russell, Sennacherib's Palace, 223ff.

military conquest. The annals were inscribed on cylinders and prisms, yet portions often became part of a standard inscription found on the walls or at the thresholds of the palace.

The datable annalistic documents for the reign of Sennacherib which mention palace construction span the period from *circa* 702 to 689 B.C.E.[6] The following discussion cannot possibly treat all the documents from Sennacherib's reign, but will limit itself to representative texts composed during the construction of the palace. The earliest inscription, BM113203, and an inscription from 694 B.C.E., BM103000, provide the most detail concerning the palace construction. Because the first was produced very early in Sennacherib's reign, and is the first which discusses palace construction, it provides the beginning point for the textual evidence. BM103000 was composed near the conclusion of palace construction and provides details of subsequent building activity on the palace. Of the texts from the intervening years, the Bellino Cylinder and the Rassam Cylinder recount site preparation, but give no real information concerning construction.[7] It is important to note these inscriptions because they refer to the palace, but since they offer no new information, these two documents will figure only briefly in the following discussion. Two other intervening texts, K1674+ and BM103214+, dated 697 and 695 B.C.E. respectively,

---

6   Specifically, the earliest is BM113203, an inscription dated "at the beginning of my reign," which gives an account only of the first campaign; the BellinoCylinder, dated 702 B.C.E., which contains information on the first two campaigns; the Rassam Cylinder, dated 700 B.C.E., which contains information on three campaigns; BM103000, dated 694 B.C.E., which gives information on five campaigns; the Taylor Prism, dated 691 B.C.E. and the Oriental Institute Prism, dated 689 B.C.E., both of which contain information on eight campaigns. While these are the only datable texts, there are several which give information on the intervening numbers of campaigns, but do not include a dating formula. Initial publication information for all of these may be found in D. D. Luckenbill, The Annals of Sennacherib, OIP II (Chicago: The University of Chicago Press, 1924), 20-21, or in Eckart Frahm's more recent Einleitung in die Sanherib-Inschriften, AfO 26 (1997).

7   They simply state, "Therein I had them build a palace of ivory, ebony, boxwood, *musukkanu*-wood, cedar, cypress, and spruce, the 'Palace without Rival,' for my royal abode."

provide new information concerning the wall reliefs and will supplement the discussion of the two primary documents.[8] Two other texts, undated building inscriptions, will provide information on the significance of particular raw materials used in the construction.[9] Finally, the Oriental Institute Prism refers to the completed palace. This document, dated to 689 B.C.E., contains a building report of the armory (*bīt kutalli*), but begins with the phrase, "At that time, after I completed the palace in the midst of Nineveh for my royal dwelling. . ." While it offers no details about palace construction, it does make general reference to the style and beauty of the palace and will be consulted as evidence of Sennacherib's own assessment of his accomplishment regarding the palace.

The primary texts for this study, BM103000 and BM113203, are arranged synoptically here in order to exhibit their similarities and differences. The categories will also provide the structure for the subsequent discussion. An overview reveals that while the later document, BM103000, contains much of the same information found in BM113203, it includes more detail about the construction of the palace and incorporates information not found in the earlier document. The palace construction was ongoing between the composition of the two documents and the later document incorporates activities and details which had not been accomplished when the first document was composed. It is interesting to note when the two documents do treat the same issue or construction element, they are virtually identical, an indication of the standardization common to Neo-Assyrian inscriptions. At the same time, the later document was freely expanded to incorporate more information as the palace construction continued.

BM113203 (702 B.C.E.)   **BM103000** (694 B.C.E.)

1. Choosing the site   1. Choosing the site

---

8   These are T10 and T11 in E. Frahm, Einleitung in die Sanherib-
     Inschriften, 66-70. The primary document numbers are those used here,
     though the full documents include several joins which Frahm has
     explained in his study.
9   Luckenbill, Annals, I9 and I13, quoted below, p. 59.

2. Description of labor force	2. Description of labor force [Interruption detailing the quarrying and transporting of the ^{d}aladlammu]
3. Preparation of the site -tearing down the former palace -changing the course of the Tebiltu -heaping up a foundation terrace -reinforcing the terrace	3. Preparation of site -tearing down the former palace -changing the course of the Tebiltu -heaping up a foundation terrace -reinforcing the terrace

4. Construction of the palace
  -materials
  -doors
  -portico
 	
-lion doorway supports
	4. Construction of the palace
	  -materials
	  -portals instead of doors
	  -arrangement of chambers and corridors within the space inside the building
	  -female colossi
	  -painting the roofing timbers
	  -adornment of walls with burnt bricks and lapis lazuli
	  -alabaster and limestone revealed by the gods for use in the palace
	  -bull and cow colossi carved in Balatai and brought into the palace

-orthostats brought in and carved	-orthostats brought in and carved
	5. Contrast of Sennacherib's abilities in working bronze with those of his predecessors
	6. Columns set up in rooms of the palace
5. Creation of the Park	7. Creation of the Park

Besides the textual outline of similarities and differences as noted above, it is also important to address the rhetorical function of the inscriptions. The inscriptions provide no clear image of the appearance of the building, so their function is obviously not an

accurate description of the building. This study presupposes that the
information contained in the building reports is influenced by their
rhetorical function. For example, one can find building reports with
no mention of the labor force, the special acquisition of rare
materials, or the details of wall sculpture. Therefore, a building
report that contains any or all of these elements does so not because
the genre requires it, but because the genre is being used to make a
specific statement. These subjects are all contained in Sennacherib's
building reports to be discussed below and are rhetorically significant
because they define and characterize his achievements in a particular
way.

The following discussion shows that the documentation for
Sennacherib's reign, particularly the annals that contain building
reports, serve several functions for the modern scholar. One function
is their position in the royal rhetoric of the Neo-Assyrian empire.
They offer accounts of the achievements of the king which express
the attributes the king desires to be associated with his reign. They
are the pathway to the characteristics associated with kingship in the
ancient world. One way the modern scholar can understand what a
Neo-Assyrian emperor is in the ancient society is through the
attributes expressed in the achievements the documents record. The
royal administration is concerned to communicate that Sennacherib
built a particular building, as well as to communicate that he was a
builder. This emperor of Assyria is a world shaper, a creator, and his
documents identify him as such.

Choosing the Site

Sennacherib chose the ancient city of Nineveh for his royal
capital. In BM113203 and BM103000 he describes the city as

> . . .the noble metropolis, the city beloved by Ishtar, where are all the
> meeting places of the gods and goddesses; the everlasting substructure, the
> eternal foundation; whose plan was designed from of old and whose
> structure was made beautiful with the firmament of heaven; the beautiful
> place, the abode of law into which had been brought all kinds of artistic
> workmanship, every secret and pleasant thing; where from of old the kings
> who went before, my fathers, exercised lordship over Assyria before me

and ruled the subjects of Enlil, and yearly without interruption, received
there an unceasing income, the tribute of the princes of the four quarters.[10]

The choice of Nineveh as the site for his royal abode is an
intentional move of the Assyrian capital to a new city. When
Sennacherib's father, Sargon II (721-705 B.C.E.), built a new city in
the north and moved his capital there from Kalhu, he used creation
rhetoric to describe his actions. Inscriptions on the back of his wall
relief slabs read:

> In my all embracing wisdom and the fertile planting of my brain, which
> thinking Ea and Bēlit-ilāni had made to surpass that of the kings, my
> fathers, following the prompting of my heart, I built a city at the foot of
> Mount Musri, in the plain of Nineveh, and named it Dūr-Sharrukîn.[11]

Sargon identifies the act as the product of the wisdom that the gods
Ea and Belit-ilani, two deities associated with creation of humanity,
had provided him. Moreover, the rest of the text gives the distinct
impression that he builds this city where there were no people, since
he inhabits his new capital with conquered people from throughout
his realm.[12]

When Assurnasirpal II (883-859 B.C.E.) moved his capital from
Assur to Kalhu, he claimed only to have rebuilt a city that had been
built by Shalmaneser, his predecessor.[13] When Tukulti-Ninurta I
built the suburb of Assur that he called Kar Tukulti-Ninurta, he did
so upon the instruction of the god Assur.[14] Sargon II identifies his
building of a new capital as an act of creation of something entirely
new, his later mentioning of Magganubba notwithstanding.
Sennacherib returns the capital to an ancient city, but recreates it in

---

10   Luckenbill, Annals, 94; see also 103.
11   D. D. Luckenbill, ARAB II, §105.
12   Ibid. One must contrast with this presentation, however, that of ARAB,
      II §§119-120, in which the king apparently admits that, in fact, there was
      a town already at the foot of Mount Musri and that he bought the land
      from the people who were already in the territory before he built his new
      capital city. Still the building report invokes the names of the deities of
      the creation stories and identifies the king as creating a new thing.
13   ARAB I §§ 492, 511, et. al.
14   ARAB I §167.

a magnificent style. Building a new city and moving the capital may be understood as one way Sargon and his son establish their own identity, express their ability to create, and make a lasting name for themselves.[15] By choosing Nineveh, Sennacherib identifies himself with the ancient traditions associated with that city. The description of Nineveh shows an awareness of the position the city held in the history of Assyria. Sennacherib establishes a continuity with that ancient past and identifies his kingship as part of the fabric of the world established at creation. The use of creation imagery and language in his building inscriptions is the introductory step to Sennacherib's identification of himself as a creator.

The second part of the description of Nineveh identifies it as beautiful and a place where there were all kinds of artistic workmanship. Yet Sennacherib lists five ways his predecessors had neglected the city: they allowed the palace site to remain too small, streets were not laid out, squares were too narrow, canals were not dug and trees were not planted.[16] In each of these Sennacherib corrects the omissions of the former kings and makes Nineveh a metropolis. His improvements are so extensive that he virtually builds a new city for his royal capital. The rhetorical devices are interdependent. Nineveh is a city steeped in ancient traditions and moving his capital there associates his reign with those traditions. Nineveh is known as a large and beautiful city, yet the greatness of Nineveh is actually a product of Sennacherib's reign. He molds an ancient cult center into his own metropolitan capital city, the center and embodiment of his empire.

---

15 These same concerns may be discerned in a text from the second millennium which recounts the goals of Yakhdun-Lim, King of Mari. See J. M. Sasson, Mari Historiography and the Yakhdun-Lim Disc Inscription, Lingering over Words: Studies in Ancient Near Eastern Literature in Honor of William H. Moran Harvard Semitic Studies 37, ed. T. Abusch, J. Huehnergard, and P. Steinkeller (Atlanta: Scholars Press, 1990), 446-447.

16 Luckenbill, Annals, 95: 68-70.

Description of Labor Force

Both documents give a brief list of the different peoples that Sennacherib had conquered and incorporated into his labor force. The lists are identical except that the later document includes the peoples of Philistia and Tyre, who had been captured in a later campaign to the west. This segment of the building reports provide a direct point of contact with the accounts of military campaigns that precede them. Here one reads what became of all the people the Assyrians took captive after defeating their cities.

This section provides no information on the king's intent for his palace, but offers strong rhetoric for the reign of Sennacherib. It is a testimony to his military prowess, and the extent of his political power, that this king was able to muster and control a vast labor force made up of so many different peoples. Naturally, the list expanded in subsequent editions as more people were conquered. The significance is clear. Sennacherib needed an immense labor force to accomplish his building programs, and he was able to maintain such a corvée because of the extent of his military prowess.

In the earlier document, the narrative moves from the description of the labor force to a description how the Tebiltu River had destroyed part of the foundation platform of the former palace. BM103000 (the latter text), however, has a fourteen line interruption of the narrative which describes the quarrying and transportation of bull colossi in Tastiate, on the other side of the Tigris. This interruption is significant because it incorporates a detailed description of the labor involved in the transporting of the colossi across the Tigris during the spring floods. It refers to the former palace, which was built by previous kings and whose site had become too small. Though the former kings had not made the palace beautiful, the text shows that they had worked hard on its construction. As Sennacherib describes it:

ba-hu-la-te-šu-un ú-ša-ni-hu ú-lam-me-nu ka-ras-si-in i-na da-na-ni ù šup-šú-qi mar-ṣi-iš ú-bi-lu-nim-ma ú-ša-aṣ-bi-tu KÁ.MEŠ-*ši-in*

> They [the former kings] made their crews strain and injure their bodies, but by might and main with difficulty they brought them and placed them by their doors.[17]

Then the document returns to the damage the Tebiltu River had done to the palace foundation platform using language very similar to the earlier document. These fourteen lines serve two functions. They allow Sennacherib to mention the bull colossi that figure so prominently in his own palace after describing the extent of his military and political control in his realm through his list of conquered peoples in his labor force.

Preparation of the Site

The preparation of the site of the new palace was a necessary first step in palace construction. The palace of the former kings had been allowed to fall into disrepair and the Tebiltu River had undermined its foundation platform. Sennacherib's work begins with the complete destruction of the former palace and addressing the threat of the Tebiltu River. Only after this was completed could he rebuild. BM113203 merely indicates that he "improved its course and made its outflow run properly."[18] BM103000 is more specific. It quotes the king, ". . .I diverted its course from the midst of the city and into the plain behind the city."[19] A bull inscription in one of the grand entrances to Sennacherib's throne room describes the work on the Tebiltu in this manner, "I changed its course, I made its outflow run properly in its low water channels."[20]

These three documents describe the work on the Tebiltu in ascending specificity. The first is general, indicating merely that the flow was corrected. The second document informs the reader to what area the water was directed. It is only the third document, and

---

17   Luckenbill, Annals, 105: 74-78.
18   Luckenbill, Annals, 96: 75
19   Luckenbill, Annals, 105: 87.
20   Luckenbill, Annals, 118: 15. Luckenbill lists this as an undated inscription, but Frahm, Einleitung, 118, proposes a date after 694 B.C.E. based upon the information it contains.

the latest according to Frahm, that describes the work within the context of the problem the Tebiltu presented. All documents describe the Tebiltu as "a raging stream."[21] BM103000 and the bull inscription, both dated to 694 B.C.E. or just after, mention that the destruction caused by the Tebiltu was because of its "great floods at high water worked havoc with its foundation and destroyed its platform."[22] It is only the bull inscription which describes the work on the Tebiltu as correcting its flow so that it remained within the low water channels and ceased from flowing against the palace walls and foundation.

Once the Tebiltu has been brought under his control, Sennacherib builds a foundation platform for his palace. He raises it higher than it had been before and reinforces its sides with slabs of limestone to guard against future erosion.[23] This description of his foundation platform, higher than all others, is a testament to Sennacherib's status as a king above all others. To prepare the site for his palace, Sennacherib changes the course of a river by gaining control of its water flow. Then he raises up a terrace of dry ground from the dry bed. He manipulates the topography of the site in order to accommodate his royal palace. The creation overtones in this passage are obvious as it describes the formation of a palace site

---

21   *a-gu-ú šit-mu-ru*; the Bellino cylinder, not under discussion here, refers to
      it as "a ragingly destructive stream," *a-gu-ú šam-ru-ú šit-mu-ru*, and
      indicates that it had destroyed royal mausoleums in addition to the
      destruction it caused to the palace. Luckenbill, Annals, 99: 46.

22   See Luckenbill, Annals, 105: 82-83 and 118: 14.

23   BM113203 gives the height as 170 *tipku*, while BM103000 gives 190
      tipku. The Bellino cylinder reports a height of 160 *tipku* which is later
      raised to 180 *tipku*. This raises the question of the differing quantifications
      throughout the palace description since overall measurements do not
      match from document to document. Russell, Sennacherib's Palace, 78-88
      has offered his estimation of the overall palace size based upon his own
      survey of the site. His concludes that the differing quantifications are
      attributable to the fact that the palace construction was ongoing and that
      subsequent documents gave the current measurements. This is also the
      conclusion of M. De Odorico, The Use of Numbers and Quantifications
      in the Assyrian Royal Inscriptions, SAAS III (Helsinki: Neo-Assyrian
      Text Corpus Project, 1995), 70.

where there had not originally been room. Sennacherib could shape the world to fit his will.[24]

Construction of the Palace

There are more noticeable differences between the two primary documents in their description of palace construction. In most cases, the differences can be attributed to the later document's inclusion of information of progress made in the intervening years. The description offered by BM103000 is far more extensive than BM113203 and it provides much more detail when describing activities merely mentioned in the earlier document.

Both refer to the materials used in palace construction. BM113203 lists ivory, ebony, boxwood, *musukkanu*-wood, cedar, cypress, and spruce. BM103000 adds to this list the finishing and decorative materials such as gold, silver, copper, carnelian, breccia, alabaster, *elammaku*-wood, *sindû*-wood, marble, lapis lazuli and other semi-precious stones. The uncommon nature of these materials is expressed in several ways. Of alabaster the reader is told:

ša NA₄-*parûtu ša i-na tar-ṣi* LUGAL.MEŠ-*ni* AD.MEŠ-*ia a-na kar-ri nam-ṣa-ri šú-qu-ru i-na sa-pan* KUR *am-ma-na-na ú-šap-tu-ni pa-ni-šu*

> Alabaster which in the days of the kings, my fathers, was precious enough for (inlaying) the hilt of a sword, they [Assur and Ishtar] revealed to me in the interior of Mount Ammanana.[25]

An inscription from the period between 697 and 694 B.C.E. tells of another precious stone.

É.GAL ᵐᵈ30-PAP.MEŠ-SU MAN GAL MAN *dan-nu* MAN SÚ MAN KUR *aš+šur* NA₄.ᵈŠE.TIR *ša* GIN₇ *še-im ṣa-ah-ha-ri ši-kin-šú nu-us-su-qu ša i-na tar-ṣi* LUGAL.MEŠ AD.MEŠ-*ia ma-la* NA₄ GÚ *šu-qu-ru i-na* GÌR KUR *ni-pur* KUR-*i ra-ma-nu-uš ud-dan-ni*

---

24   The literary motif of building a city or structure because the king himself
       desired to do so is quite old in the Ancient Near East. See, for example,
       J. M. Sasson, Mari Historiography, 446.
25   BM103000, Luckenbill, Annals, 107: 54-56.

a-na ^fAB.ZA.ZA-*a-ti ú-še-piš-ma ú-šal-di-da qé-reb* URU *ni-na-a*

Palace of Sennacherib, the great king, the mighty king, king of the universe, king of Assyria. NA$_4$.^dŠE.TIR whose splendid surface (made it seem) as if (it were) of kernels of *sahhar*-grain, which in the time of the kings, my fathers, was solely valued for necklaces, made its appearance at the foot of Nipur mountain, I had female colossi made of it and transported into Nineveh.[26]

And finally, another building inscription describes the basalt seats for palace door posts:

NA$_4$-*ka-šur-ru-u a-qa-ra ša* KUR-*šu ru-u-qu ú-ra-am-ma* DIŠ SIG *ṣir-ri* GIŠ.IG.MEŠ KÁ.MEŠ É.GAL-*ia ú-kin*

. . .costly basalt, whose land (mountain) is distant, I brought and placed it under the door-posts of the gates of my palace.[27]

The valuable nature of these materials is indicated by their use in jewelry, by their discovery only with the help of the gods, or by the fact that they had to be brought from a great distance by immense expenditure of labor. The difficulty of acquiring the materials naturally adds to their value, but it also indicates the status and power of the king. Only Sennacherib is in the position to receive such secret knowledge from the gods who favor his reign. Furthermore, only Sennacherib has the military might and capability to control vast territories where natural resources not found within Assyria itself can be garnered for use in his palace. He is able to construct his Palace without Rival because he is the unequaled king of the world who controls all the resources within his reach.

---

26 This is Luckenbill, Annals, 127: I9; Russell, Sennacherib's Palace, Appendix I, 276 provides a new transliteration and translation of this text, followed here. Russell, 90, opts for the later dating while Frahm, Einleitung, 140-141, proposes the earlier dating right after the campaign to Mt. Nipur in 697. The name of the stone itself is made up of signs that designate the grain god Ashnan = ^dŠE.TIR (EZINU) identifying it as a divine substance.

27 Luckenbill, Annals, 127: I13, 3-6; see also Frahm, Einleitung, 141.

    Sennacherib adds to the incomparable nature of his palace in the way he uses the materials he gathers from throughout his realm. As the above quotes indicate, he selects stone that had previously been used only for inlay and jewelry and creates massive sculptures from it. Stone whose rarity had made it valuable for small scale adornment is discovered in abundance with the help of Assur and Ishtar and is used by this king for large scale decoration of his palace. The site becomes the Palace without Rival in part through the way Sennacherib incorporates jewel stone and semi-precious materials into its construction.[28]

    The actual construction of the palace described in the texts follows a peculiar order. BM113203 begins with the ceiling beams of cedar from Mount Amanus, then describes the doors. Considerable space is devoted to the description of the adornments for the palace entrances. Large pillars resting on lion colossi supported the doors. Mountain sheep as protective figures decorated the doorways. Then the text describes the wall reliefs.

> *as-qup-pat*NA₄ *pi-i-li rab-ba-a-ti da-ád-me na-ki-ri ki-šit-ti* ŠU-*ia*
> *ki-rib-ši-in is-si-qa a-sur-ru-ši-in ú-ša-as-hi-ra a-na tab-ra-a-ti*
> *ú-ša-lik*

> I engraved great slabs of limestone with the dwelling places of the enemy, the capture of my hands, I set them around its (the palace's) ground floor walls, I made them objects of astonishment.[29]

---

28   Another, more elaborate, example of the choice of materials having more than decorative qualities has been proposed by J. M. Russell, Sennacherib's Palace Revisited: Excavations at Nineveh and in the British Museum Archives, Assyria 1995, ed. S. Parpola and R. M. Whiting, (Helsinki, 1997), 295-306. Russell offers a new translation of a document concerned with the *bīt nakkapti* built by Sennacherib in Nineveh. The document refers to the use of breccia, a stone described as "effective for assuaging throbbing in the temple and which as a charm stone brings joy of heart and happiness of mind." The word for temple (on the side of the head) in Akkadian is *nakkaptu*, so the building is explained by Russell as a space inside which one might have found protection against a certain type of headache by virtue of the materials used in its construction.

29   Luckenbill, Annals, 97: 86 translated this passage " the enemy tribes, whom my hands captured, dragged (the limestone slabs) between them

The texts shows no interest in following the order of construction, making the rhetorical function more important. Most of the description is concerned with the adornment of the doorways. The figures that flanked Sennacherib's palace doorways were indeed one element that made his palace unique, and they will occupy much of the following discussion concerning the building. Sennacherib's texts that mention these figures contain a literary innovation. The sign KAL has the two readings $ALAD_2$ and $LAMA_2$, which normally have the Akkadian meaning *šēdu* and *lamassu*, respectively. These are combined to produce a unique Akkadian word, ^{d}*aladlammû*.[30] This term, which is used as a specific reference to the human headed winged bulls, is abandoned by his successors for the terms used by Sennacherib's predecessors. This literary modification, the creation of a new word for these figures, combined with the unique use of these ^{d}*aladlammû* at significant passages throughout the palace indicate their importance in Sennacherib's literary and visual presentation of his reign. The ^{d}*aladlammû*, whether with regard to their protective strength or with regard to their ever watchfulness, characterized the reign of Sennacherib like no other decorative element.

(the doors)" deriving the verb *is-si-ha* from *nasāhu*, "to pull," even though this verb is u/a (*issuh*). Translating the same passage in K1674+, Frahm, Einleitung, 82, follows the proposals of von Soden, AHw, 249a, and Russell, Sennacherib's Palace, 299 n.18, and reads the verb as being *esēqu*, "to engrave on stone," even though he notes problems with both of their proposals in his comments on BM113202: 86, Einleitung, 45.

30 CAD, A/1 s.v. *aladlammû*, explains that the innovation uses KALxBAD to write ALAD. This sign is designated $ALAD_3$ in Labat's Manuel d'épigraphie akkadienne, 147:323. For $ALAD_3$ the BAD sign is infixed between the second and third vertical strokes of the KAL sign. This new sign is combined with the KAL sign for the new reading, ($^dALAD_3$-$^dLAMA_2$). KAL also has the reading *danānu*, "be strong," while BAD might also be read *bēlu*, "to be lord or ruler." These are states represented by the cuneiform signs and may express the abstractions that lie behind the concept of protection.

BM103000 describes the palace construction following a different order from BM113203. Beginning with portals [31] opposite the doorways to the palace, the document describes the roofing beams of cedar and cypress which were brought from Mount Amanus and used in these portico areas. Afterward, doors of cedar, cypress, pine and *sindû*-wood were built and plated with silver and copper. Once the doors were completed, BM103000 states that doorways were erected for the doors. The inner space of the structure is addressed only after the entryways were completed.

Interestingly, the work on the palace began outside the structure, on the portals that presumably led to some sort of entry courtyard. Then the doorways were made for the doors. The doorways appear to have been part of the construction of the exterior walls of the palace and are treated as an outside element. Their appearance at this point may be for a different reason, however. It could very well be that the doorways and doors are described first because these were the passages into the palace, as if the entries had to be described before the rest of the structure could be explained.

Doorways throughout the palace were adorned with different protective images. The female colossi (^{d}*šēdātu*) are described as "clothed in strength and vigor, full of splendor," and were made from alabaster and ivory.[32] There were also ^{d}*aladlammû* made from one large slab of white limestone quarried in Balatai. In addition to these, BM103000 mentions ^{f}*apsasātu*, which were representations of some sort of animal as doorway guardians.[33] These were made of

---

31   The Akkadian, *bīt mutirrite* means "house of double doors" and refers possibly to a double doorway with an ante-chamber of some sort. These are described as patterned after a Hittite style palace, so they are a western architectural form which Sennacherib incorporated into his palace comparable to the *bīt hilāni*.

32   The Akkadian is the same signs as the *šēdu*, but prefixed by the feminine determinative: MÍ.DINGIR.ALAD$_2$.MEŠ

33   Written MÍ.ÁB.ZA.ZA, these were first identified as a "wild cow," understanding the ÁB syllable as a determinative meaning "bovine," and rendering the word as *zazatu*. CAD A/2 allows for the colossus to be some other animal, possibly a sphinx, and indicates that the earliest reference to these figures as palace fixtures occurs in the texts of Sennacherib. J. M. Russell, *Sennacherib's Palace*, 99, states that these were the female sphinxes in the form of winged lions described by A. H. Layard,

both alabaster and white limestone from Balatai. Bronze lions, open at the knees were cast and placed at doorways to support large columns made of cedar and overlaid with bronze and lead. In all, BM103000 gives a total of twelve lions, twelve ᵈ*aladlammû*, and twenty two ᶠ*apsasātu* stationed at the palace entrances.

These figures again present Sennacherib the opportunity to distinguish himself from his predecessors. The white limestone from Balatai used for the ᵈ*aladlammû* and the ᶠ*apsasātu* was discovered with the aid of the god and was brought to adorn the palace only by the expenditure of a great deal of labor. It is his description of his bronze works, however, where Sennacherib truly set himself apart. After describing the difficulty that had always attended the casting of bronzed images, he boasted,

> *ia-a-ti* ᵐᵈ30-PAP.MEŠ-SU *a-ša-rid kal mal-ki mu-di-e šip-ri ka-la-ma dim-me* URUDU GAL.MEŠ *ur-mah-hi pi-tan bir-ki šá ma-nam-ma la ip-ti-qu* LUGAL *pa-ni mah-ri-ia i-na uz-ni ni-kil-ti šá ú-šat-li-ma ru-bu-ú* NIN.IGI.KUG *i-na ši-tul-ti ram-ni-ia a-na e-piš šip-ri šú-a-tu ra-biš am-tal-lik-ma i-na me-lik te-me-ia ù me-riš ka-bit-ti-ia pi-ti-iq* URUDU *ú-ba-aš-šim-ma ú-nak-ki-la nik-la-su*

> But I, Sennacherib, first among all princes, wise in all craftsmanship, great pillars of bronze, swift lions, which no king before my time had fashioned, through the clever understanding which the noble Ea had given me, and in my own wisdom, I pondered deeply the matter of carrying out that task, following the advice of my will and the prompting of my heart, I fashioned a work of bronze and cunningly wrought it.[34]

After a brief description of the formation of clay molds and the pouring of (molten) bronze into them, Sennacherib listed again all the magnificent creatures he made for the doorways of his palace. Within the chambers of the palace he created colonnades using wood

---

Discoveries in the Ruins of Nineveh and Babylon (London: John Murray, 1853), 445-446. It should be noted, however, that Layard referred to these figures as "bulls" in his notebooks recently transcribed and published in J. M. Russell, Layard's Descriptions of Rooms in the Southwest Palace at Nineveh, Iraq 57(1995): 81.

34 Luckenbill, Annals, 109: col. VI line 80-col. VII line 8.

columns coated with silver and other metals. Finally, he briefly
mentions the orthostats of breccia and alabaster with which he lined
the walls and "made them astonishing objects."[35]

Clearly, Sennacherib understood his ability to work the materials
into the forms he desired as that which truly set him apart from other
kings. His own craftsmanship and skill was unsurpassed and he was
able to create any form using any material he chose.

The concluding statements regarding the palace construction found
in BM103000 make clear Sennacherib's designation and intent for
his palace.

> É.GAL.MEŠ *ša-ti-na ú-ša-lik as-me-iš si-hir-ti* É.GAL *a-na tab-rat
> kiš-šat* UN.MEŠ *ul-la-a ri-ši-ša* É.GAL *ša-ni-na la i-šú-u ni-bit-sa
> az-kur*

> I beautified those palaces around the large palace. For the
> astonishment of all peoples I raised its top, I called its name "the
> Palace without Rival."[36]

After completing the palace, Sennacherib began work on the armory
(*bīt kutalli*) adjacent to the palace. The Oriental Institute Prism
contains a building report of the armory which opens with an
assessment of his accomplishment with the palace.

> At that time, after I had completed the palace in the midst of
> Nineveh for my royal residence, had filled it with gorgeous
> furnishings to the astonishment of all people...[37]

Each of the documents discussed above includes a statement that
Sennacherib also built in Nineveh a great park described as "like
Mount Amanus." Mount Amanus is in northeast Syria and was the
source for many of the cedar and cypress logs used in the
construction of the palace. In this garden Sennacherib planted trees
and plants from throughout his realm and devised an innovative
watering system. The incorporation of plants and animals from his
entire realm effectively made the garden in Nineveh a microcosm of

---

35   *a-na tab-ra-a-te ú-ša-lik*, lit. "I/he made them suitable for admiration."
36   Luckenbill, Annals, 110:49-111:52
37   Luckenbill, ARAB II: §424

the empire. The intricate detail found in Sennacherib's documentation, plus the fact that no such structure is described in Neo-Babylonian documents, much less found in the archaeological record, has led S. Dalley to propose that Sennacherib's park in Nineveh is the historical source of the legend of the Hanging Gardens which is later misidentified with Babylon by the classical authors.[38] If she is correct, this is further evidence of Sennacherib's innovative approach to construction and shaping his environment.

Conclusion

The documents that describe Sennacherib's palace building do not explain precisely what the palace looked like or how he achieved every decorative element. The structure of the presentation does not even follow what one could consider advisable building procedure. In fact, reading the two documents together, one is struck that the order follows a pattern influenced by a walk through the structure. The tour begins at the portals and doorways, with considerable space spent describing the fantastic creatures stationed as the door posts. Only after the entryways are clearly described do the documents offer information on the interior of the palace. The eye is drawn to doorways, ceilings, doors, pillars, walls, ceilings, doorways, columns and walls again. The description of palace construction is a textual tour of Sennacherib's palace written as if one were walking through the structure.

The reader/viewer is reminded repeatedly in this textual tour that Sennacherib, who created this palace, surpassed all his predecessors in his creative ability and his innovative approach to old problems. The materials described in the palace came from throughout his realm and made his royal dwelling truly a structure built from all the elements of the empire. Areas that may not have contributed raw materials no doubt contributed labor, making the royal palace, as it

---

38   See her discussion in Nineveh, Babylon and the Hanging Garden: Cuneiform and Classical Sources Reconciled, Iraq 56 (1994): 45-58, where she also indicates that the device known as Archimedes' Screw may have actually been developed by Sennacherib and his engineers in the Neo-Assyrian period, some four hundred years earlier than Archimedes.

is described in the documentation, *the* aggregate building of the empire.

The rhetoric of the documentation reveals a clear intent throughout. The texts use description of palace construction to set the king apart from all who went before. There is not enough information in the documents to reconstruct the appearance of the palace, and indeed this is not the point of the documentation. At each stage of the building reports it is clear that the palace is evidence for the king's status and power. Through his special relationship with the gods he was granted military ability and artistic creativity, both of which were necessary to maintain his realm and complete his palace. The literary description of palace construction thus identifies the king behind the palace. The Palace without Rival was the product of Sennacherib's creativity and was evidence for his status in the world.

The Building

Sennacherib's palace at Nineveh has been excavated since the middle of the eighteenth century, yet knowledge of its structure and appearance is still incomplete. Part of the reason for this lies in the fact that any upper floors to the palace were completely destroyed in antiquity, leaving only the ground floor. Yet not even the ground floor is completely available because of incomplete excavation due either to loss of area by erosion or inadequate funding for such a project. Ultimately, however, though there is no evidence for the façade or upper floors, and only partial evidence for the ground floor, Sennacherib's palace remains one of the most extensively excavated Neo-Assyrian palaces to date. It provides sufficient evidence for the floor plan and the decorative program for a built environment study of the structure.

Art historians have explained the palace as an element in royal rhetoric that identifies key characteristics the king and his administration wanted to be associated with his reign.[39] This rhetorical function is achieved through the use of an intentional decorative program which consists of images of the king depicted engaged in various activities in bas relief on the palace walls. The images aid the identification of desirable characteristics with the royal person. A built environment approach to the palace incorporates art historical information regarding the decorative program and its significance for the meaning of the structure with another element of the building not addressed by art history. Coming as it does from an environmental psychology background, built environment analysis incorporates the study of the effect of the spatial layout and the decorative elements on human behavior in order to understand more fully how the palace functioned as a building. Spatial arrangement, which is essentially the spaces defined by the placement of boundaries (walls) and accesses (doorways) within a building, is one manner of controlling the movement within a structure. The control of access to certain areas is significant for understanding social structure and the flow of social activity within a building. The ancient palace of Sennacherib responds well to a study that focuses both on its spatial arrangement and its decorative elements.

This study of Sennacherib's palace concentrates on two distinct areas in order to highlight two elements of Sennacherib's royal rhetoric. Courtyard VI is an outer courtyard area which is the connecting point for four different suites of rooms. Room XXXVI lies at the center of a suite of rooms to the south of Courtyard XIX. Both of these areas of the palace are the focus of previous studies, but those studies do not apply the type of spatial analysis used in this

---

39   Representative discussions include I. J. Winter, Royal Rhetoric and the
      Development of Historical Narrative in Neo-Assyrian Reliefs, Studies in
      Visual Communication 7, 2 (1981): 2-38; idem., The Program of the
      Throne room of Assurnasirpal II, in Essays on Near Eastern Art and
      Archaeology in Honor of Charles Kyrle Wilkinson, ed. P.O. Harper and
      H. Pittman (New York, 1983): 15-31; idem., Art *in* Empire: The Royal
      Image and the Visual Dimensions of Assyrian Ideology, Assyria 1995,
      359-381; J. M. Russell, Sennacherib's Palace; M. I. Marcus, Geography
      as Visual Ideology: Landscape, Knowledge and Power in Neo-Assyrian
      Art, Neo-Assyrian Geography, ed. M. Liverani (Rome, 1995): 193-202.

examination.[40]   These domains represent contrasts of spatial arrangement, one easily accessed and the other less so. They provide evidence for the function of spatial arrangement within a structure as it affects the flow of activity within the palace and the impact of decorative material.

These areas are also chosen because of the content of the relief programs they exhibit and the fact that presenting them in tandem highlights the complimentarity of the military and construction aspects of Sennacherib's reign. They also provide the opportunity to set forth several ways in which Sennacherib's spatial arrangement and relief program are distinctive from his predecessors and successors, furnishing clear evidence of his uniqueness among the Assyrian monarchs.

Courtyard VI Spatial Arrangement

Neo-Assyrian palaces follow a standard general arrangement of internal space. The interior of the palaces is divided into suites of rooms that surround a central courtyard area. These courtyards are large areas, possibly open to the sky, that provide a common zone of connection between the suites. Courtyard VI is surrounded by suites on all sides, with the throne room (I) in a suite to the northwest of the courtyard.

Surrounding the courtyard are entryways to the different suites. The walls on the southeast, southwest, and northwest of the courtyard contain three doorways each: a central main entry and two side entries. The doorway that leads to the throne room is a single door to Room V, through which one reached Room I. The central, main entries are each flanked by a pair of colossal ^d*aladlammû*. Standing in the center of the courtyard, a visitor was surrounded by these threshold guardians.

---

40   Russell, Sennacherib's Palace, 94-116, 202-209, 252-257; idem., Bulls for the Palace and Order in the Empire: The Sculptural Program of Sennacherib's Court VI at Nineveh, Art Bulletin 69 (1987): 520-539. See also D. Ussishkin's The Conquest of Lachish by Sennacherib (Tel Aviv: Tel Aviv University Institute of Archaeology, 1982).

The area of the courtyard is clearly an intermediate space. It is a connector and a focal point in between the different suites and other areas of the palace. It belongs to no one suite, but is an area held in common by them all. Whether a passage in between, or a gathering point where one waited to enter the suite, anyone in the courtyard during its full glory rested under the watchful eyes of the ^{d}*aladlammû*.

The Reliefs

The reliefs on one side of Courtyard VI present in detail the quarrying and transportation of an ^{d}*aladlammû*, and include an epigraph identifying the quarry as located in the region of Balatai. This is a rare example of an actual construction scene since no previous Assyrian king gave so much time and wall space to the depiction of his construction project. While there are a few problems with the scenes, primarily associated with those reliefs for which there are only drawings available for study, they clearly present the importance the king placed upon his new palace and its construction in the presentation of his reign.[41] What is more significant for this study, however, is the king's choice of the ^{d}*aladlammû* as the subject of his construction reliefs. With so many elements from which to choose, Sennacherib characterizes the artistic nature of his constructive ability through reliefs depicting the quarrying and transport of these mighty protective figures.

The choice of the ^{d}*aladlammû* as representative of his creativity is important. The ^{d}*aladlammû* embody the protective deities that guard the thresholds of the palace and are invoked in inscriptions for constant presence and watchfulness against evil spirits that might enter the palace to harm the king and/or his reign.[42] Sennacherib displays on the walls of Courtyard VI the vast amount of labor necessary to quarry and transport just one of these protective figures

---

41   For detailed discussion of the issues associated with the reliefs, see Russell, Sennacherib's Palace, 94-116.

42   See, for example, Luckenbill, Annals, 117-125, note particularly 125: 52-53.

into Nineveh. Significantly, this relief presentation appeared in an area where a visitor was surrounded by no less than eight of these colossi. The contrast of viewing such an expenditure of labor for one colossus and then seeing eight of them in one place, all facing the courtyard, must have had a sobering effect.

The reliefs present the intense labor required to build the palace by exhibiting the many different tasks that engage the labor force as they quarry and transport the ^{d}aladlammû across land. Sennacherib's annal from the year 694 B.C.E. (BM103000) tells of bringing one colossus from Tastiate, on the other side of the Tigris, and the struggle to complete the task.[43] These reliefs present an even greater effort in image form. They communicate in still life that Sennacherib's construction of the Palace without Rival is completed only by the hard labor of a captured force working under the taskmaster's whip and the watchful supervision of the king himself.

The ^{d}aladlammû, ^{f}apsasātu and the other lion figures are not the only protective images Sennacherib incorporates into his palace wall reliefs. He also includes depictions of other protective images throughout his palace, particularly beside the doorways in association with the three doorpost figures. According to Russell, there are many more of these apotropaic figures on the walls of Sennacherib's palace than on other Neo-Assyrian palaces.[44] He even uses forms in his reliefs that are traditionally reserved for threshold and foundation deposits. Russell concludes:

> One wonders whether the absence of any reported figurine deposits in Sennacherib's palace might be because nearly all of the traditional figurine types were instead prominently displayed on the reliefs of various doorways. Whether or not this is the case, it appears that in decorating his doorways, Sennacherib made visible that which had previously been invisible--that is, he displayed on the door jambs powerful apotropaic figures that had formerly been buried under the pavement.[45]

---

43   See the discussion above, p.60.
44   See Russell's discussion, Sennacherib's Palace, 179-187.
45   Ibid., 186.

The reliefs and arrangement of Courtyard VI may be characterized, using Russell's terminology, by Sennacherib's tendency to make visible what previous kings had left invisible. He presents a vast construction project in the main courtyard near his throne room, depicting himself as the direct overseer of the activity. This makes visible a direct connection between the king and his protective guardians while illustrating the first person narratives in the annals. Secondly, Sennacherib makes other protective figures visible to palace visitors. Figures that are traditionally buried in the floors, out of sight, confront palace guests, repeatedly reminding them that the kingship of Sennacherib is under the watchful protection of the divine realm. These reliefs are not merely decorative. They clearly present the person of the king as creatively gifted and completely protected, while his texts indicate that he received his creative ability as a gift of the gods.

Interpretation

In Courtyard VI, the height, width and length of the area must have made a strong impression on the visitor in comparison to the other, non-monumental structures of the city. The ability to enclose such a comparatively large space within the walls of one building, given the construction techniques of the seventh century B.C.E., is no ordinary feat. This large area is bounded on one side by images of scores of people hard at work, first in the quarry and then in row after row in front of a large sledge, upon which lay the colossus. The king is presented high above the labor, but directly overseeing its progress. The redundant use of human form after human form gives the images depth and emphasizes the ponderous labor involved.

The walls are punctuated by bearded faces of the colossi under horned crowns, gazing down upon the visitor. Steadfastly they watch as the visitor views the still narrative of their creation and transport. They communicate Sennacherib's power and status. His power because only a king who controls vast territories could muster the labor force necessary to create these colossi. His status because only a king favored by the gods has the knowledge and creativity necessary to bring them into the palace, where they guard against any threat. In the face of such a presentation the viewer is aware of his own insignificance before this powerful monarch.

Though the reliefs stand in the British Museum exhibiting only the color of the stone from which they are carved, when they adorned the walls of Courtyard VI they were no doubt quite colorful.[46] The Assyrian kings use color extensively in the decoration of their palaces and official buildings and show a distinct fondness for reds and blues as primary colors with white and black used for outlines and backgrounds.[47] Assyrian use of color has been characterized by modern viewers as "possessing none of the characteristics of original inspiration . . ."[48] and as having a "garish" effect,[49] yet it is indeed strong contrast to the modern appearance of the reliefs and images. Color on the reliefs heightens their effect on the viewer considerably, giving the entire scene more realism, as well as highlighting the details of the redundant images in the reliefs themselves.

The interaction between the reliefs and spatial arrangement creates a domain in which the building prowess of Sennacherib is established in stone and space. The expanse of the courtyard, roughly 80 feet

---

46   A. H. Layard indicated that many of the reliefs from the palace still bore flakes and hints of color when the dirt was first removed from them. See his description in Nineveh and its Remains, vol. 2 (London: John Murray, 1849), 238-243.

47   For examples of the use of color in ninth century Assyrian palaces at Nimrud see A. H. Layard, Monuments of Nineveh (London: John Murray, 1849), plates 84, 86, and 87. These are reproduced in J. M. Russell, From Nineveh to New York (New Haven and London: Yale University Press, 1997), 49-50, figs. 28-31. For eighth century Assyrian palaces see F. Thureau-Dangin and M. Dunand, Til Barsib (Paris, 1936), 45ff. The seventy feet long Til Barsib mural that shows Tiglath-pileser III holding court in the throne room is reproduced in A. Parrot, Nineveh and Babylon, trsl. S. Gilbert and J. Emmons (Thames and Hudson, 1961), 100-112. For the buildings at Khorsabad see G. Loud, Khorsabad I: Excavations in the Palace and at a City Gate, Oriental Institute Publications 28 (Chicago: University of Chicago Press, 1936), 60, fig. 72.

48   Owen Jones, The Grammar of Ornament (London: Day and Son, 1856), as quoted by Russell, From Nineveh to New York, 51.

49   Henri Frankfort, The Art and Architecture of the Ancient Orient, 5th edition (New Haven and London: Yale University Press, 1996, first published 1954), 171.

wide and 120 feet long, is necessary for the depiction of this vast labor project. The large number of laborers in the quarry, along the road back to Nineveh and in the river in the background require a large open space to allow for the full effect of the reliefs.

Another characteristic of the relief program which is accommodated well by the courtyard setting is the geography. The epigraphs and Sennacherib's annals locate the quarry in the area of Balatai. Russell, citing an unpublished letter of Rawlinson, identifies this quarry with Tell Jikan, some 50 kilometers up the Tigris from Nineveh.[50] After the images are quarried they are transported south to Nineveh. The figures in the reliefs move from right to left along the entire northern wall of the courtyard. The length of the courtyard provides an appropriate setting for the depiction of such a long journey over land on foot and enhances the plodding struggle of the laborers as they drag the colossus from the quarry to the palace. The intensity of the labor required to move the statues is emphasized through the vast extent of the relief series dealing with one subject in progressive stages.

The military conquests in the east, which are the subject of the reliefs opposite the construction reliefs, clue the viewer to the source of this labor force working in the quarries and on the palace. The annals tell of military conquest and the acquisition of foreign captive labor. The reliefs show them at work. These military images connected with the construction images link the two inseparably. The king and his administration establish a rhetorical connection between the military and construction activities by placing them in the same courtyard. The king controls a vast labor force that he acquired through his own military might. His status as a king above others is evident in the depiction of him supervising the capture of his hands in the labor of his own design.

The expansive, open area of the courtyard is emphasized by the height of the space and the redundancy of the relief images. The spatial dimensions and the reliefs work in tandem to produce the desired effect on the viewer. Within its ancient time and place, the achievement depicted in the reliefs and evidenced by the staring colossi surrounded the visitor with the all-knowing mastery of

---

50   Sennacherib's Palace, 98-99.

construction this Assyrian king possessed. The expansiveness of the courtyard and the iterative nature of the image of the labor force acting at his will communicates Sennacherib's status in the human world to the viewer. Moreover, if the courtyard is indeed an area open to the sky, the play of sunlight on the reliefs would provide the additional effect of motion. The shifting shadows of the figures in the reliefs would give the workers and their taskmasters life. It would provide the same effect for the colossus being moved from quarry to palace.

The presence of protective figures that are normally found in foundation and threshold deposits is another method Sennacherib uses to indicate his own status. Foundation and threshold deposits are placed in the ground for the benefit of the unseen realm of the deities and the divinities of both good and evil intent. By making these figures visible in the human realm, Sennacherib makes the domain of his palace inseparable from the divine realm. He moves through the palace in the constant company of his divine protectors and they are visible not only to the king, but also to any who would plan injury for the royal person.

Room XXXVI: The Lachish Room Spatial Arrangement

A study of the spatial arrangement of Room XXXVI must begin with the entryway. Courtyard XIX is an inner courtyard in the southern corner of the excavated portion of Sennacherib's palace. Like Courtyard VI, it is surrounded by suites of rooms. The spatial arrangement of the southwestern suite, which centers on Room XXXVI, is unique to this palace. The arrangement of this suite of rooms is a symmetrical ordering of two broad rooms (Rooms XXIX and XXXIV) which run perpendicular to the axis of entry. Behind these are three small rooms at the back (Rooms XXXV-XXXVII). On either end of the two broad rooms are more room suites. The right suite (Rooms XXXVIII-XLI) is fully enclosed, while the left suite (Rooms XXX-XXXIII) accesses what may have been another courtyard area (LX).

The walls that divide Room XXIX from Courtyard XIX contain three doorways, as do the walls that divide Rooms XXIX and

XXXIV. These three doorways provide axes of entry for Rooms XXXV-XXXVII. Since Room XXXV is not fully excavated it is impossible to determine whether that is a single straight axis of entry from Courtyard XIX. The axis leading to Room XXXVII is not a straight axis since the three doorways (*g, e, c*) are not in line with one another. This leaves the central axis of entry through doorways *h, l,* and *b* as the only triple entryway lying on a single axis of movement. Spatially, this emphasizes the central entryway as the primary path into the suite.

The first doorway is flanked by a pair of 18 feet tall ^{d}*aladlammû*. Beyond them, and on the same axis, stand another pair of ^{d}*aladlammû* which are shorter than the first. Finally, beyond this second pair, flanking the doorway of Room XXXVI is a third pair which are 12 feet tall.[51] The placement of the entryway on a single axis and the consistent reduction of the height of the protective figures as one moves further from the courtyard produces an optically accelerated perspective which gives the appearance of much greater distance than is actually the case. No other room in any excavated portion of a Neo-Assyrian palace is accentuated in this manner.

Though this type of triple threshold entryway is not found in any other Assyrian palace excavated thus far, it is known elsewhere in Assyrian architecture in monumental city gateways and in temple architecture. Monumental city gateways were developed to impede progress into the city by allowing entrance to the city only in stages. They have two chambers on either side of the path of entry which creates a total of three thresholds to be crossed in order to enter the city. Typically, only the outermost threshold have a protective ^{d}*aladlammû*, while the second and third function for military

---

51 Russell, Sennacherib's Palace Revisited, 296, has recently indicated that this last pair, which flank the doorway of Room XXXVI, may actually have been winged *lions*, rather than winged bulls. Though Layard described them all as bulls in his Discoveries, 445, Russell has found that Layard referred to the pair in entrance *b* as lions in his manuscript. Other doorways in the suite have the ^{f}*apsasâtu* flanking them (doorway *p*, for example) which Layard described in his notes as "bulls" but in his publication as "lions," so it is not inconceivable that Layard's 1853 publication misrepresents the figures in doorway *b* as bulls.

advantage.[52] The triple threshold, in addition to its military function, is a clear physical marker between the world outside the city and the world inside.

There are two types of approaches common in temples in the ancient world. The long-room temple is entered on one of the short sides and the cella is on the same axis of entry, though at the far end. In this type of temple the cella and the statue of the god are typically shielded behind at least one more threshold.[53] These temples are also designated "straight-axis" since the cella stands on a straight axis with the entryway and the worshiper is not required to turn in either direction to face the statue of the deity. The broad-room temple entry is on one of the long sides and requires the worshiper enter and make a 90 degree turn to the right or left in order to face the cella. They are also termed "bent-axis" temples since full entry requires a bent axis approach to the deity.

In both cases the clear division between outer world and the inner world of the temple is expressed architecturally. In the straight-axis approach the individual must cross several thresholds, each significant of moving deeper into the world of the temple and away from the outer world of society. In the bent-axis approach the individual must turn off the path of entry in order to face the deity, thus separating from the path taken from the outer world.

---

52   See G. Loud, Khorsabad I, and M. E. L. Mallowan, Nimrud and Its Remains, 3 Volumes (Aberdeen, 1966) for diagrams of chambered city gates. For representations of the style of city gates at Nineveh, see D. Stronach, Notes on the Fall of Nineveh, Assyria 1995, 312, fig.2, where he indicates the Halzi, and Shamash gates were two chambered (three thresholds) while all others were single chambered (two thresholds). Stronach also explains how the defensive ability of these gates were compromised by their having been so spread out along the city wall, as well as the fact that the gateways themselves had to be narrowed when the city was threatened in 612 B.C.E. in order to make them more defensible.

53   It should be noted that, on occasion, the threshold was nothing more than a few steps which must be ascended in order to reach the raised floor level of the cella. Several of the palace temples at Khorsabad have this type of division between the entry hall and the cella. See Loud, Khorsabad I, and D. Oates, Balawat (Imgur Enlil): The Site and its Buildings, Iraq 36 (1974):176, note particularly the plan of the Temple of Mamu, Plate XXV.

Many scholars have studied Sennacherib's palace and made comment on the triple use of the bull colossi in this suite of rooms, but have given no attention to the spatial arrangement of the suite with regard to the axis of entry and the relationship between Courtyard XIX and Room XXXVI.[54] The triple threshold entry functions in two ways. The three thresholds divide the space into three domains, two of which must be crossed to reach the third. The thresholds also emphasize the depth and inaccessibility of the inner chamber that sits at the heart of this suite. Depth is an indicator of power and status and Room XXXVI in the Palace without Rival is a spatial presentation of power and status.[55] The spatial composition of this suite places Room XXXVI at the innermost location and therefore in the most reserved position of the rooms. A visitor could reach this room only by crossing three thresholds, each of which is guarded by the protective colossi. The entryway separates the inner space of Room XXXVI from the outer space of the courtyard and the rest of the palace. Anyone entering this area from the courtyard would clearly be aware of moving from the unrestricted open area of the courtyard into a more restricted, less accessible space. The triple threshold thus functions as a three-fold boundary between Room XXXVI and the world of palace business.

At the same time, the three thresholds delineate a distinct path of entry. The three pairs of protective figures standing along the same axis practically require a visitor to the palace to venture further/deeper into the suite. This arrangement of boundary and access serves the double function of inviting and prohibiting; they invite the visitor to follow the straight entry into the room while guarding each threshold from the entry of evil intent.

Understanding this spatial arrangement as invoking that of the straight-axis temple places Room XXXVI in the precise position where one would find the cella and the statue of the deity. Given the pride of place afforded Room XXXVI in Sennacherib's palace, it stands to reason that this room serves a function quite distinct from

---

54   See the descriptions found in A. H. Layard, Discoveries in the Ruins of Nineveh and Babylon (London: John Murray, 1853), 445; Russell, Sennacherib's Palace, 252; as well as that found in M. T. Larsen's The Conquest of Assyria (London and New York: Routledge, 1994), 270-272.

55   See Markus' comments, Buildings and Power, 16.

those around it or in adjacent suites. The unique spatial arrangement in this suite of rooms requires that it be understood as a significant space in the palace. Spatial analysis, however, cannot tell all the secrets of this suite when used in isolation. It must be combined with other specific information on the room itself in order to produce an interpretation that considers all the options on the basis of all the evidence at hand. More evidence on the significance of Room XXXVI comes from the bas-reliefs that lined the walls of the room. The reliefs of Room XXXVI illustrate a specific event in the reign of Sennacherib and were placed in this central location in order to highlight the military characteristics of this king.

The Reliefs

Having reached the final doorway in the entry to Room XXXVI, a visitor would have seen the sharp upward angles of the siege ramp against the walls of the doomed city of Lachish. To the left, horsemen and charioteers, then three ranks of archers, arrows nocked in their bows drawn and aimed up toward the men who fight from the top of the city walls. In front of the archers, siege towers with battering rams approach the city walls on wheels. From above, flaming torches rain down upon the siege machinery and the archers. Men in the siege towers pour pails of water on the battering rams to keep them from catching fire due to the downpour of fiery torches.

The city itself is a heavily fortified stronghold surrounded by a double wall system with towers. Directly below the raging battle, men with slingshots and piles of stones prepare to aid in the fight. Just behind (below) them, three casualties from the city are impaled on upright poles. To the right of the city are the results of the battle: two rows of people moving away from the city. The rows consist of Assyrian soldiers bringing the spoils of war to the king. Among the spoils are captives from the city and their livestock. Some of the soldiers pull a chariot, others carry furnishings.

The train moves to the right leading the viewing eye toward the goal of this queue. There, on the right wall of Room XXXVI, is Sennacherib, King of Assyria. He sits upon his throne wielding the bow and arrows that are signs of his military prowess, with the mountains behind him as a backdrop. Before him is a royal official, flanked by soldiers, with his hand raised before him in a gesture of obeisance.[56] The captives and the spoils of battle are directly behind the soldiers. An inscription over the head of the official reads:

[md]30-PAP.MEŠ-SU MAN ŠÚ MAN KUR *aš+šur ina* GIŠ.GU.ZA
né-me-di ú-šib-ma šal-la-at URU *la-ki-su ma-ha-ar-šu e-ti-iq*

Sennacherib, King of the world, King of Assyria, sat on a *nēmedu* throne while the booty of Lachish passed in review before him.[57]

Behind the throne are two attendants who fan the king. Directly behind these attendants is the tent of Sennacherib. Below the tent, and thus in the foreground of the picture, is the battle chariot of Sennacherib and his charioteers, some of whom hold replacement horses for the chariot. Behind these is a second chariot which appears more ceremonial than the first because of the elaborate harness on the horses and the decorations on the wheels.

Even further to the rear of the throne is a fortified camp. The wall around the camp has towers at regular intervals. Inside the camp are seven tents, five of which are presented in cross-section, revealing activity within. In the upper section of the camp there is a ceremonial chariot which stands adjacent to an altar. A fire on the altar is tended by two priests. This chariot has two staffs rising from the body indicating that it is the chariot of the god.[58]

Starting again at the extreme left and panning to the right, the storm of battle grows to a resounding crescendo in a still life of the siege of Lachish. Continuing the circuit of the reliefs, the tumult

---

56   Hammurabi takes the same posture before the god Shamash on the top of the obelisk that contains his law code. This "hand in front of the face," is a common posture for a human to take before someone of higher status and may be a method of indicating one's unworthiness to look directly at that person.

57   Russell, Sennacherib's Palace, 276, my translation.

58   These staffs are no doubt the *urigallu* discussed by F. A. M. Wiggermann, Mesopotamian Protective Spirits (Gronigen: Styx, 1992), 70ff, as the symbols of the god on chariots that accompanied the Assyrian army. They were originally gateposts, or threshold markers, which came to symbolize the portable presence of and access to the god.

calms again as the spoils of that battle make their way before the victorious King of the world, King of Assyria. The reliefs of Room XXXVI lead the viewer's eye from left to right. The action points the direction for the unknowing and leads to a direct encounter with the image of the victorious king, but only after experiencing his military might.

Interpretation

Room XXXVI is a much smaller space than Courtyard VI. Yet, in order to understand the full significance of this room it is necessary to include the entryway from Courtyard XIX. Again, the combination of spatial arrangement and relief program produce an effect upon the viewer that could not be achieved by either one alone. The triple threshold entry incorporates an architectural form reminiscent of the long room temple and placed Room XXXVI in the position of the cella. The recessed placement of the room and the use of three thresholds as physical markers of different domains to be crossed create a concrete area that is open only to limited access. The use of the protective colossi at each of the thresholds is one way the relief program is integrated with the spatial arrangement. The decreasing height of each subsequent pair of colossi, their redundant pairing and the fact that they stood on the same axis all contribute to the optical impression of even greater depth for the room.

Once inside the room, the relief program is a depiction of Sennacherib's military might. It is a still life of power. Moreover, the relief program within the room forces movement. The viewer enters the room facing the raging battle for Lachish, but the motion of the reliefs forces the eye to move to the right, where the viewer faces the image of Sennacherib enthroned. In this manner the relief program of Room XXXVI turns the straight-axis of entry into a bent-axis approach to the image of the enthroned, victorious king. Here, the combination of spatial arrangement with relief program allows Sennacherib to create a truly unique domain in Assyrian architecture. The entryway and reliefs of Room XXXVI compose a spatial unit which was *both* a straight-axis and a bent-axis approach to the image of Sennacherib, King of Assyria.[59]

At this point one may speculate as to the choice of the town of Lachish as the subject matter of the focal area of this suite. The town is specifically named in the epigraph over the head of Sennacherib, and yet does not appear in any extant copies of the royal annals. With reference to this campaign to the west, Sennacherib merely states that he captured forty six of Hezekiah's fortified towns and shut the king of Judah within his capital city. One might consider Babylon a more fitting subject matter for such a treatment within an Assyrian palace. Yet Babylon is not depicted in the reliefs that survive from the palace. Upon consideration, there is a striking contrast between Babylon and Lachish. Military matters concerned with Babylon are treated extensively in the royal annals, and indeed have quite the tone of domestic difficulties. Lachish, by contrast, is far to the west, in fact, it is nearly to the sea that marked the western extremity of Sennacherib's control. The question naturally arises why Sennacherib would devote such decorative and rhetorical energy to a relatively minor city in the west and ignore the opportunity to elaborate on his great victory over the capital city of an enemy. One reason may be chronology. Sennacherib's defeat of Babylon is achieved long after the palace is completed. But there could be other reasons as well. Lachish is not mentioned in the annalistic documentation of Sennacherib's reign, but it offers testimony to Sennacherib's military power and prowess in the far distant periphery of his realm in the relief narrative of Room XXXVI. The pictorial account may have made a verbal account of the extent of the king's political control unnecessary. Furthermore, as is explained below in chapter four, the issue of what to do about Babylon becomes a treacherous undertaking later in the reign of Sennacherib,

---

59   A. L. Oppenheim pointed to the similarity of spatial arrangement between Assyria throne rooms and bent-axis temples in Ancient Mesopotamia: Portrait of a Dead Civilization, rev. ed. By Erica Reiner (Chicago: University of Chicago Press, 1977), 328. Note however that Sennacherib's own throne room (Room I) had a wall niche opposite the main entrance, possibility indicating that Sennacherib's throne could be moved in line with the main entrance to the throne room, hence straight-axis. See Russell's discussion, Sennacherib's Palace, 47-48.

and may have already been an issue that the king considered it best to leave aside.

The function of Room XXXVI may indeed be lost to the centuries that separate the modern viewer from its creator. Yet a built environment analysis is capable of reassembling its significance through the documentation and study of the spatial arrangement and decorative elements. As described above, spatially there can be no doubt that the contours of the suite centered on Room XXXVI invoke a straight-axis temple arrangement. Furthermore, the combination of this with the decorative program, which invokes a bent-axis arrangement, leaves little room for denial that this suite is structured as a temple or sanctuary. This places Sennacherib's military might and the image of him enthroned victoriously as the focal point of this spatial arrangement.

Royal shrines are not unknown in Neo-Assyrian palaces. Russell recently made the case for a royal shrine in the palace of Assurnasirpal II (883-859 B.C.E.) at Nimrud.

> If this interpretation is correct, then the east wing could be the location of royal rituals that involved liquid offerings to Assyrian deities, offerings that are depicted in the two outer rooms and that may actually have been made in the smaller back rooms that were lined with apotropaic figures.[60]

Moreover, at Khorsabad, Sargon built a series of temples adjacent to his palace in the citadel. While these were dedicated to various gods and were not technically part of the palace, these two situations are precursors to Sennacherib's innovative construction. The suite of rooms focused on Room XXXVI has all the markings of a sacred, separate area within Sennacherib's palace devoted to the veneration of his military proficiency and status in the world.

---

60   J. M. Russell, From Nineveh to New York, 22.

Conclusion

The documents BM113203 and BM103000 maintain a bilateral presentation of the royal activity of Sennacherib in the form of his military exploits and his construction activity. The annals begin with long recitations of year by year military campaigns which demonstrate continued control over the borders of the empire. Though some areas are visited more than once, the overall image is of a king progressively expanding the resources under his control through the exercise of military might. Regardless of the region where Sennacherib goes to battle, the litany is consistent. The enemy kings and their armies are overcome with fear when they view his terrifying royal aura and often flee before the battle is engaged.

The military image of Sennacherib in his annals is that he moves to and fro upon the earth, roaring like a lion, bellowing like the tempest, laying siege to fortified cities, conquering them, counting all their people, animals, and materials as spoil of battle, impaling those who do not recognize his might and surrender, and placing heavy tribute upon the offending cities. This accomplished, he returns to his capital city having once again established his military superiority and his right to rule. The next year the cycle begins again.

At the end of the recitation of military campaigns, the documents describe the building of the palace in the capital city. The natural resources of conquered regions are incorporated into the palace structure and the labor force is increased with the influx of new captives. The relationship between military campaigns in distant lands and building programs at home is not entirely rhetorical. Since the Assyrian homeland is actually bereft of many of the precious materials used in palace construction, the only way for the king to acquire these items is by military action. The elaborate building programs could not have continued without the yearly forays to replenish materials and labor. The great builder is able to be so only by also being a great military leader. Sennacherib is both and the lines of his annals present clear and inspiring images of him as victorious military leader and skillful builder.

The textual presentations of the building programs are, admittedly, all of the same voice. The information is presented in the first person, as though Sennacherib himself speaks to the reader and recounts his achievements. The lack of testimony from other social groups or from anyone who actually saw the palace is characteristic of the period. Writing was a tool of business and politics. Only the elite could afford scribes and their services. The nature of the evidence is a function of social norms of the time, and though it limits the depth of the image, it is a characteristic of Neo-Assyrian life. It is to be expected that the only voice would be that of the royal administration.

The documents do not present a clear image of the palace itself. They give very little specific information about the layout of the structure or of activities within particular areas of the palace. The information recorded in the annals, such as the materials used, the great distances they were brought, or the skillfulness of the king's use of the exotic materials, all point to the status of Sennacherib rather than seeking to communicate something specific about the appearance of the structure. Ultimately one must conclude that the palace itself is not the point of the documentation. The rhetorical concern is the person of the king and his standing in Assyrian social structure. The documents use descriptions of palace building as a device to set the king apart not only from the people of Assyria but also from his predecessors.

The palace is the dwelling of the king and the royal family. More than this, it is the place of royal business and the point from which imperial decisions are sent forth. The contribution of the built environment analysis is that it recognizes that buildings are more than dwellings and centers of political life, they also communicate information regarding social structure and the relationships of status and power within the society. The way that space is structured and decorated in a building provides a concreteness to the metaphorical notions of power, honor, kingship, servanthood, etc.[61] The structure of the spatial units delineates social interaction while the decorative program communicates unspoken cultural cues for behavior and interaction. All of these elements are found within the evidence for the physical structure of Sennacherib's palace at Nineveh.

---

61   As Markus explained, "they [buildings] organize people, things and ideas in space so as to make conceptual systems concrete." Buildings and Power, 19.

While art historical discussions provide invaluable information concerning the development of relief styles and use in Neo-Assyrian palaces going back to the time of Assurnasirpal II (883-859 B.C.E.), they approach the palaces and their decorative elements with a method that relies on the textual metaphor. The use of spatial analysis as a category of evidence and its incorporation with the art historical discussion yields more information concerning the function of the building as a building, without treating the building as a text. It provides the opportunity to investigate the function of the building as a built environment which not only is influenced by the intent and desire of the builder, but also influences the social behavior within it through nonverbal cues. In Sennacherib's palace these cues exist in the form of the relief program and the spatial arrangement used in tandem to create domains that both praise the king for his unparalleled creativity in palace building and raise his military ability to the status of divinity without actually claiming that he was himself divine.

The first point is made explicitly in the royal annals as they describe the palace construction. Courtyard VI exhibits Sennacherib's constructive creativity through the combination of an expansive spatial arrangement and the reliefs depicting a vast labor force carrying out his royal direction. The fact that the quarry site is revealed by the will of the gods places divine favor upon his activities. Moreover, that Sennacherib is the only Assyrian king who makes his construction activity a central element in his royal image, indicates that the built environment method is particularly suited for studying this king. The reliefs of Courtyard VI call for those who would understand the significance of Sennacherib in the history and tradition of the Neo-Assyrian Empire to approach him through his buildings and other construction projects.

The second point is never stated explicitly; no Assyrian king ever claimed divine status in his documentation. Yet, in the formation of the spatial units surrounding Room XXXVI, the way Sennacherib arranges the boundaries and the permeability of access from one room to another, he provides spatial cues to the high status he associates with his royal person. Furthermore, the arrangement of the reliefs in Room XXXVI elicits additional movement once one enters the room. The ninety degree turn to the right to face the enthroned king is a resounding cue to the prestige of Sennacherib.

The materials used in palace construction are the physical evidence of the narrative of the annals and the events recorded in the wall reliefs. Once the palace is completed, it is truly an embodiment of the empire. The king lives in a building that is made from precious materials brought from throughout his realm and constructed by his defeated subjects. The Palace without Rival at Nineveh is the product of long military campaigns to distant lands. Each new material incorporated into its structure is another piece of the world added to Sennacherib's control. The palace is the physical make-up of the entire realm brought together at one place, at the center of the empire, and in this manner an embodiment of the empire of Sennacherib.

Yet the palace must be placed in the context of Sennacherib's other building projects. It is a multifaceted structure that incorporates the king's developing notions of his status and identity as ruler of the Assyrian empire. Though his reign ends with his assassination, there are approximately ten years between the completion of the palace and the death of Sennacherib. The last ten years is a period of continual construction and military victory. The rhetoric of Sennacherib's royal administration continues to increase in this last decade and the claims of his palace are made far more explicit in his later years. Establishing the palace in the context of Sennacherib's wider building program clarifies the significance and the innovative nature of his early claims. In chapter four we will return to the palace and recognize the early, almost tentative, beginning of the religious and political reform Sennacherib attempts.

Chapter 3

Solomon's Temple in Jerusalem

YHWH intended to dwell in the thick cloud. I have indeed built you a lordly house, a fixed place for your eternal dwelling.

I Kings 8:12-13

But will God indeed dwell on earth? Surely, the heavens, even the highest heaven cannot contain you, much less this house which I have built.

I Kings 8:27

But listen to the supplication of your servant and your people Israel which they pray toward this place; when you hear in your dwelling place in heaven, listen and forgive.

I Kings 8:30

In the study of the description of Solomon's temple, biblical scholars usually propose that the primary significance of the text is to provide information necessary for a visual reconstruction of the temple. Literary scholars lend credibility to this endeavor when they speculate regarding possible source materials that stand behind the biblical text. Archaeologists also contribute by offering comparative evidence from temples excavated at sites other than the mount in Jerusalem, suggesting that the excavated temples and the Jerusalem temple described in the book of I Kings are of the same architectural type. The preponderance of this type of study suggests that even though there is no recovered physical evidence for the actual temple in Jerusalem, modern scholars are quite certain of its appearance and are able to reconstruct the temple built by Solomon.

There are, however, flaws in this image of modern certainty regarding Solomon's temple. It has long been recognized that the description of the temple in I Kings 6-7 lacks important details for a reconstruction, even though it appears to be a very detailed narrative about the building of the temple. For this reason, scholars turn to the temple descriptions found in II Chronicles 3-4 and Ezekiel 40-42 to provide information on the thickness of walls and the foundation platform for the structure to have the data necessary for a reconstruction.[1] Clearly, the text of I Kings 6-7 is not a self-contained temple description that is useful for a complete reconstruction of the temple. But the use of other texts in the biblical material to fill in the details, without first carrying through a study of their function and significance within their own context, is problematic.[2]

Archaeological excavations have not produced a temple within the boundaries of Iron Age Israel that is comparable to that of the biblical description of the temple in Jerusalem. Most of the Iron Age temples used for comparison are found in the territory of modern Syria. More significantly, archaeology is unable to provide the caliber of physical evidence one would expect for the period of Solomon, which supposedly flourished with royal building

---

1   This may be seen in the works of L. Waterman, The Damaged 'Blueprints' of the Temple of Solomon, JNES 2 (1943):284-294; as well as G. E. Wright, Biblical Archaeology, abridged edition (Philadelphia: Westminster, 1976, originally published 1960), 80-83. T. Busink, Der Tempel von Jerusalem von Salomo bis Herodes, 1. Band, Der Tempel Salomos (Leiden: E. J. Brill, 1970), 23-26, discusses the necessity of using the descriptions in Chronicles and Ezekiel when reconstructing the appearance of the temple.

2   It should also be noted that there is the occasional reference to Josephus' Antiquities of the Jews, Book VIII, as well as to tractate Middoth of the Mishnah for information regarding measurements and arrangements within the temple precinct. These two sources of information are from a time period much later than the biblical narrative in I Kings and the time of Solomon. More significantly, their value as sources for the appearance of Solomon's temple is compromised by the fact that Josephus' work exhibits a considerable dependence upon the narrative of the Chronicler, particularly with reference to his description of Solomon's building of the temple, while Middoth appears to be based upon the measurements and quantifications found in Ezekiel 40-44. Based upon this I do not consider these late documents any more helpful in clearing up the gaps of information found in I Kings than are the narratives of Ezekiel or II Chronicles.

programs.[3] Given this state of the physical evidence for the temple, one must inquire as to the propriety of the continued use of the biblical material to recreate an image of a structure for which there is no physical evidence.

The lack of physical evidence and the lack of necessary information in the description are overcome by the application of a new theoretical model to the temple description. In the preceding chapter the archaeological and literary evidence for the palace of Sennacherib is interpreted using the analytical categories of built environment studies. If one were to grant that the biblical description of the temple is based upon actual archival documents composed by eyewitnesses to its appearance, and therefore is an accurate description, a study of the temple according to the built environment approach is still the only approach able to provide an interpretation of the significance of the structure based upon its spatial arrangement and decorative program. Even though there is no physical evidence for the appearance of the temple available, built environment analysis remains an appropriate method for the temple description for two reasons. One reason is that built environment analysis elucidates the subtle cultural cues present in a building.

Another reason these categories remain appropriate rests upon the assumption that the author of the temple description has not made a mistake or left out information that should have been included. Rather, it trusts the document is an accurate presentation of the information the author intends to communicate to the reader. The application of built environment analysis to the information provided yields a different understanding of the significance of the temple description of I Kings 6-7, which is based solely on the information the author includes and does not gather other data from different biblical texts. Without physical evidence to interpret the meaning of

---

3   G. Barkay, The Iron Age II-III, in The Archaeology of Ancient Israel, ed. A. Ben-Tor, trsl. R. Greenberg (New Haven and London: Yale University Press, 1992), 366 indicates that the excavations in Jerusalem have produced no finds which reflect the "grandeur of Solomon's day." Y. Aharoni, The Archaeology of the Land of Israel: From the Prehistoric Beginnings to the End of the First Temple Period, trsl. A. F. Rainey (Philadelphia: Westminster Press, 1982), 227 bemoans the lack of discovery of a temple comparable to that of Jerusalem.

the structure, the text is presented as a verbal icon of the temple and is interpreted as the literary embodiment, if not creation, of that space. Once the significance is placed on the description of the space and not the actual structure, then many of the problems associated with the details and the sources of the description fall away leaving only the clarity of the icon.

Issues of Historicity

One assumption of most previous studies of Solomon's temple, the historicity of the king and of his construction, is currently under discussion. Hotly debated are issues that surround the dating of the so-called Solomonic gateways at Gezer, Megiddo, and Hazor, which up to now have been the primary physical evidence cited for the building program at the beginning of the reign of Solomon in the tenth century B.C.E. Since many previous studies of the temple description assume the historical accuracy of the biblical material, it is important to highlight the current debate on what is meant when scholars refer to the historical evidence, and precisely what may be considered evidence for the historical accuracy of biblical material. Naturally, one element of the discussion between archaeologists and biblical scholars is the relationship between the data of their two disciplines and how one should or should not use the data of the other as an interpretive key. The current state of this discussion sheds light on the flaws of past approaches. We therefore begin with a complete analysis of the evidence for the existence of Solomon and the temple, and then analyze past approaches in light of what is known. Finally, those studies relevant and helpful to the proposed new approach are highlighted.

The studies that consider the reign of Solomon and his building of the temple as historical events place them in the tenth century B.C.E. primarily on a chronology built from references to later Israelite and Judahite kings in extrabiblical documents from Moab and Assyria.[4]

---

4   The earliest extrabiblical references date to the ninth century B.C.E. and
      mention the Israelite kings Ahaz and Jehu in the annals of Shalmaneser III

In addition to these extrapolations from extra-biblical texts, archaeologists use the monumental gateways excavated at Megiddo, Hazor and Gezer as evidence for Solomon and his building activities. All of these structures are usually dated to the tenth century, based upon the typological evidence of the pottery discovered in association with the gateways. Having such unshakeable foundations in ancient literature reinforced with physical evidence, Solomon's place in the mid-late tenth century B.C.E. has appeared quite secure.

Recently, however, the evidence for the tenth century dating of the gateways has been questioned and gaps are forming in the arguments, leading some scholars to propose a different understanding of the significance of the gateways and therefore for Solomon himself. [5] The mention of Israelite kings in ninth-century documents from Assyria and Moab is incontrovertible, but there is no mention of a king of Israel named Solomon in any extant record from neighboring societies, and therefore no independent witness to the existence of this king. This leaves the biblical narrative as the sole literary witness to his reign. The principal weak point in the structure of a Solomonic kingship in the tenth century is the dating

---

(858-824 B.C.E.), the latter identified as the son of Omri; and the mention of Omri and an unnamed son in the inscription of Mesha from Moab. For translations of these texts see D. D. Luckenbill, Ancient Records of Assyria and Babylonia I, §§590, 611, and 672; A. Dearman, ed., Studies in the Mesha Inscription and Moab (Atlanta: Scholars Press, 1989), 97ff. The earliest reference to a specific Judahite king is Azariah of Judah in the annals of Tiglath-pileser III (745-727 B.C.E.), see Luckenbill, ARAB I, §770. The Aramaic inscription from Tel Dan is also dated to the ninth century, but is not helpful in this regard. Outside of its interesting mention of the house of David, it provides no unbroken mention of specific names.

5   Two recent volumes have been dedicated to the discussion of the evidence for Solomon. BASOR 277/278 (1990) is dedicated to the reevaluation of the archaeological evidence for Solomon and L. K. Handy, ed., The Age of Solomon: Scholarship at the Turn of the Millennium (Leiden: Brill, 1997) is dedicated to the discussion of the historicity of Solomon from the perspectives of literary criticism, archaeology, and sociology. A good summary discussion of the question of Solomon may be found in G. N. Knoppers, The Vanishing Solomon: The Disappearance of the United Monarchy from Recent Histories of Ancient Israel, JBL 116/1 (1997): 19-44.

of the gateway structures that are attributed to his reign in the biblical account. Thus, the biblical account of the events of the tenth century is called into question based upon continued literary study as well as disagreements among archaeologists over the dating of the gateways. It is necessary to review here the evidence scholars depend on to reconstruct the reign of Solomon and to evaluate the usefulness of these approaches for historical reconstructions.

Archaeological Evidence for the Reign of Solomon

The gateways at Megiddo, Gezer and Hazor have stood for forty years as the quintessential physical evidence believed to confirm the accuracy of I Kings 9:15, as well as the existence of Solomon.[6] I Kings 9:15 states, "Now this is the forced labor that King Solomon raised in order to build the house of YHWH and his house, and the millo, and the wall of Jerusalem, and Hazor, and Megiddo, and Gezer." The similarity of the form of the gateways at Hazor, Megiddo, and Gezer, in conjunction with this single statement is interpreted to mean that these towns are part of the royal building program of Solomon. This position is not without its detractors, however. In 1990 the archaeological debate over evidence for Solomon was reinvigorated by the challenge issued by G. Wightman.[7] Noting that the archaeological evidence for dating the gateways has always been the associated pottery, Wightman indicates that there has been considerable disagreement through the years over the dating of the pottery. His discussion makes it clear that the problem is focused on the type of data with which one begins. Archaeologists who use the biblical material as an interpretive key for their dating will always face the problem that the literature is unable to provide an absolute chronology for the material remains they excavate. For instance, P. L. O. Guy dated the pottery he excavated at Megiddo to the tenth century because of its

---

6   It was Y. Yadin who first identified these gateways as having been built "from the same blueprint," Solomon's City Wall and Gate at Gezer, IEJ 8 (1958): 80-86.

7   G. J. Wightman, The Myth of Solomon, BASOR 277/278 (1990): 5-22.

association with the monumental gateway, which had previously been attributed to Solomon.[8] Later, K. Kenyon dated the same style pottery at Samaria to the ninth century because of its association with the citadel walls supposed to have been built during the reign of Omri (I Kings 16:24).[9] Both of these datings, it must be admitted, are based at least in part on biblical narrative rather than stratigraphy or other physical evidence, and therefore do not provide a strong archaeological argument for dating the pottery types.[10]

Wightman proposes a revision of the chronology of the sites of Samaria, Hazor, Megiddo, and Gezer. He bases his proposal on the stratigraphy of the sites, the chronology of the red slip pottery, historical discussion of the situation at Iron II Samaria, and the information in I Kings 9:15. He concludes that the levels and the material remains, particularly the monumental gateways at these sites should be dated down to the ninth century rather than the tenth. This would, of course, place the construction of the gateway structures in the reigns of the later kings and relieve the difficulty of the Solomonic attribution based only on the biblical narrative.[11]

Two Israeli archaeologists, D. Ussishkin and I. Finkelstein, make their own arguments against a tenth century date for the monumental

---

8   P. L. O. Guy, New Light from Armageddon, Oriental Institute Communications No. 9 (Chicago: University of Chicago Press, 1931).

9   See her discussions in J. W. Crowfoot, G. M. Crowfoot, and K. M. Kenyon, Pottery: Early Bronze and Israelite, The Objects from Samaria (London: Palestine Exploration Fund, 1957), 90-134; and in Megiddo, Hazor, Samaria and Chronology, Bulletin of the Institute of Archaeology, University of London 4 (1964): 143-156.

10   Wightman, Myth of Solomon, 7-8 offers the strongest critique of Guy's archaeological method describing it as an assumption based solely on the biblical narrative. Guy asserted that what he found at Megiddo was Solomonic and then used that same material as proof of the narrative. Wightman charges that this circular method "went unchallenged and had considerable influence over later scholarly thinking, particularly within the American and Israeli schools." By the time of the discovery of the chambered gateway at Hazor in Stratum X, the monumental chambered gateway had become a recognizable form of Solomonic architecture and the gateway was dated tenth century without corroborative dating evidence.

11   See his discussion in Myth of Solomon, 5-22.

gateways in the same volume of BASOR.[12] Ussishkin points out that
the attribution of the destruction levels at Megiddo to the campaign
of Shoshenq I (biblical Shishak) is also a key to the chronology that
places the monumental gateways in the days of Solomon. He
recognizes the importance of the red-slip pottery, but concludes that
there is no precise way to date this important linchpin for the
chronology of these gateways.

> The conclusions regarding Shoshenq I's stele found in Megiddo add
> to the difficulty of accurately dating this pottery in Megiddo, and
> hence elsewhere. Thus the pottery associated with the fortifications
> of Gezer could date to the reign of Solomon, but it could equally
> well date later, to the end of the tenth or first part of the ninth
> century, B.C., after the division of the United Monarchy.[13]

With the archaeological evidence so thoroughly questionable,
Ussishkin concludes that the only information left that supports the
attribution of the fortified gateways to Solomon is the biblical
reference in I Kings.

Finkelstein's contribution to the volume is a discussion of the
methods used in the re-excavation of Gezer and an evaluation of the
conclusions the archaeologists draw regarding their new evidence.
He critiques Dever's lack of separation between archaeological
evidence and historical assumptions and concludes that Dever's work
at Gezer exhibits "another example of 'classic' biblical
archaeology."[14]   Finkelstein remains critical of the way Dever
maintains the Solomonic dating for the gateways, even though the
physical evidence points to the need for revision.

---

12   D. Ussishkin, Notes on Megiddo, Gezer, Ashdod, and Tel Batash in the
     Tenth to Ninth Centuries B.C., BASOR 277/278 (1990): 71-91; I.
     Finkelstein, On Archaeological Methods and Historical Considerations:
     Iron Age II Gezer and Samaria, BASOR 277/278 (1990): 109-119.
13   Ussishkin, Notes, 76.
14   Finkelstein, Methods, 113-114. The "historical assumptions" Finkelstein
     cites are, placing the Outer Wall in the Amarna Age, even though there is
     no archaeological evidence for this dating, and Dever's belief that all four
     entry gateways were built in the tenth century, even though this type of
     gateway has been discovered at the seventh century site of Tel 'Ira.

Finkelstein concludes that Wightman also practices "traditional biblical archaeology." Though Wightman rejects the attribution of the gateways to Solomon based merely on the I Kings 9:15 statement, he accepts the ninth century dating of the Samaria sherds based on the passage in I Kings 16:24. Finkelstein indicates that the distinctions between the pottery types are far too vague to provide a clear chronology based solely upon ceramic data and agrees with the assessment of Ussishkin that the primary data for Iron II chronology is still the biblical narrative. Finkelstein recognizes that archaeologists will continue to use the biblical narrative as an interpretive key for their excavated materials and cautions that greater care is taken in assessing exactly what sections of the narrative may be considered historical evidence.[15]

The strongest response to these challenges is that of W. G. Dever, who charges that Wightman's essay misses the crucial point of the dating discussion among archaeologists.[16] The main concern for archaeologists is how to convert the relative chronology, which is the developmental relationship between different pottery types (i.e., a typology) into an absolute chronology (i.e., a datable sequence) for a particular site. It is one thing to be able to extrapolate a sequence of development in a series of different pottery types, and yet another to be able to associate that sequence with a specific period in time. Only by making this association is archaeology able to identify individual builders with the excavated material culture.[17]

---

15   Finkelstein, Methods, 117, proposes that "scholars must cautiously take a middle path between total reliance on the biblical text and complete dependence on purely archaeological evidence." This proposal has been echoed by biblical scholars who specialize in literary approaches to the material. See the literary discussion below.

16   W. G. Dever, Of Myths and Methods, BASOR 277/278 (1990): 122.

17   Dever, Myths and Methods, 122 also explains that it is significant whether an archaeologist dates a floor or ground level by the pottery in the fill, i.e., that which is below the level of the ground, or by that which is above the ground level, and therefore part of the use-phase of the site. Dever favors using the use-phase pottery to date the gateways, following the arguments of G. E. Wright. It should be noted, however, that while the fill is only able to establish a *terminus post quem*, the use-phase may be contaminated with later forms, and therefore only be able to establish a *terminus ante quem*.

Herein lies the difficulty and the primary point of contention among archaeologists. Up to this point the only material that provides any connection with historical events, and therefore a doorway between relative and absolute chronology, is the Shoshenq stela found at Megiddo and the biblical narrative about Solomon's work at these sites. Both of these texts have difficulties associated with them that preclude simple identification.[18] While the Shoshenq stele is an indicator that this Egyptian king captured the city, it does not aid in determining the date for the destruction of Stratum VA-IVB at Megiddo or the pottery assemblages sealed beneath that destruction debris. As Ussishkin notes, it was standard practice to set up victory stelae in towns that continued to exist, not in those that were destroyed. A later date for the destruction level at Megiddo requires a later date for the gateway, which moves its construction well after the period associated with Solomon.

The debate continues among archaeologists. Some hold to the Solomonic identification for the monumental gateways and others date the gateways to levels later than Solomon.[19] The loss of the monumental structures at Gezer, Megiddo, and Hazor from the tenth century leaves no material remains to be identified with the reign and building program of Solomon as narrated in I Kings. This is a serious problem for archaeology only insofar as it considers part of its role to be the recovery of physical evidence for the biblical narrative. There is no question that monumental gateways were built for these cities, but monumental gateways of this type are found throughout the ancient world over a very wide range of time and cannot be limited to a particular period. Archaeology is as yet unable

18 See Ussishkin's discussion of the stele in BASOR 277/278 (1990): 71-74, and the discussion below concerning the problems associated with the use of biblical material as a historical source.

19 Dever's optimism about Solomonic dating exhibited in his earlier discussions continues in a recent essay, Archaeology and the 'Age of Solomon': A Case Study in Archaeology and Historiography, in The Age of Solomon: Scholarship at the Turn of the Millennium, Studies in the History and Culture of the Ancient Near East, XI, ed. L. K. Handy (Leiden: Brill, 1997), 217-251. John Holladay supported the 10th century dating with his quantitative analysis of pottery in his Red Slip, Burnish, and the Solomonic Gateway at Gezer, BASOR 277/278 (1990): 23-70.

to provide conclusive evidence for the existence of Solomon and must find solutions to its own methodological issues before it appeals to the biblical narrative as an interpretive key for archaeological evidence.

Literary Evidence for the Reign of Solomon

Discussion of the literary evidence is primarily concerned with whether the biblical narrative is an accurate presentation of the events of the early Iron Age. Literary criticism has long questioned whether the narrative can be verified as historical. The recent archaeological debate has instigated considerable discussion among biblical scholars regarding the existence of Solomon.

J. M. Miller calls for biblical studies and archaeology to carry forth their research and interpret their evidence each without reference to the other. Criticizing the use of biblical narrative as an interpretive key for archaeological discoveries, as well as the use of archaeological evidence to support particular interpretations of the text, Miller proposes that the two disciplines work independently and only compare their results after the interpretive work is completed. He offers a challenging question to archaeology,

> . . . is the emerging archaeological picture such that, even if there was no Hebrew Bible and archaeologists had no prior knowledge of Solomon, would they likely have hypothesized by now something on the order of a Solomonic empire and golden age to explain their findings?[20]

Dever responds affirmatively that the archaeological remains are such that if there was no knowledge of Solomon, archaeologists would indeed have to "invent a 10th century B.C.E. Israelite king by another name."[21] The problem with such a blanket response from an archaeologist is that there is so much dissention in the ranks of archaeology that biblical scholars cannot be expected to accept this

---

20   J. M. Miller, Separating the Solomon of History from the Solomon of Legend, in The Age of Solomon, 20.

21   Archaeology and the 'Age of Solomon,' 251.

as a pat answer to the problem. Archaeology must get its own
theoretical house in order before it can offer biblical studies this type
of confirmation.

A. Millard proposes that the ability to reconcile the biblical
description of various elements of Solomon's reign with what is
known about monarchical practices in the ancient world should be
considered solid evidence that the narratives present an accurate
account.[22] Using documents from ancient societies surrounding
Israel as comparative evidence for activities and practices of ancient
monarchs, Millard identifies the material in I Kings that narrates the
activities of Solomon's reign as fitting well within the context of
these other sources. He offers a theoretical explanation for his
method, "Were the Solomon Narrative a hitherto unknown writing
embodied in a recently excavated manuscript some two thousand
years old, a primary mode of evaluation would be contextual . . ."[23]
This may be, but one must be quick to note that the biblical
narratives are not recently excavated manuscripts. On the contrary,
they are narratives that have been worked and reworked by human

---

22   See his discussion in A. Millard, King Solomon in his Ancient Context,
     in The Age of Solomon, 30-53; this essay is an expansion of his earlier
     discussion, in King Solomon's Shields, Scripture and Other Artifacts:
     Essays on the Bible and Archaeology in Honor of Philip J. King, ed. M.
     C. Coogan, J. C. Exum, and L. E. Stager (Louisville: Westminster John
     Knox Press, 1994), 286-295.

23   Ancient Context, 30. Millard's method is to show that the narratives about
     Solomon could fit well in tenth century B.C.E. context and then to claim
     that they must be dated to that time period. This method is similar to that
     formerly used by biblical scholars in their discussions of a second
     millennium dating for the patriarchs based on the assumption that certain
     elements of the narratives, such as names, social customs and lifestyles,
     fit with what was believed to be common for second millennium societies
     based upon documents from places like Nuzi, Mari, Alalah, and Ugarit.
     A comprehensive discussion and critique of this approach to the patriarchs
     may be found in J. Van Seters, Abraham in History and Tradition (New
     Haven and London: Yale University Press, 1975), 7-103; cf. also the
     discussion of T. Thompson, The Historicity of the Patriarchal Narratives:
     The Quest for the Historical Abraham BZAW 133 (Berlin: Walter de
     Gruyter, 1974).

hands throughout the millennia and to set them forth as such an equivalent clouds the important issues involved in literary study.

This point aside, Millard's presentation of the reality of ancient monarchs' use of gold and decorative elements exhibit the difficulties inherent in his argument. The illustrations he cites to supply a context for accuracy in the text come from Egypt between the fifteenth and the twelfth century, from Assyria in the seventh to the sixth century and from Greece in the fifth century.[24] His discussion of shields used in palace furnishings mentions examples from the reign of Sargon II of Assyria in the eighth century and Simon the Maccabee in the second century.[25]

It is clear from the dating of the majority of Millard's contextual markers that one cannot limit the context of the biblical narrative about Solomon to the tenth century. He is quite correct to indicate that a written work will include cultural and contextual information from the period of its composition, but what is not clear from his examples is precisely when this description was composed. Since many of his examples appear in materials that are in fact much later than the tenth century, one cannot rule out these later centuries as the proper context for the narratives about Solomon.[26] The author presents Solomon as a great king in Israel's past and describes his greatness in terms of royal activities common to kings in the ancient East over a very long period of time. Nothing in the narratives or in Millard's comparative material fixes the events of the narrative in the tenth century. Simply because the narrative could fit the tenth century is not evidence that it does fit that period.

The literary supports for attributing large sections of the biblical material to the reign of Solomon in the tenth century have fallen just as drastically as have the archaeological supports for the dating of the

---

24   Ancient Context, 33-36.

25   Ancient Context, 37n18.

26   Millard's proposal, Solomon's Shields, 287-293 that later texts may preserve much earlier practices, and his appeal to the example of the histories written by Pausanius and Herodotus is simply not convincing. There are simply far too many variables in this type of argumentation that one cannot conclude that his is the only viable explanation. This type of ambiguity undermines confidence in historical accuracy of the material.

monumental gateways to the tenth century. With both the literary and the archaeological evidence for the existence of Solomon in such a questionable state, one must consider the implications for understanding the narratives as they now stand in the biblical material.

Previous Approaches to Solomon's Temple

Previous studies of the description of Solomon's temple as described in chapter one are characterized by an assumption of historicity of the narrative. This assumption leads to the search for source materials to stand behind the narrative and the investigation of archaeological data for comparative evidence for the appearance of the temple. Other studies of the temple description assume the historicity of the narrative and interpret the structure of the temple, along with its decorative program and the implements in the courtyard, as symbolic of the religious belief and conceptions of the ancient Israelites. Each of these approaches attempts to provide the background and information necessary for an understanding of the meaning and significance of the temple description, yet leave serious questions unanswered.

The Search for Sources

Since B. Stade's identification of the temple description as part of a building report (Baubericht) from the time of Solomon, commentators on the material have identified various possible source documents that might have provided the detailed information found in the description.[27] In the middle of the twentieth century, J. Montgomery's assessment that the material came from actual

---

27   B. Stade, Der Text des Berichtes über Salomos Bauten, 1Kö. 5-7, ZAW
       3 (1883): 129-177. See also the later comments of C. Watzinger,
       Denkmäler Palästinas I (1933), 88, who also thought that the description
       must have been based upon documents from the time of the construction.

archival sources added fuel to the growing consensus that the description of Solomon's temple must be based upon contemporary source documents.[28] After Montgomery, M. Noth proposed that the source for the temple description was a Book of the Acts of Solomon. Noting the use of technical terms and the attention given to the measurements of the structure, Noth said that the Book of the Acts of Solomon had gotten its information from the actual instructions given to the artisans and craftsmen who had worked on the temple.[29] Subsequent works have proffered various permutations of the basic thesis that the temple description is based upon contemporary documents that had been maintained in the royal or temple archives.[30]

The proposition that the temple description depends on contemporary documents, which were subsequently maintained in royal or temple archives, provides an air of authenticity to the material, but does little to advance our understanding of the significance of the temple, not to mention the text. In fact, it relegates the temple description to a secondary position in the interpretive process and sets forth the object to which the text is supposed to be a witness, i.e., the temple, as the primary object of concern. It is true that the use of what appear to be technical terms, many of which are *hapax legomena*, contributes to the sense of architectural accuracy. But to say that this usage points only to the employment of archival documents presumes that later writers could not have known or understood the technical terms. The problem remains, however, that many scholars use the terms "archive" and "annalistic" to describe the proposed source documents without

---

28 J. Montgomery, The Books of Kings, International Critical Commentary, ed. H. S. Gehman (Edinburgh: T. & T. Clark, 1951), 33-38, see also his comments on 142 and 145 regarding the archival character of the material.
29 M. Noth, Könige, BKAT 9/1 (Neukirchen-Vluyn: Neukirchener Verlag, 1968), 104-108.
30 See, for example, J. Gray, I & II Kings, 2nd ed., Old Testament Library (Philadelphia: Westminster Press, 1970), 23-24, 157-158; E. Würthwein, Das Erste Buch der Könige, Kapitel 1-16, Das Alte Testament Deutsch 11,1 (Göttingen: Vandenhoeck & Ruprecht, 1977), 57-59; S. DeVries, 1 Kings, Word Biblical Commentary 12 (Waco, TX: Word Books, 1985), 92-93.

carrying through the necessary investigation to understand the existence and use of such materials in the ancient world.

An exhaustive study of the creation, maintenance and use of annals, chronicles, and other archived documents in the ancient world has been done by J. Van Seters.[31] After a careful study of the different genres of archived materials in the ancient world, he concludes that history writing does not necessarily develop from genres such as annals, royal inscriptions, or chronicles, nor were these materials available to historiographers when writing their histories. In a more recent summation of the use of archived documents in the ancient world Van Seters states, "In antiquity, there was never a body of official or religious documents preserved for posterity, to be consulted by later historians for their curiosity."[32] The evidence clearly indicates that the proposition of source documents for the temple description in I Kings 6-7 does not agree with what is now known about the use of archival documents in the ancient world. While there is an indication that archival documents may have been useful for administrative concerns, there is no illustration of their use by historians as sources for the composition of a narrative history or as a support for the accuracy of such a history.

A more promising approach to the compositional history of the temple description may be that of A. Hurowitz.[33] Hurowitz undertakes a form critical study and seeks his comparative data from the building inscriptions discovered in Mesopotamia and the Levant. After a comparison of the description of Solomon's temple building with the royal inscriptions from these other cultures, Hurowitz concludes that the narrative of I Kings 5:15-9: 25 was influenced by the building inscription genre as it developed in Assyria.[34] The

---

31   J. Van Seters, In Search of History: Historiography in the Ancient World
       and the Origins of Biblical History (New Haven and London: Yale
       University Press, 1983).
32   J. Van Seters, Solomon's Temple: Fact and Ideology in Biblical and Near
       Eastern Historiography, CBQ 59 (1997): 49.
33   A. Hurowitz, I Have Built You an Exalted House: Temple Building in the
       Bible in Light of Mesopotamian and Northwest Semitic Writings, JSOTS
       115 (Sheffield: Sheffield Academic Press, 1992).
34   Hurowitz, Exalted House, 316.

difference in Hurowitz' approach from those which identify specific source documents is that he does not outline a direct dependence of this narrative upon Assyrian materials, but rather explains the literary form as influenced by the (apparently) widely known form of royal building inscriptions. He explains that the information in the description is based upon "original documents--the letters, administrative records, chronographic records, dedicatory inscriptions, building plans and prayers-- . . ."[35] This information is shaped into this building report form by the Deuteronomistic historian when he composes his description of King Solomon building the temple.

Hurowitz has marshaled a large collection of material from the Ancient Near East and provided the clearest discussion of this literary form in the ancient world. He may be right in stating that the composition of the temple description is structured following the pattern of this genre, but some of his conclusions are questionable. Though he indicates that the I Kings narrative follows the Assyrian inscriptions most closely, there are real differences between them for which he makes no account. Assyrian building inscriptions follow the form of the annals of a particular king and follow a long list of the yearly campaigns of the king. There is nothing like this in the biblical text. The Assyrian inscriptions used in his comparison end with a section of blessings and curses that would befall later kings who encounter the inscription, depending upon how they treated the inscription itself. Again, the biblical text does not contain this element.

Hurowitz admits that the level of detail found in the I Kings narrative is rare in Assyrian materials, yet he maintains the closeness of the forms. In fact it is very unusual for a Mesopotamian inscription to give details of the appearance of the structure, while the I Kings text is mostly a detailed description of the temple.[36] If

---

35   Hurowitz, Exalted House, 319.

36   J. Van Seters, In Search of History, 310 suggests that the lack of detail would be expected when the building was present and could be seen and that such a detailed description would only be necessary if the structure were far off or no longer extant. Hurowitz addresses this by indicating that the Sennacherib inscriptions that describe his Palace without Rival in Nineveh provide the more detail about the appearance of the structure than

one adds to these difficulties the recognition that Assyrian inscriptions usually treat palaces, while Babylonian building inscriptions have a much higher interest in the construction of temples, then Hurowitz conclusion that the biblical narrative is more akin to Assyrian than Babylonian inscriptions seems less likely. Moreover, Assyrian kings who recount their temple building are typically those like Esarhaddon and Assurbanipal, who had a true affinity for things and customs Babylonian. These facts, combined with the acknowledgment that his comparative materials for the dating formulas in I Kings 6 come from late sources, bring the dating of the biblical description down to a period later than that proposed by Hurowitz.[37]

Two recent studies of this text take a new angle on the issue of source materials. Noting the similarities in the description of the sea and columns of the temple in I Kings 7 and in the destruction of the temple in II Kings 25, Van Seters understands the author to be connecting the temple at the end of the kingdom with the great temple built by Solomon at the beginning of the kingdom.[38] Moreover, Van Seters identifies the temple description in I Kings 6-7 as based upon the appearance of the temple in the days of the Deuteronomistic historian at the end of the kingdom rather than having its source in the time of Solomon.[39] This is an innovative way of understanding the material which is quite plausible, given the similarity of the description of the vessels, and does not require the supposition of source documents for which there is no extant evidence. If the source for the description of the temple is the appearance of the temple at the end of the kingdom of Judah, then the description in I Kings 6-7 is completely separated from any connection with the time of Solomon. The historian's identification

---

any other Assyrian text, and that these were public texts while the palace was still standing. This argument is not particularly helpful since it ignores related issues of literacy in Assyrian society, as well as questions about who would and would not have been allowed to view the palace.

37   Hurowitz, Exalted House, 230, admits to late dating of his comparative material and the questionable use of this as evidence for comparison, but considers it evidence for the form nonetheless.

38   Van Seters, Solomon's Temple, 55.

39   Van Seters, Solomon's Temple, 56.

of the vessels as those which were made by King Solomon for the house of YHWH (II Kings 25:16, cf. also Jeremiah 52:20) and the description of the temple as it was built by Solomon (I Kings 6-7) both should then be understood as literary constructs that serve the historian's purposes, rather than as accurate accounts of the appearance of the temple constructed by Solomon or that destroyed by Nebuzaradan and his troops. Van Seters concludes that the temple description in I Kings 6-7 and the description of the courtyard vessels and implements in II Kings 25:15-17 identify the temple with the conditions stated in I Kings 9:1-9, which include the divine judgement that destroyed it in II Kings 25.[40]

N. Na'aman follows Van Seters' suggestion that the temple description is patterned after the temple of the historian's own time.[41] Na'aman dates the composition to the reign of Josiah and indicates that the historian uses the temple of his own time as his pattern in order to establish continuity between the great reign of Solomon and that of Josiah. The detail and accuracy in the temple description are, in Na'aman's view, attributable to the historian being an eyewitness to the structure he is describing. It is not the actual temple built by Solomon, but rather the one renovated by Josiah.[42]

In each of the above approaches to the description of the temple of Solomon, one consistent problem remains. Whether one seeks sources for the description of the temple in contemporaneous archival documents used by the historian in the composition of his national history, or in the memory of eyewitnesses (including the historian) to the appearance of the temple in its last days, there remains the question of why the historian provides this type of description of the appearance of the structure. I Kings 6-7 does not furnish enough of the necessary details for a reconstruction and

---

40 Van Seters, Solomon's Temple, 57. Note particularly the language of I Kings 9:7-9, which describes the rejection of the house and the reaction of passersby when they see what has happened because the royal house turned after other gods. The ideological significance of the temple will be discussed fully below.

41 N. Na'aman, Sources and Composition in the History of Solomon, in The Age of Solomon, 57-80; idem, Royal Inscriptions and the Histories of Joash and Ahaz, Kings of Judah, VT 48,3 (1998): 333.

42 Na'aman, Sources and Composition, 75.

therefore could not have been a pattern upon which a restored temple was based. While Van Seters' conclusions are most helpful insofar as they concentrate on the ideology of the historian as the controlling factor in the description, there is still no explanation for such a detailed description in I Kings. It would seem then that the most useful next step is to set aside issues of sources and accuracy and take up issues of the ideology and conceptual world of the historian describing this structure.

Interpretive Approaches to Solomon's Temple

Interpretive approaches to the description of Solomon's temple also accept the narrative as an accurate presentation of the temple and interpret the implements and the decorative program as symbolic of religious beliefs and concepts in ancient Israel. For instance, the religionsgeschichtlich approach assumes that the narrative is an accurate presentation of events and finds within it information on the development of religious belief and practice in ancient Israel.[43] Scholars such as Schmid and Rupprecht suggest that the temple was built on the site of a preexisting Jebusite sanctuary dedicated to El-Elyon and that Solomon's choice of this site was part of an attempt to unify Israelites and Jebusites of Jerusalem through an association of YHWH and El-Elyon.[44] This approach offers no discussion of the significance of the temple description itself except as evidence for the historical and religious development of Israel.

E. Bloch-Smith, while also assuming the accuracy of the biblical description of the temple in I Kings 6-7, addresses the specific descriptions found in the text by offering an interpretation of the symbolism of the various implements and the decorative program of

---

43 H. Schmid, Der Tempelbau Salomos in religionsgeschichtlicher Sicht, in Archäologie und altes Testament: Festschrift für Kurt Galling, hg. A. Kuschke and E. Kutsch (Tübingen: Mohr Siebeck, 1970), 241-250; K. Rupprecht, Der Tempel von Jerusalem, Gründung Salomos oder jebusitisches Erbe? BZAW 144 (Berlin: Walter de Gruyter, 1977).

44 Schmid, Tempelbau Salomos, 249-250; Rupprecht, Tempel von Jerusalem, 100-105.

the temple.[45] She concludes that the temple decoration recalls the paradise story in which the cherubim are stationed to guard the path to the tree of life. The implements in the courtyard are symbolic of YHWH's victory over chaos at creation and his triumphal entry to his temple to be enthroned above the cherubim.[46]

While this type of interpretive approach moves away from discussions of sources for the biblical narrative and focuses more on the symbolism within the text, it is still problematic. On the one hand, Bloch-Smith's approach focuses on the structure of the temple rather than the literary structure of the text and understands the text to be merely a witness to the appearance of the temple. On the other hand, her dependence upon the myth-ritual pattern in which the deity, victorious over the powers of chaos, is enthroned on his holy mountain (as in the Baal cycle from Ugarit) is unconvincing for two reasons. First, it applies a foreign interpretive key to a biblical narrative. A better founded interpretive approach to the temple description is one that interprets the significance of the text within the parameters of other Deuteronomistic texts. There is no clear tradition in the biblical material of the creation of the world being achieved through a battle with chaotic powers. This motif is known from surrounding cultures, but is not clearly part of Israelite mythic traditions. Second, the narrative development of the Baal cycle is not clearly established. It is evident that there is a battle between Baal and Yamm, however, its purpose in the narrative is not creation, but rather the limited exaltation of Baal as king.[47] Further, the order of

---

45   E. Bloch-Smith, "Who is the King of Glory?" Solomon's Temple and its Symbolism, in Scripture and other Artifacts: Essays on the Bible and Archaeology in Honor of Philip J. King, ed. M. D. Coogan, J. C. Exum, and L. E. Stager (Louisville, KY: Westminster John Knox Press, 1994), 18-31.

46   Bloch-Smith, "Who is the King of Glory?" 26-27.

47   M. S. Smith, The Ugaritic Baal Cycle, Vol. I: Introduction with Text, Translation and Commentary of KTU 1.1-1.2, VTSup 55 (Leiden: E. J. Brill, 1994), 318-324 for text and translation of KTU 1.2 IV, 324-361 for commentary on the same material. Interestingly, later in the narrative it appears that the defeat of Sea (Yamm) was accomplished by Anat and not Baal, cf. M. D. Coogan, Stories from Ancient Canaan (Philadelphia: Westminster Press, 1978), 92-93. For a more general critique of the problems associated with the use of this pattern to understand Israelite

the tablets is not without controversy, a situation which introduces serious questions regarding the development of the pattern.[48] The use of the Ugaritic material to interpret a biblical text is not a satisfactory method as long as there is such debate regarding the order and significance of the narrative of the Baal story. While there may be similarities in the general range of symbolic elements, this does not indicate a similarity of belief or conceptualization of the divine realm.

Within the above interpretive approaches the text is generally considered to provide a reliable account of the construction and appearance of the temple and is used as a witness to that structure. The difficulty is that they relegate the text itself to secondary status as pointing to an object for which there is no physical evidence. What is needed is an approach that understands the primary nature of the text as a verbal icon.

Archaeological Approaches to Solomon's Temple

Archaeological approaches usually carry out excavations in order to provide physical evidence in the form of material culture that can then be interpreted. This is not the case with Solomon's temple. No excavations are allowed in the area believed to have been the site of Solomon's temple, so retrieving physical evidence for the appearance of the temple is foreseeably not a possibility. Given this set of circumstances, archaeologists take a different approach to the temple of Solomon. Excavated temples from other sites are cited as comparative evidence for the appearance of the Jerusalem temple.[49]

---

religious symbolism and descriptions of theophany, see J. Van Seters, The Life of Moses: The Yahwist as Historian in Exodus-Numbers (Louisville: Westminster John Knox Press, 1994), 257-259.

48   M. S. Smith, The Ugaritic Baal Cycle, 2-25.

49   See, for example, the discussions of W. G. Dever, Monumental Architecture in Ancient Israel in the Period of the United Monarchy, in Studies in the Period of David and Solomon and other Essays, ed. T. Ishida (Winona Lake, IN: Eisenbrauns, 1982), 269-306, particularly 295-304; and A. Mazar, Temples of the Middle and Late Bronze Ages and the Iron Age, in The Architecture of Ancient Israel from the Prehistoric to the

This approach also assumes the accuracy of the biblical text and seeks to confirm its accuracy by comparing that description with the actual floor plans of excavated structures.

This has been a problematic enterprise from the start. A. Mazar indicates that the Iron Age temples that have been excavated within the boundaries of ancient Israel do not match the description of Solomon's temple. The symmetrical long room temples, of which the Jerusalem temple is an example, appeared in the last century of the Middle Bronze but did not continue in use into the Iron Age.[50] The Iron Age temples are most often of the form known as broad room, though Mazar admits that the excavated structures exhibit such a wide variety of forms that it is nearly impossible to categorize them.[51] The most commonly cited example for comparison with the Jerusalem temple is that of the palace-temple complex at Tell Tayinat. But there are discrepancies in the details when this temple is compared with the description of the Jerusalem temple.[52]

Archaeology can establish that the form of the temple described in the biblical narrative was known in the ancient world, even if it cannot be verified by excavations within Iron Age Israel, but archaeology cannot offer confirming evidence for the appearance of the temple in Jerusalem. Without physical evidence that confirms the appearance of Solomon's temple in Jerusalem there is no actual structure with which to compare the description. Therefore, the function of the description within the literature is more significant than a recreation of a historical edifice through the use of comparative structures. The literary description of Solomon's temple is an important element in the Deuteronomistic History of the nation

---

Persian Periods, ed. A. Kempinski and R. Reich (Jerusalem: Israel Exploration Society, 1992), 161-187, particularly figure 14 on page 163 where Mazar includes a reconstruction of the floor plan of Solomon's temple for comparison with those of other actually excavated temples.

50 Mazar, Temples, 164.

51 Mazar, Temples, 181.

52 See the comments of Y Aharoni, The Archaeology of the Land of Israel: From the Prehistoric Beginnings to the End of the First Temple Period, trsl. A. F. Rainey (Philadelphia: Westminster Press, 1982), 227-228, where he indicates that the two temples have certain clear differences though they belong to the same general type.

of Israel. Its purpose in that history, however, may not be the presentation of an accurate description of that temple. Recent studies of other temple descriptions in the biblical material offer an important shift in focus with regard to such compositions and are informative for the approach of this study.

Literary Approaches to Temple Descriptions

Literary approaches to temple descriptions offer a promising new perspective in the way they take seriously the contexts of the material related to the temple. As indicated in the introduction to this chapter, because the description of Solomon's temple in I Kings 6-7 does not include all the necessary details for a reconstruction, scholars turn to the descriptions found in   II Chronicles 3-4 and in Ezekiel 40-42 in order to provide that information. For instance, Busink's delineation of sources for Solomon's temple includes the descriptions in Chronicles and Ezekiel.[53] This practice is more common before M. Noth's commentary and his cogent arguments against such usage. He argues that the description in II Chronicles is clearly dependent upon that in I Kings and the description in Ezekiel is patently a vision and not a description of an actual temple.[54]

Recently, J. Z. Smith has studied the temple description in Ezekiel without attempting a reconstruction of it as an actual structure.[55] Noting that the description gives more information about the temple precinct than about the temple itself, Smith reads the description as

---

53   Busink, Der Tempel von Jerusalem, see his discussion 23-24 in which he maintains that there is information that is useful for reconstruction of the temple in these two descriptions even though he is aware that many scholars consider these descriptions to be based upon structures later than that of Solomon.

54   Noth, Könige, 106-107. Noth does allow that the temple described in Ezekiel could be based on the structure in Jerusalem just before the exile, but maintains that one should not consider this description in any way based upon the temple from the time of Solomon.

55   J. Z. Smith, To Take Place: Toward Theory in Ritual (Chicago and London: The University of Chicago Press, 1987), 47-73.

a literary presentation of ideological maps. The architectural arrangement of boundary and access in the temple precinct mirrors the social arrangement of status and power based upon the dichotomies of sacred/profane and pure/impure.[56] The temple precinct is divided into domains within which different social groups may move. For instance, the Zadokite priests have access to the innermost domain, the Most Holy Place, because of their status as the purest in society. Smith explains that the description of the precinct is more concerned with the description of social status and power than with giving an accurate presentation of the appearance of the temple structure. The ideology of the author is a major factor in the form the description takes. Following Smith's conclusions regarding the literary maps embodied in this temple description in Ezekiel, it is certainly inappropriate to reduce Ezekiel's temple description to an amplification of the description in I Kings 6-7.

The second temple description, II Chronicles 3:3-4:22, has long been recognized as having used the description in I Kings 6-7 as its starting point. The recent study of J. Van Seters surmises that the Chronicler reworked this material by incorporating elements from the priestly description of the tabernacle in Exodus 25-30.[57] Modifying the temple description of I Kings in this manner, the Chronicler established a continuity between the temple of his own time, after the exile, and that of Solomon and the tabernacle of Moses. Thus the description in II Chronicles is less concerned with providing an accurate description of the temple as it appeared in Solomon's day, than with establishing an ideological continuity that reached from his own time back to the founding days of the people of Israel.

The conclusions of these two studies are similar, even though they come from different perspectives. In each case the narrative is recognized as ideologically motivated and the goal of the studies is to elucidate the ideology embedded in the narrative. If these two scholars are correct in their readings of these important biblical texts

---

56   See particularly Smith's discussion in pages 56-65.
57   J. Van Seters, The Chronicler's Account of Solomon's Temple-Building: A Continuity Theme, in The Chronicler as Historian, JSOTS 233, ed., M. P. Graham, K. G. Hoglund and S. L. McKenzie (Sheffield: JSOT Press, 1998), 283-300.

and if Ezekiel and the Chronicler have ideological concerns that override any intention of providing an accurate description of an actual structure, then this material should not be used to provide details not found in I Kings 6-7. However, there are enough similarities in the structure and rhetoric of the temple descriptions of I Kings, II Chronicles, and Ezekiel to conclude that the I Kings text is also motivated by the author's ideology rather than concern for an accurate presentation of the temple's appearance. Understanding these temple descriptions as ideological literary creations requires a new consideration of how one might approach a literary temple.

Solomon's Temple in I Kings: The Text

The following discussion is a presentation of the standard commentaries and their explanation of the description of Solomon's temple and its implements in I Kings 6-7. It has long been clear that the temple description is problematical in its structure and usage of vocabulary. Much of the work performed by the commentaries is the investigation and discussion of linguistic elements that provide true obstacles to modern understanding of the temple description. In some cases they clarify the meaning of a passage, but in others the reconstructions offered by the commentaries create other problems which need further clarification.

I Kings 6:2-36: The Description of the Temple and its Decoration

The text that describes the temple presents the reader with several problems which are attributable to the fact that many of the words are *hapax legomena* and their meanings are obscure at best. In addition, there are also scribal errors in the text that compound the difficulty of reading the description as a clear presentation of the appearance of Solomon's temple. A comparison of several commentaries on the text reveals that scholars rarely agree on exactly how one should understand these troublesome terms or how to reconstruct the text so that it presents a clear description. In what follows we will concentrate on those sections of the description on which the commentaries offer differing opinions in order to highlight the problematic nature of the text.

The description of the temple begins by giving the overall measurements of the elements that make up the temple, the main structure (הבית) in verse 2, the portico (האולם) in verse 3, and the side chambers (הצלעות) in verses 5-6, 8, and 10.[58] It is in this section, which gives the dimensions of the building elements, that the difficulties inherent in this description first come to light. Verse 2 gives the dimensions of the house as 60x20x30 cubits, but gives no information about whether these measurements include the walls, are the external dimensions, or the internal dimensions measured within the walls of the building.[59] There is no information given for the thickness of the walls of the structure. Though not symmetrical, the measurements exhibit an interesting relationship between the dimensions for the main chamber. Its length is three times its width and its height is half its length. The fact that no measurements are given for the wall thickness is a real problem so long as one considers an accurate architectural presentation of the structure to be the intent of the text. This requires that one secure information from Ezekiel to be able to imagine the wall thickness. Rather than appealing to Ezekiel, if one accepts the I Kings 6 description on its own merits, then giving only internal dimensions, without wall measurements, may indicate a concern solely for the internal space of the temple. The author does not provide measurements for the thickness of the wall because the walls are important merely as boundaries that delineate this internal space. It is the ideological proportions, not the actual measurements that are important.

The dimensions of the porch provide another difficulty. The Hebrew text of I Kings 6:3 reads,

והאולם על־פני היכל הבית עשרים אמה ארכו על־פני
רחב הבית עשר באמה רחבו על־פני הבית

---

58   There is some discussion concerning the use of the term צלע and יציע
      (Ketib = יצוע) in the description of the side chambers. We will return to
      this problem below.
59   This dilemma is ultimately clarified in verses 16-17, see below.

The portico upon the front of the great chamber of the House was twenty cubits in length upon the front of the width of the House; its width was ten cubits upon the front of the House.

The misunderstanding of this verse stems from the use of the words "length" (ארך) and "width" (רחב). In verse 3, the portico is described as half as wide as the house and as having a length that is twice its width. Most commentaries change the reading so that the portico dimensions indicate that the portico was the same width as the house and only ten cubits long from front to back.[60] These changes are based primarily on comparison of the LXX translation and an appeal to comparative evidence.[61] Yet this ignores the fact that everywhere else ארך is used in this description it indicates dimensions from front to back, while רחב indicates dimensions from side to side.[62] The portico is still symmetrical if one follows the Hebrew text, it merely exhibits a different type of symmetry.

---

60 Cf. Montgomery, Kings, 144; Würthwein, 1. Könige 1-16, 60, 62; Gray, I & II Kings, 161. Noth, Könige, 95, translates ארך as „Länge" but understands the length to run along the width of the house, „und die Vorhalle . . . hatte 20 Elle Länge entlang der Breite des Hauses . . ." Only DeVries, 1 Kings, 85 understands the length of the porch to be longer than its width.

61 Gray, I & II Kings, 164, notes the LXX describes the אולם as flush with the side walls of the house and shapes his translation of the text in that way. LXX, however, appears to be a fairly slavish translation of the Hebrew of MT: καὶ τὸ αιλαμ κατὰ πρόσωπον τοῦ ναοῦ, εἴκοσι ἐν πηχει μῆκος αὐτοῦ εἰς τὸ πλάτος τοῦ οἴκου καὶ δέκα ἐν πηχει τὸ πλάτος αὐτοῦ κατὰ πρόσωπον τοῦ οἴκου. Noth, Könige, 111 explains his translation by stating that comparative evidence from excavated temples indicates that the porch was formed by an extension of the side walls of the main chamber, which would make a porch that was the same width as the main structure. The primary comparative material comes from Tell Tayinat, where the side walls extend to the porch, but there are other problems with using the Tell Tayinat structure as an interpretive key for the temple description of I Kings. For further comments regarding the temple at Tell Tayinat, see above, 123 n.52.

62 These are from the perspective of one facing the house and are constant throughout the description. For a further example of this consistency see the comments on verse 6 below.

Verses 5-6 begin the description of the building of the side-chambers all around the house with the statement that Solomon first made a platform upon which to build the addition.

ויבן על־קיר הבית יצוע סביב את־קירות הבית סביב להיכל
ולדביר ויעש צלעות סביב: היצוע התחתנה חמש באמה רחבה
והתיכנה שש באמה רחבה והשלישית שבע באמה רחבה כי
מגרעות נתן לבית סביב חוצה לבלתי אחז בקירות־הבית

> Then he built against the wall of the house a platform surrounding the walls of the house all around the main chamber and the inner chamber, and he made stories all around. The lowest story, its width was five cubits, and the middle, its width was six cubits, and the third, its width was seven cubits, because he placed recesses all around the outside of the house so as not to connect to the walls of the house.[63]

The appearance of היצוע at the beginning of verse 6 appears to be a scribal error for הצלע. This may be confirmed by a comparison of verse 6 with verse 10. Verse 6 indicates that the structure under discussion was made of three levels (stories) and that each one was wider than the one below it.[64] The outer wall of the house had recesses upon which the floors of the side-chambers could rest. This was done in order to allow for the structure to meet the outside wall of the house without actually being attached to it. If one understands

---

63   The text has יצוע but should be read יציע. יצוע means "bed, couch," while יציע is only a Qere and is taken to mean a "flat surface." Montgomery, Kings, 144; and Würthwein, 1. Könige 1-16, 60, take it to refer to the addition as a whole that was built on the outside wall of the temple. Most other commentaries take it to refer to the foundation platform upon which the side-chambers were built.

64   The lowest was five cubits wide, the middle was six cubits wide, and the third story was seven cubits wide. Each of these widths are from the perspective of a viewer standing facing the temple, so the width described is from the point where the chamber meets the outer wall of the temple to the point to the left or right of that, depending upon which side of the temple one is viewing. This would normally be considered the length, or depth, of the room if one were standing at the doorway to that particular chamber. This is another example of the use of רחב to describe width from the perspective of one facing the temple structure.

the term היצוע to refer to the side-chambers, then verse 10 is a direct
contradiction to verse 6 since it indicates that the יצוע was attached
to the house, not to mention that it describes the height of the יצוע as
only five cubits.[65] היצוע may refer to the platform upon which the
side-chambers were built. It would have been five cubits high and
gone around the entire temple. No height would therefore be
indicated for the stories of the side-chambers.[66]

Verse 7 is an addition to the text which incorporates the idea that
no metal tools were heard within the precinct of the temple. It offers
no information on the structure and interrupts the description of the
side-chambers.

Verse 8 picks up the description of the side-chambers and
describes how they were accessed. A doorway on the right side of
the temple entered the lowest story. The text indicates that they
could reach the upper stories by means of something referred to as
לולים. These have for some time been considered a winding
staircase (so the NRSV). Stade preferred to understand this word as
referring to "trapdoors," and he has been followed by many
commentaries in this.[67] There is only one door of access and one
stairway up to the chambers which provides a most awkward mode

---

65   ויבן היצוע על־כל־הבית חמש אמות קמתו ויאחז את־הבית בעצי
     ארזים: Then he built the platform upon all the whole temple; its height
     was five cubits and it connected with the house by means of cedar beams.

66   It is only Montgomery, Kings, 144, and his comments on 147, and
     Würthwein, 1. Könige 1-16, 60, who maintain that the term יצוע refers to
     the side-chambers. This leads Montgomery to misunderstand the ledges on
     the exterior walls as modifications made so as not to have insets in the
     walls of the house, as though the controlling factor was the width of the
     chambers. It is clear in the text, however, that the width of the chambers
     was the result of the ideological requirement that they not connect to the
     house. Montgomery and Würthwein both understand the five cubit height
     to refer to five cubits for each story, i.e., fifteen cubits total height for the
     addition. Cf. also B. Stade, Der Text des Berichtes, 139.

67   Stade, Der Text des Berichtes, 140; Noth, Könige, 96, 99; Gray, I & II
     Kings, 162, 166. Stade first objected because no such winding stairs were
     known from the ancient world. L. Woolley discovered winding stairs at
     Acbatana and removed this objection. Noth and Gray maintain "trap-doors"
     based on post-biblical (Rabbinic) Hebrew usage. The verb of access is יעלו
     from עלה, "go up," which fits nicely with the idea of stairs.

of access through which one would have to start on the south side of the building, walk all the way to the back (west) wall, turn north and walk to the left side of the building before turning east and reaching the side-chambers on that side of the temple. Even though it has been proposed that there were at least two such doorways, one on either side, that led to the side-chambers, this is based on Ezekiel's description and does not clarify this text.[68]

The side chambers are not easily accessed and according to the description are not reached from within the temple, since this would require that they in fact be attached to the temple building and the description takes care to explain that they are not. Even though this makes for awkward movement between the temple and the side chambers, it maintains the distinctive nature of the two domains. They are clearly presented as entirely separate from one another. This element seems obviously ideological. Ease of access to the side chambers and the items that may have been stored in them would no doubt have been part of the floor plan of the temple. Had the side chambers no points of access from within the temple it would have been far too awkward to store items in them and their usefulness would have been seriously compromised. Maintaining their separateness is part of the ideology of the historian and does not present the reader with an accurate image of the structure of the temple storage complex.

Verse 9 is a summarizing statement that Solomon completed the main structure by roofing it over with cedar beams. Verses 11-13 are a post-deuteronomistic insertion since they interrupt the description in order to say something about the role of the house as the place where YHWH will dwell in the midst of the people as long as the king (Solomon) remains wholly committed to the statutes and commandments of YHWH. It does not advance the description of the structure, but rather seeks to make the deuteronomistic ideology of obedience explicit, as well as offering a foreshadowing of the significance of the temple in Jerusalem. Verse 14 resumes the description by repeating the summary statement of verse 9 that he completed the building of the main structure.

---

68   This was the proposal of L. Waterman, The Damaged 'Blueprints' of the Temple of Solomon, JNES 2 (1943): 288.

Verse 15 describes the wood paneling of the inside of the house from the floor to the ceiling.[69] Verses 16-20 describe the construction of the inner chamber (דביר) within the space of the main structure (בית). The MT exhibits some confusing structure which may be attributable to scribal errors. What follows is a reconstructed Hebrew text which relies on changes based upon LXX.

ויבן את־עשרים אמה מירכותי הבית בצלעות ארזים מן־הקרקע
עד־הקירות ויבן לו מבית לדביר לקדש הקדשים: וארבעים באמה
היה הבית הוא ההיכל לפני הדביר: וארז אל־הבית פנימה
מקלעת פקעים ופטורי צצים הכל ארז אין אבן נראה: ודביר
בתוך־הבית פנימה הכין לתתן שם את־ארון ברית יהוה: הדביר
עשרים אמה ארך ועשרים אמה רחב ועשרים אמה קומתו ויצפהו
זהב סגור ויעש מזבח ארז לפני הדביר ויצפהו זהב סגור:

And he built twenty cubits from the back of the house with cedar planks from the floor to the ceiling and he built it within as an inner chamber, the Holiest Place. And the house, which was the main chamber was forty cubits in front of the inner chamber. And the cedar on the inside of the house was carvings of cones and blooms of flowers; the whole was cedar, no stone was visible. He established an inner chamber in the midst of the house to place the ark of the covenant of YHWH there. The inner chamber was twenty cubits long and twenty cubits wide and twenty cubits was its height, and he plated it with reserved gold, and he made a cedar altar in front of the inner chamber and he plated it with reserved gold.[70]

---

69   Cf. Montgomery, Kings, 153; Noth, Könige, 99; Gray, I & II Kings, 168, who reconstruct עד־קורות הספן with LXX, which reads, καὶ ἕως τῶν δοκῶν καὶ ἕως τῶν τοίχων, ". . . to the rafters of the ceiling," in place of MT קירות, "walls." The reconstruction is not necessary if one understands קירות to refer to the "inner surface" of the ceiling, a usage which is attested when קירות is used in conjunction with other terms, see BDB 885a, s.v. קיר.

70   Verse twenty begins with ולפני הדביר. The critical apparatus suggests omitting the first word and beginning the verse והדביר. Also, MT mentions a cedar altar in the last phrase as being plated with gold. This is the first mention of the altar, which seems strangely out of place in this context. Noth, Könige, 100, suggests reconfiguring the verse so that the initial words ולפני הדביר refer to the placement of the altar in front of the inner chamber. Würthwein, 1. Könige 1-16, 61; and Gray, I & II Kings, 168 follow Noth's suggestion. The reconstruction offered here follows the

The text initially describes the wall that divides the inner chamber and the main chamber (היכל) as built twenty cubits from the back of the house. This leaves forty cubits for the main chamber, which is completely paneled in cedar that is engraved with carvings of bulbs (cones?) and blooming flowers. Verse 19 indicates that the inner chamber is a place for the ark of the covenant of YHWH. Only in verse 20 are the actual dimensions for the inner chamber given. It is a perfect cube of twenty cubits that is completely plated with reserved gold.

Again the dimensions provided require some explanation. In this section it would appear that the dimensions that are given for the building in verse 2 are the internal dimensions; they are the measurements from wall to wall and floor to ceiling. Though that issue is now clarified, another problem arises from the dimensions given for the inner chamber. The twenty cubit cube is delineated within the space of the house which leaves forty cubits of length for the main chamber (היכל). This, however, leaves no room for the wall and door that separates the inner chamber from the main chamber. Moreover, the inner chamber is evidently constructed only by the construction of the separating wall since the width is the same as the rest of the house. The ten cubit difference between the height of the inner chamber and the rest of the building is not explained in the description and does not agree with the description of the wall separating the דביר from the היכל being constructed from floor to ceiling.[71] There is either an empty space above the inner chamber, or its floor is raised ten cubits from that of the rest of the building. Both options are problematic. The former is problematic because the description indicates the wall is constructed from floor to rafters, while the latter has the problem that no stairs are indicated in this temple description. All of these points of difficulty are evidence that the description is ideological and not a physical description of the structure of the temple. Only when the reader understands that the controlling agenda is ideology and not accuracy and begins an

---

LXX which reads καὶ ἐποίησεν θυσιαστήριον κατὰ πρόσωπον τοῦ δαβιρ καὶ περιέσχεν αὐτὸ χρυσίῳ.

71   On this rendering of הקירות, see 118n69, above.

investigation to perceive the ideology of the author are the difficulties resolved.

The lack of clarity with regard to the dimensions of the house and its constituent elements is a characteristic of the description. This lack may be more apparent than actual, and may be a product of modern scholars' attempts to use the description in inappropriate ways. If one follows the emphasis of the description, it is clear that such clarity is not necessary for an understanding of the description. The author explains the inner chamber as carved out of the existing space of the building. His initial emphasis is on the space and the boundaries and accesses are the elements which demarcate that space. The author of this description is constructing spatial domains and the apparent lack of clarity does not exist when the reader follows the author's lead rather than pushing the text to fit modern concerns.

Verses 21-22 complete the description of the decoration of the temple by indicating that the entire structure is plated with reserved gold, as is the altar in front of the inner chamber. While Montgomery cites texts from the Neo-Assyrian and Neo-Babylonian kings that describe their plating the inside of sanctuaries with gold in order to show that this is not an unusual practice in the ancient world, this type of evidence does not confirm the accuracy of the biblical description.[72] It could just as well indicate the author's awareness of such a practice and have been incorporated to equate the sanctuary he describes with some elaborate sanctuaries of which he is aware. In the description presented here, the use of gold certainly marks the space as privileged and entirely distinct from the mundane world of the human realm. The use of gold in the temple forms an important element in the interpretation of the significance of this verbal icon, as will be clear in the discussion below.

Verses 23-28 indicate that two cherubim are made and placed within the inner chamber. Their height and the length of their wings are given, but there are no details of the appearance of these creatures other than that their wings reach to the outer wall of the inner chamber and touch in the middle. Verse 29 describes the decoration of the walls of the house, both the inner chamber and the

---

72   See Montgomery, Book of Kings, 150-151.

main chamber with engravings of cherubim and palm trees with blooming flowers in a repeating pattern. Verse 30 says that even the floors of the inner chamber and the main chamber are plated with gold.

Verses 31-35 describe the construction of the doorways and doors for the inner chamber and the main chamber of the temple. The commentaries disagree on how one should understand the description of the doorways. The doorway to the inner chamber is usually understood to be shaped like a pentagon with a peaked lintel.[73] Others understand the doorway to be made of a five-part rebatement.[74] The latter seems the better sense of the description when one takes into consideration the basic meaning of the final phrase of verse 31, האיל מזוזות חמשית. The Hebrew word איל refers primarily to a pilaster or some type of projection on either side of an entrance. Montgomery and others have understood it to refer to an upward projecting lintel (i.e., a peaked lintel) which would give the doorway a pentagon shape. If one maintains its basic meaning, and the next two words describe the pilasters on either side of the entryway to the inner chamber, Würthwein's translation, that the pilasters were doorposts with a five-part rebatement, seems probable. Again, the difficulty stems from the fact that the first term, האיל, is used only here and in the temple description of Ezekiel. Though the term is not used in the description of the doorway to the main chamber in verse 33, those doorposts may be understood as a four-part rebatement.

Verses 32 and 34-35 describe the doors for these entryways. They are folding doors with cherubim and palm trees with garlands of blooming flowers engraved around them. Both sets of doors are plated with gold. Verse 36 concludes the description of the temple structure by explaining how Solomon builds the inner courtyard, which is just outside the temple.

---

73   Montgomery, Kings, 157-158; Gray, I & II Kings, 173; and DeVries, I
       Kings, 86, 88.
74   Noth, Könige, 102 understands the doorposts to be "fifthed," or "five-
       part," but this does not clarify the sense of the description. Würthwein, 1.
       Könige 1-16, 61, offers that the doorposts were made of five levels or
       ledges.

It is clear that the differing opinions of the commentaries regarding so many of the elements of the temple description indicate that the text presents serious problems to the reader who seeks to reconstruct the appearance of the temple. There are far too many of the elements for which there is no definitive understanding of precisely what is meant. This often leaves one in the position of simply having to choose a meaning without knowing for certain if that meaning is the one intended. This type of approach to the temple description leaves too many gaps in our understanding and does not solve the underlying desire to know the significance of the description. For that one must turn to a method that brings a different set of analytical tools to bear on the description.

I Kings 7:13-50: The Description of the Temple Vessels and Furnishings

After the intervening description of the construction of Solomon's palace and the associated structures, 7:13 begins the description of the making of the implements, vessels and furnishings for use in the temple.[75] The vessels and implements of the temple are made of bronze and include the two pillars, the sea, the lavers and their stands. The furnishings are made of gold and include the table, the lampstands, the altar, and the snuffers and tongs used inside the temple. Noth explains that the text treats the bronze objects first before describing the gold objects, understanding that the description moves from the more common metal to the more precious.[76] It may also be stated that the description treats the implements outside the temple before it describes those that were placed inside the main chamber.

The two bronze pillars are the first elements described. Their description is straightforward and clear, but their significance is not. The text does not indicate that they serve any architectural purpose,

---

75   LXX rearranges the verses so that 7:13-50 follow directly after 6:36, and 7:1-12 follows 7:13-50. In this arrangement the description of the temple vessels and placement is completed before the historian describes palace construction.

76   Noth, Könige, 146.

i.e., they do not support a lintel of any kind, which leaves them as free standing pillars on the porch. There is comparative evidence, well cited in the commentaries, which indicates that pillars of this type were well known in the ancient world.[77] There are examples of pillars which are supports for a lintel as well as those which are free standing. What provides the most fodder for discussion with regard to the two pillars is the fact that the text indicates that they are named. The one on the right is Jachin and the one on the left is Boaz. Since the work of R. B. Y. Scott, it has become acceptable to understand these names as the first words in an inscription borne by each of the pillars.[78]

The symbolism of the pillars has been explained as indicating the presence of YHWH in the temple through appeals to W. R. Smith's idea of the pillars as cressets and W. F. Albright's citation of other examples of pillared cressets.[79] While this is an often cited explanation, few commentaries take this position. The more plausible understanding for the pillars is the identification of them as symbolic gateposts which mark the threshold between the outer world and the inner world of the temple. This position is taken by some scholars who claim much more for the significance of the

---

77   See the various comments of Montgomery, Kings, 172-178; Gray, I & II Kings, 189-193; Noth, Könige, 161-162; and Würthwein, 1. Könige 1-16, 74-82.

78   R. B. Y. Scott, The Pillars Jachin and Boaz, JBL 58 (1939): 143-149. Scott reconstructs two possible inscriptions, one a dynastic promise based upon the use of the verb כון in the promise to David in II Samuel 7, and the other a confession of YHWH's power at creation. For the latter Scott has to reconstruct $be^{c}\bar{o}z$ in place of $b\bar{o}{}^{c}az$ for בעז. It must be stated that Scott's explanation, as well as those who follow his approach, are completely speculative and do not offer any conclusive information regarding the function of the pillars.

79   See W. R. Smith, Lectures on the Religion of the Semites (New York: D. Appleton and Company, 1889), 468-469; W. F. Albright, Two Cressets from Marisa and the Pillars of Jachin and Boaz, BASOR 85 (1942): 18-27. It is Gray, I & II Kings, 187, who most clearly takes up this interpretation and identifies the pillars as symbolic of YHWH's presence in that they may stand for the "pillar of fire by night and the pillar of cloud by day" as the fat of the offerings were burned in the bowl-like capitals on top of the pillars.

pillars than can be supported from the text or current knowledge about the use of twin pillars in the ancient east.[80] It is more probable that the pillars are threshold markers along the lines of the *urigallu* known from Mesopotamian ritual texts and wall engravings from Neo-Assyrian palaces.[81] These twin standards are symbols of the moveable threshold of the deities, and therefore provide access to the deity or divine power whenever the king is away on military campaigns. The twin pillars Jachin and Boaz may be understood as a more fixed version of the threshold marker and be indicative of the threshold of the divine realm in Jerusalem.

There is little or no disagreement among the commentaries regarding the descriptions of the bronze vessels that are placed in the courtyard and on the porch of the temple. Most consider the vessels to have symbolic significance, though there is some disagreement about whether the sea and the lavers might also have a practical function. The problem revolves around the assumption that water sources would be important in the temple courtyard where priestly ablutions and other forms of cleansing might be necessary and the concomitant recognition that the sea and the lavers are of too great a size and volume to make such a function practical.[82] The Chronicler describes the function of the sea and the lavers as water sources in the courtyard and some scholars ignore the impractical

---

80   C. Meyers, Jerusalem Temple, ABD VI, 361, interprets the pillars as gateposts, but then adds that they symbolize "the legitimizing presence of Yahweh in the Temple to all subsequent onlookers." This, evidently, because they symbolize the gateposts between which the ark was carried into the temple. This is similar to a statement made by E. Bloch-Smith, "Who is the King of Glory?" 19, 21, who identifies the pillars as symbolic of YHWH's entrance into the temple as well as of YHWH's blessings to the king and people through the inscriptions she supposes were on the pillars. Noth, Könige, 154, supposes that the pillars could be symbols of lordship, as he understands twin poles and pillars to be in ancient Assyria, following W. Andrae, Das wiedererstandene Assur, second edition (Munich: Beck, 1977, first edition, 1938), 54, 106ff.

81   See the discussion of F. A. M. Wiggermann, Mesopotamian Protective Spirits: The Ritual Texts, Cuneiform Monographs 1 (Gronigen: Styx & PP Publications, 1992), 70-73 and the reliefs he cites.

82   Montgomery, Kings, 178.

dimensions and follow the Chronicler's explanation.[83] The preference among the commentaries that follow the symbolic approach is to understand the sea as a symbol for the cosmic sea that was defeated at creation, which stands in the courtyard of the temple as a reminder that YHWH is the god who tamed the chaotic powers in order to establish the regular order that pervades the universe.[84] Others trust the description of the lavers and understand them as symbols having some connection with YHWH as the provider of rain for the people.[85]

It is noteworthy that all symbolic interpretations of the sea and the lavers consider the significance of the vessels as connected to mythological meanings identified as "non-Israelite." Whether discussing the sea as the chaotic power in the cosmos, or the lavers as symbols of rain-making power, the interpreters explain this connection by appealing to texts and traditions that come from Ugarit, Mesopotamia, or even Greece. When reference is made to the Psalms and creation imagery which includes imagery of YHWH as taming the sea or defeating the great serpent, it is explained as coming from an ancient Near Eastern notion of creation as a divine battle, which is symbolically presented in the vessels of the temple in Jerusalem.

---

83   II Chronicles 4:6; Josephus, Jewish Antiquities, VIII, 87 accepts the Chronicler's explanation and says that the sea was for the priests to wash their feet and hands, while the lavers were for cleansing the animals to be offered as sacrifices. Gray, I & II Kings, 193 believes that the lavers were functional and discounts the dimensions given in the text as unreliable.

84   See the discussions cited in note 80 above, particularly Bloch-Smith, "Who is the King of Glory?" 18-31, and the discussion of her approach above, pages 120-122. It is interesting to note, however, that the only indication of a sea as part of the vessels within a temple court area comes from Herodotus, Histories, VIII.55, who mentions a sea and an olive tree in the shrine of Erechtheus on the acropolis in Athens. Herodotus explains that the Athenians identified them as placed there by Poseidon and Athena as "tokens of their contention for the land." Note, however, that W. Burkert, Greek Religion, trsl. J. Raffan (Cambridge, MA: Harvard University Press, 1985), 86 discusses the sea on the acropolis as important as a water source within the temple precinct.

85   Noth, Könige, 161; Würthwein, 1. Könige 1-16, 82.

The gold implements inside the main chamber do not exhibit the same symbolic difficulty as the bronze vessels of the courtyard. The table and the implements mentioned in 7:48-50 all seem to have an obvious function in the sanctuary. They are furniture and tools necessary for the operation of the cultic activity within the chamber. The statement that the lampstands were placed on either side of the entrance to the inner chamber, five on the south and five on the north, reminds the reader of the lavers and their stands in the courtyard, five to the south of the entrance to the main chamber and five to the north. This symmetrical placement provides a balanced presentation in both the courtyard and the main chamber of the temple. Symmetry is very important in the historian's presentation of the spatial arrangement and decoration of the temple, yet this characteristic is never noticed by the commentaries or interpreters of the temple description.

Current State of Interpretive Approaches to the Temple Description

The preceding discussion shows that interpreters of the biblical text operate under the assumption that the text points to the appearance of the temple and its implements with the intent of providing an accurate presentation that enables scholars to recreate the sacred precinct visually and/or conceptually. The text stands in a secondary position to the reconstruction, and the goal of interpretation is either to provide the reader with a visual image of the structure or to interpret the vessels and the structure so that the reader understands the symbolic value of the various elements that inhabit the sacred precinct.

There is much that is helpful in previous studies of the temple description. The text critical analysis of the commentaries is indispensable in making sense of an admittedly difficult text. The discussions of the meanings of the various technical terms and the *hapax legomena* are firm foundations upon which to proceed with any study of the significance of this material. The interpretive explorations of the significance of the various implements and accoutrements of the temple courtyard and the main chamber engage the reader with the conceptual realms within which the author perambulates. But what remains lacking in these explanations is an understanding of the text, the temple description itself, as the primary icon.

With all the textual analysis and the discussion of technical terminology, there remains a considerable realm of unknowing, a vast chasm of imprecision in this document lauded as dryly detailed and masterfully precise. If the author intends to present nothing more than a simple physical description of the temple built by Solomon, and if the author has at his disposal official documents that communicate the clear details of its construction, how could he not produce a clearer presentation? Perhaps the answer to this question is that a clear visual presentation of the appearance of the structure is not the author's goal, even if he has documents before him, or if he uses the temple of his own day as his pattern for the description. In spite of the overwhelming amount of attention that is given to textual details and to the interpretive possibilities in light of the conceptual world of the ancient east, something important is yet overlooked.

What is never mentioned in the previous discussions, what is never even alluded to, is the movement within the text. None of the preceding studies gives attention to the way in which the author moves the reader through the structure in the same style as the textual tour of the temple in Ezekiel 40-44. In the Ezekiel text movement is overt and conspicuous. The prophet is given a tour by a divine messenger who provides him with the measurements and arrangement of the entire precinct. In I Kings the movement is covert and woven within the fabric of the narrative. It is more subtle, but it is there nonetheless.[86]

---

86   As indicated above, J. Z. Smith, To Take Place, 47-66 explains the description of the temple in Ezekiel as a map of social structure based upon power and status. The different social relationships that Smith elaborates are not present merely in the description, but primarily in the ability of the different elements of society to move within the realm of the temple precinct. The prophet is taken by his divine guide through the entire structure of the temple precinct. Prophet and divine guide exist outside of the social structure presented. In much the same manner, the historian of I Kings 6-7 offers the reader information on the appearance of sections of the temple that, presumably, no layperson would have seen.

A second element that is not attended to in the preceding studies is the way in which the spatial units of the structure are arranged and ordered. To be sure, there is considerable discussion of the tripartite plan and the long room style of the structure, but it is concerned with the arrangement of the walls. There is no real attention given to the space that is delineated by those walls. One insurmountable problem of the preceding studies is the lack of information on the thickness of the walls, and the fact that there is no room at all for a wall between the main chamber and the inner chamber. If the author is concerned to present only the spaces, then the thickness of the walls, not to mention the foundations and the empty space above the inner chamber, is simply irrelevant to that goal. It only becomes a problem when the reader misunderstands and thinks that the author intends to be precise with regard to structural details.

Finally, the third element that receives very little, if any, attention in the preceding studies is the arrangement of the implements within the temple court and the main chamber. For all the debate on the symbolic or functional significance of the different vessels and implements, there is virtually no discussion of their placement within these different domains. If the reader attends to this detail, it quickly becomes apparent that there is considerable structure to the arrangement, and that this is an important element in the general make up of the verbal icon.

Any new study of Solomon's temple must proceed with the realization of the current state of Solomonic research in mind. With the serious questions that have been raised regarding evidence for the reign of Solomon, one can no longer read the description of the temple as it is read in previous studies and assume that it refers to a specific structure that would be recognizable to any ancient Israelite who might happen to see this description. Visual reconstructions based upon information gathered from the temple descriptions found in Ezekiel and II Chronicles are fraught with problems associated with the differing contexts and meanings of these descriptions. What is necessary is an approach that brings a new model of understanding the temple description to bear on the text.

M. Dick is correct to understand at least some of the writing prophets as composers of literary works, using the analogy of craftsmen and icons.[87] Quoting Greek poets, Dick understands the texts composed by the prophets as created works, the products of craftsmanship; he proposes that the written text is an icon and that the writing prophet who creates it is, in fact, an image maker.[88] He highlights the irony that the prophets make the very things against which they preach, but what is significant for the purposes of this study is his identification of the ability of a text to function as an icon. This identification opens the possibility of reading the temple description as something other than a mere representation of the appearance of the structure.

It is reasonable to posit the same model for the creative activity of the historian who composed the Deuteronomistic History. This author creates a description of the temple in Jerusalem that stands apart from any attempt to force it to provide an accurate and clear image of the appearance of the structure because that is not its purpose. As a verbal icon it presents a conceptual sacred space created by its author and structured in order to manifest the author's own ideas concerning proper worship and relationship with the deity. Each of the elements which are lacking in the preceding studies are important indicators in this verbal icon and move boldly into the light when the text is approached using the categories of built environment analysis. Dick's innovative study of prophetic material, followed by the important precedent set by the studies of J. Z. Smith and J. Van Seters, clearly prepares the way for an understanding the biblical text as an ideological presentation in which the writer embodies his own construct of reality in order to influence the developing social world of his own time.[89]

The combination of these recent studies with the theories of W. J. T. Mitchell form the foundation upon which the use of built

---

87 M. Dick, Prophetic *Poiesis* and the Verbal Icon, CBQ 46 (1984): 226-246.

88 Dick, Prophetic *Poiesis*, see his comments on pp. 235, 236, and particularly 240-246.

89 See the discussion above of J. Z. Smith, To Take Place, and J. Van Seters, The Chronicler's Account, and Solomon's Temple, for a presentation of these novel approaches to the biblical descriptions found in the text.

environment analytical categories is based.[90] Mitchell explains that
a text may be understood to function as a verbal icon when the
images that it exhibits are no longer defined "as a pictorial likeness
or impression, but as a synchronic structure in some metaphorical
sense."[91] Once the temple description is no longer approached with
the creation of a visual reconstruction as the goal, one is able to read
the text as a literary creation of the historian structured by the
ideology of the author. The structure and arrangement of the temple
functions iconographically to present the reader with a particular
image of the deity and how one should relate to the deity.

In the following discussion it is important first to explain the
temple description and the way the historian structures his
presentation of sacred space. Afterwards it will be necessary to place
the temple description within the broader context of the national
history composed by the Deuteronomist. The historian not only
structures the temple description in accordance with his own
ideology but also provides a context that influences the reader's
understanding of the significance of the temple through an
association of the structure with the covenant mediated by Moses and
the reigns of King David and King Solomon. The temple and the
kings are iconic elements in the reform theology of the historian. His
use of these figures in connection with the Mosaic tradition, which
Dtr considers foundational, shows how his reform incorporates the
ancient past in order to establish its legitimacy in the present.

Built Environment Analysis of the Temple Description

The application of the built environment categories of height,
color and redundancy, as well as attention to the formation of
boundaries and access in the temple may seem unusual since these
categories are usually applied to actual structures. While there is no
actual building, approaching the temple description as a verbal icon

---

90   W. J. T. Mitchell, Iconology: Image, Text, Ideology (Chicago and
     London: The University of Chicago Press, 1986).
91   Mitchell, Iconology, 21.

for such a building makes the use of built environment analysis applicable, with a few minor modifications. Since the description concentrates attention on the overall dimensions and not just upon the height of the structure, the interpretative discussion focuses on the use of dimensions in the description of the different domains of the temple and their relation to each other. Furthermore, the only reference to what might be considered color in the description is to the metals used in the decorations and the implements, i.e., gold and bronze. Attention to redundancy in the verbal icon reveals a repetitive pattern of the description of decorative elements in a way that maintains a particular view of the individual domains and dovetails with the use of boundary and access to preserve the conception of the different segments of the temple as entirely separate domains. Finally, the arrangement of boundary and access in the verbal icon forces a distinct manner of movement through the structure.

Height and Dimensions

There is a clear rhetoric of measurement that enforces the historian's conception of the temple as a construction of separate domains. This rhetoric is most evident in those situations where modern scholars perceive inadequacies in the description. The overall measurements of the building are given without a clear indication of their precise extent. When it appears in I Kings 6:16-17 that these are internal dimensions, it creates further difficulties. The overall length of the building is described as sixty cubits. The inner chamber is described as twenty cubits and the main chamber as forty cubits. This leaves no room for the wall that should divide them. No measurements are given for any of the walls in the temple structure. Moreover, no explanation is given for the difference between the height of the inner chamber and the main chamber.

The rhetoric of the dimensions of the porch maintains its status as a separate domain. Its length and width are on the front of the house but not part of the house. It is clear that the unusual arrangement of the dimensions highlights the separateness of the porch. If one understands the porch as having the same width as the house, and therefore created by an extension of the side walls as described by Noth, then why are the overall dimensions not given as 70x20x30?[92] Describing the porch as only ten cubits wide along the front of the house preserves its status as a separately constructed domain that is not merely an extension of the main chamber.[93]

The third area of the temple that has presented dimensional difficulty for the modern scholars is the construction of the side chambers. Each level has a different width (as viewed from the front of the temple) because of the ledges upon which the floor beams of subsequent stories rested. This maintains the integrity of the temple in relation to the side chambers; they could not be part of the divine realm. However, if one understands the height given in I Kings 6:10 to refer to the height of each story, as many commentaries do, the overall height would be fifteen cubits, one half the height of the main building. Recognizing that the dimensions given for the main building are internal dimensions limits the usefulness of considering the overall height of the side chambers as fifteen cubits since no measurements for wall or roof thickness are given.

The primary significance of the dimensions given for the temple is not to provide an actual measured plan of the structure but rather to emphasize that each domain is a separate unit. The description of dimensions moves from the main building to the external additions, the porch and the side chambers, and then inside to the inner chamber. Care is taken in each case to distinguish each new element from the main structure and to preserve each as distinct architectural units. The inner chamber is kept separate from the main chamber through the disagreement in height. The author presents these architectural segments that make up the whole temple as discreet spheres of activity and the rhetoric of the measurements reinforces that separateness. Furthermore, the lack of interest in wall thickness and clarity regarding the height of the inner and main chambers

---

92   Y. Aharoni, The Archaeology of the Land of Israel, 226 gives the overall measurements of the house as 70x20x30 cubits, understanding the porch to be formed by an extension of the side walls of the house.

93   A further indication that the porch is not part of the main building is the description of the construction of the inner chamber to be discussed below. It was delineated from within the overall space of the house, while the porch was not.

indicates these were not elements important to the author. The author is concerned with the creation of space through the description of spatial units. The rhetoric of dimensions presents separate spatial units without interest in the structural boundaries that keep them separate.

Color

Color, as explained in chapter one, is a decorative element that is often indicative of status and/or power when they are commodities that are not easily acquired.[94] The only color mentioned in the description of the temple is the use of gold to plate the interior of the structure and the bronze and gold used to make the furniture and the implements.[95] The extravagance of plating the entire inside of the structure with gold highlights the exceptional and exalted nature of the building.[96] More to the point, it sets the interior apart from the mundane world outside. The author describes the dwelling of the deity as a domain completely coated with gold, one of the most precious substances available for decorations. Though understood by some as an extravagance on the part of the king that shows his devotion, the use of gold to plate the interior sets the inside space apart from the everyday world and identifies it as divine.[97]

The gold is overlaid on top of cypress and cedar, two very costly wood products for which Solomon would have had to pay dearly. The walls of the main structure are built of large carved stones, and

---

94   See discussion on pp. 6-8 above.

95   I Kings 6:20, 21; 7:15, 27, 38, et. al.

96   II Chronicles 3:6-7 further exagerates the decorations by indicating that Solomon also inlayed the walls with precious stones and plated the beams, rafters and thresholds with gold as well.

97   A. Millard, King Solomon in His Ancient Context, in The Age of Solomon, 38-41, insists that one should consider the amounts listed in Solomon's construction and decorative program as accurate. Montgomery's citations of other ancient texts which include the same kind of elaborate use of gold in his Books of Kings, 151, do not aid in the understanding of the significance of this material for the historian's verbal icon.

the inside is then paneled so that "no stone was visible." (6:18) On the surface of the wood paneling is overlaid gold; even the floors are described as overlaid with gold. In this way the inside of the house is triply insulated from the outside world with three materials of increasing value, first stone, then cedar, and then gold. The triple barrier between the divine domain within and the mundane world without made of materials of increasing value thus define the space created by the author as entirely separate from the outside world.

Redundancy

The decorative elements on the walls of the main and innermost chambers, as well as on the doors of the two chambers are described in verses 18, 29, 32, and 35 as consisting of carvings of bulbs and blooming flowers and palm trees with garlands of flowers around them flanked by two cherubim. The redundant use of the same imagery throughout the structure surrounds the reader with the repeated pattern of palm trees flanked by cherubim and again sets the domain apart as privileged space. The occurrence of this, or a similar motif, in the ancient world is usually associated with ritual and/or sacred space.[98] Standing inside the main chamber of the temple, the reader is faced on all sides by the watchful cherubim performing their guardian rituals for the palm trees.

The innermost chamber is surrounded by the same imagery, but this is dwarfed by the pair of cherubim standing ten cubits high. These and the ark of the covenant are the only implements described

---

98   See the representations of repeated patterns of mixed form creatures flanking stylistic sacred trees in the Neo-Assyrian palace of Assurnasirpal II in R. D. Barnett and A Lorenzini, Assyrian Sculpture in the British Museum (Toronto: McClelland and Stewart, 1975); and discussions of their significance in B. N. Porter, Sacred Trees, Date Palms and the Royal Persona of Assurnasirpal II, JNES 52 (1993): 129-139; P. Albenda, Assyrian Sacred Trees in the British Museum, Iraq 56 (1994): 123-134; and J. M. Russell, From Nineveh to New York: The Strange Story of the Assyrian Reliefs in the Metropolitan Museum and the Hidden Masterpiece at Canford School (New Haven and London: Yale University Press, 1997), 19-22.

in the inner chamber. They are the divine attendants that spread their wings and form the throne of God within the inner chamber.[99] It may also be that the arrangement of the implements inside the inner chamber is a translation of the decorative carvings found on the walls and doors of the temple into a specifically Israelite composition. The pattern of the stylized sacred tree flanked by mixed form creatures is found throughout the ancient near east. The tree is often understood as symbolic of divine presence.[100] If one understands the ark as the container for the covenant, following the Deuteronomic concept, then the association of the cherubim and the ark is equivalent to a three-dimensional presentation of the two dimensional decorative pattern on all the walls. The Israelite modification presents the covenant (text) as the central icon of YHWH's presence by placing it in the position normally held by the sacred date palm tree. The reader is prepared through the decorative engravings for an encounter with the divine in the innermost sanctuary, which in Deuteronomistic ideology is presented in the form of the covenant YHWH made with Israel at Horeb.

Whether or not the inside walls of the temple and the inner chamber ever bore such engraved images is not relevant to an understanding of the iconic function of placing such images in the verbal icon of the divine realm. The historian takes the reader right into the divine realm and presents it as a domain that is entirely unlike the outside world. Attributes of watchfulness and protectiveness, are embodied in the mixed form images that encompass the boundaries of that realm. The change made in the historian's description, which places the ark of the covenant in the innermost chamber rather than an image of the deity as would have

---

99 For more discussion of YHWH as enthroned on the cherubim see T. Mettinger, YHWH SABAOTH -- The Heavenly King on the Cherubim Throne, in Studies in the Period of David and Solomon and Other Essays, ed. T. Ishida (Winona Lake: Eisenbrauns, 1982), 109-138, and the references listed there. It is interesting to note, however, in contrast to ideas of the cherubim throne that Isaiah 6 makes no mention of cherubim, but rather focuses on seraphim as the divine attendants.

100 Both B. N. Porter, Sacred Trees, 129-139; and P. Albenda, Assyrian Sacred Trees, particularly 132-133, identify the date palm as associated specifically with Ishtar.

been the case in most temples of the ancient world, highlights the
centrality of the covenant relationship in the historian's view of an
encounter with the divine. This modification and placement of the
covenant as the central element is indicative of the Dtr reform
theology and will be discussed more fully in chapter four below.

Boundary and Access

Boundaries and accesses in a building prohibit and facilitate
motion between domains. Specifically they are the walls, doors, and
doorways of the structure. They divide the general space into
specific spatial units. The doorways are boundary units since the
threshold is not part of either of the spatial units it connects but is in
fact its own liminal domain between larger units. Boundary and
access, then, are about movement, and movement is a key element in
this verbal icon.

This description of the divine realm requires movement on the
part of the reader.[101] The movement of the reader in the narrative is
connected with the description of each segment of the building as a
distinct domain, a completely different spatial unit. It begins on the
outside with the overall measurements of the structure, the porch and
the side chambers. Then the reader is taken inside the structure to
"view" the internal decorations and the construction of the inner
sanctuary. Once the description of the construction of the inner
sanctuary is complete, the reader is taken inside this innermost
sanctuary and its decorations, including the engravings on the walls
and the construction of the cherubim, are described. The reader is
then escorted out into the main chamber, where its decorations are
described in greater detail. The last elements of the temple described
by the narrative are the doorways and the doors. Once these are
portrayed, the reader is moved back to the outside of the building and

---

101 See the treatment of the Neo-Assyrian texts that describe the construction
     of Sennacherib's palace in Nineveh in the preceding chapter, where I
     propose that the texts themselves are literary tours of the palace and make
     comments regarding the structure the tour takes when the reader follows
     its order of presentation.

the construction of the inner courtyard completes the literary tour of the temple structure.

In each case, the narrative completes one section before moving to the next and is careful to note that each section of the building stands apart from the others. The reader is presented with a description of a building that is, in fact, four separate structures: the main structure, the side chambers, the porch, and the inner structure. Even though they may be interconnected, they are yet separated in such a way that an activity occurring in one spatial unit is not occurring in any other at that moment. The separate domains that make up the structure of the temple are divided by their boundaries. The doorways and the doors of the inner sanctuary and the main chamber are treated separately from the domains into which they lead. They stand apart as the passageways, the thresholds between one domain and another, yet they parallel the boundaries in an interesting way. As indicated above, the boundary walls between the divine domain and the outer world are insulated in a triple fashion using three materials of increasing value. In like manner the innermost chamber, the room where one would encounter the divine, is reached by passing over (through?) three thresholds; the porch threshold marked by the two pillars, Jachin and Boaz, the four-part rebated doorway of the main chamber, and the five-part rebated doorway of the innermost chamber. Three barriers prohibit free access while three thresholds allow access in a particular order and fashion. Access to the innermost chamber is gradual and requires one to pass through two previous domains that heighten the awareness of moving into privileged space.

The access to the side chambers requires further comment. The narrative describes a single doorway that leads to a staircase by which the chambers are reached. Waterman's suggestion that there were two doorways and that these were accessed from inside the temple makes the side chambers much more functional, and follows Ezekiel's description.[102] However, it must certainly be rejected as an explanation for the I Kings description since it obliterates the division that the narrative maintains between all the spatial units. If one follows the text in I Kings, it is clear that the author allows

---

102   L. Waterman, The Damaged "Blueprints," 288-289.

access to the side chambers through an exterior door on the south side of the building, and that there is no access to the side chambers from within the temple. The side chambers are not structurally connected to the main building and the awkwardness of access to them preserves that separateness.

Furnishings

At the end of the literary tour of the building, the reader is again in the courtyard. The description of the implements for the temple again begins outside of the temple.[103] The two columns, as indicated above, mark the threshold between the courtyard and the porch of the temple. They function as the *urigallu*, the poles that were movable threshold markers for the Assyrians. Just as the *urigallu* were understood as portable symbols for the presence of the deity, the pillars Jachin and Boaz may be understood as permanent markers of the access to divine presence in the temple.[104] The sea and the ten lavers and stands all stand in the courtyard in front of the temple. At the conclusion of the description of the making of the sacred vessels, the narrative describes the placement of those implements that belonged inside the main chamber.

Again the motion of the narrative moves from the outside to the inside of the temple. The outside implements are set in place as they are made, but the implements for the inside are only set in place at the final phase of the construction. The description of their placement moves the reader inside and then back out. 7:48 indicates that all the vessels of the house of YHWH are put in place by Solomon. The placement of these vessels presents a balanced symmetry with the same number of menorahs and stands on either side of the doorways and the same number of tables on either side of the main chamber. Finally, the description mentions the gold sockets

---

103 The description of the implements begins in 7:13 after an intervening section that narrates the building of the palace and other royal buildings and fortifications.

104 See F. A. M. Wiggermann, Mesopotamian Protective Spirits: The Ritual Texts (Groningen: Styxx, 1992), 70-72 for a more thorough discussion and explanation of these implements in Neo-Assyrian art.

for the doors of the inner sanctuary and then for the entrance to the main chamber of the temple. The reader is conducted into the main chamber, to the very doors of the inner sanctuary, and then back out to the doors of the main chamber of the building.

Movement is a key element in the verbal icon presented here. Whether describing the construction, decoration, or furnishing of the temple, the order of presentation requires constant movement on the part of the reader throughout the structure. The author leads the reader in and out of the temple, at one moment standing in the very innermost sanctuary before the cherubim and the ark of the covenant, and the next moment in the courtyard outside the temple.

Interpretation of the Verbal Icon

Stating that the text is an icon that promotes consideration of the being of God requires that one then make some determination about what precisely the icon connotes about the deity. The text structures the realm of the deity as three times removed from the realm of the sacred precinct, which is itself removed from the realm of mundane existence. The innermost chamber of the temple is separated from the courtyard by its own threshold as well as by the thresholds of the main chamber and the porch. The porch threshold is marked by the pillars Jachin and Boaz, the threshold of the main chamber is marked by a fourfold doorpost and lintel, and the threshold of the innermost chamber is marked by a fivefold doorpost and lintel. In each case, crossing the threshold is indicative of passing from one domain to another and each crossing moves one closer to the deity and further from the outside world.

The innermost chamber is also insulated from the outside world by the materials used in the temple construction. The ascending value of materials, from stone to cedar to gold, suggests the increasing singularity of this domain. One need not imagine the logistics of the use of so much rare gold for interior decoration; the author presents the inner walls as coated with the only substance appropriate for surfaces that border the realm of the deity. The rarity of the substance indicates the extraordinary character of the domain.

The decorative elements of the walls and doors of the structure are idiomatic. It is the sum of their association in that place more than their individual presentation that is meaningful. The juxtaposition of palm trees with blooming garlands of flowers flanked by cherubim is more suggestive of their significance than either one would be alone. There is enough evidence from other structures to identify these images as characteristic of sacred spaces or of spaces associated with deities and kings. Within the literature of ancient Israel the cherubim are associated with the deity as the divine throne and means of mobility. The use of mixed form creatures allows for the incorporation of desirable characteristics of different species within one creature, and as such they are the divine attendants and associates that accompany the deity. The use of cherubim and palm trees in the decorative program of the textual temple, as well as the appearance of the cherubim and the ark in the inner sanctuary, defines the space as the divine realm.

The structure of the temple, as presented by the historian, is a spatial arrangement that communicates the completely separate nature of the divine realm from that of the mundane world. The verbal icon inspires a conceptualization of the deity as the inhabitant of such a realm, and therefore, completely distinct from humanity. This wholly other sphere is not impenetrable, however. There are approaches through which the divine may be encountered. As noted above, there are doorways through which one could enter the main chamber and the inner sanctuary. There are no other entrances to the temple. The description makes it quite clear that one could not gain access to the temple or the inner sanctuary from the side chambers. Through this arrangement of boundary and access the historian creates a textual temple which could only be entered by walking a prescribed path. The textual temple is an icon of the presence of the deity within the realm of humanity which maintains the singularity of the essence of the divine while not diminishing its accessability.

The iconographic function of the temple description is its presentation of the dwelling of God, the central sanctuary, as a symbol for Israel's relationship with YHWH, as imagined by the historian. The people cannot approach YHWH in all the various ways through which they might approach other deities. YHWH may be accessed only through specific paths. This conceptualization of the realm of God coincides with the Deuteronomistic notions concerning the proper access to YHWH. Deuteronomy 12 prohibits the Israelites from worshiping YHWH in any of the ways that the Canaanites worshiped their deities.[105] They should rather follow the statutes and practices that YHWH commanded. They may indeed approach YHWH, but only in the specified pathways of the covenant.[106] Moreover, the covenant stands as the primary icon of the presence of YHWH among his people. In the innermost chamber, the central placement of the ark of the covenant reinforces the Deuteronomistic notion of the centrality of that document for a proper relationship, as well as an encounter with the divine presence.

The temple description stands as a literary manifestation of the divine realm and as such it is an icon through which one may ponder the divine. The structure of the temple is shaped not by concern for an accurate presentation of the appearance of the temple built by Solomon but rather by the concern to present a structural arrangement that reinforces the Deuteronomistic idea that YHWH is a deity who is wholly separate from the human realm but not disconnected from it. In this way the Deuteronomistic temple description is no different from the typical structure of temples in the ancient near east. Temples are usually arranged so as to indicate a separation between the divine and the human realms. In other temples, however, one would find an image of the deity in the innermost chamber. The historian places the covenant as the central element in his verbal icon, a covenant that prohibits the creation of images as a representation of YHWH. The historian creates a verbal icon of proper relationship and places at its center the text that symbolizes the requirements of that relationship. This placement is an innovation of the historian and is indicative of his attempt to reform the theological assumptions of exilic Israel. Textuality and

---

105 Dt. 12:4, 29-31.

106 Cf. also II Kings 23 and the reforming activity of Josiah. One of his actions is the removal of various implements that are part of the temple of YHWH at that time but which are dedicated to other Baal and Asherah, as well as the sun and the moon and the astral deities. This type of purification of the worship of YHWH is cause for high praise for King Josiah, II Kings 23:25.

the creation of verbal icons are the historian's way of imagining the relationship between YHWH and Israel.

The Context of the Verbal Icon

The Deuteronomistic Historian places his verbal icon in the particular context of the reign of Solomon, where it serves two clear functions. First, the textual temple serves in the context of the national history as the central place for the worship of YHWH required in the book of Deuteronomy. This connection is secured by the use of terminology that binds the introduction to Solomon's temple building with the command in Deuteronomy 12. Moreover, the language is the same that appears in II Samuel 7:1 when David makes his plans to build a house for YHWH. In Deuteronomy, the people are to come to the central place when YHWH has given them rest from all their surrounding enemies. In II Samuel, David is given such rest and considers building a house for YHWH. In I Kings, Solomon introduces his intent to build a house for YHWH by stating that YHWH has given him rest all around and that he has no adversary or trouble.

Deuteronomy 12:10	II Samuel 7:1	I Kings 5:18
ועברתם את־הירדן		
וישבתם בארץ אשר יהוה		
אלהיכם מנחיל אתכם	ויהי כי־ישב המלך	
<u>והניח לכם מכל־איביכם</u>	בביתו ויהוה	
<u>מסביב</u> וישבתם בטח	<u>הניח־לו מסביב</u>	<u>הניח יהוה אלהי לי</u>
	<u>מכל־איביו</u>	<u>מסביב</u>
		אין שטן ואין פגע
		רע

The language of I Kings is modified slightly to fit the story of Solomon. In Deuteronomy, the context is that the people are told to enter the land and defeat enemies. In II Samuel, David comes to the throne and has to establish his control over the surrounding kingdoms. Solomon, however, comes to a throne that is secure from any foreign power, and therefore has no enemies. The mention of having no adversary (שטן) no doubt anticipates the adversaries that YHWH will raise against Solomon in I Kings 11 as a judgement against his going after the foreign gods worshiped by his many wives. The author modifies the language in order to tailor it to the story of Solomon while still identifying the temple he would build as the central sanctuary required in Deuteronomy.[107]

The second function of the verbal icon is the more notable for the purposes of this study. The closing bracket of the context for the verbal icon is the dedication ceremony of chapter eight. M. Noth long ago said that the only way to understand the significance of the temple described in I Kings 6-7 is to study the dedicatory prayer in I Kings 8.[108] It is in the dedicatory prayer of Solomon in 8:12-53 that the historian makes his clearest statement of the significance he places on the verbal icon of Solomon's temple. The crux of the prayer may be understood in the contrast of the two statements:

יהוה אמר לשכן בערפל: בנה בניתי בית זבל לך מכון לשבתך
עולמים:

YHWH intended to dwell in the thick cloud. I have indeed built for you a lordly house, a fixed place for your eternal dwelling. (8:12b-13)[109]

כי האמנם ישב אלהים על־הארץ הנה השמים ושמי השמים לא
יכלכלוך אף כי־הבית הזה אשר בניתי :

---

107 One of the important contributions made by V. (A.) Hurowitz, Exalted House, is the identification of the literary form in which building reports follow directly after reports of the yearly campaigns in the annals of Neo-Assyrian kings. In this instance the Hebrew narrative follows closely the literary form of the establishment of a building program after the successful completion of military battles. The Deuternomistic Historian modified that form in order to highlight the establishment of the central sanctuary for the worship of YHWH.

108 M. Noth, Könige, 129.

109 For the translations of אמר as "intended," see BDB, 56a; and of בית זבל as "lordly house," see the comments of Gray, I & II Kings, 212. He proposes "royal" following the cognate usage in Ugaritic materials.

But will God indeed dwell on the earth? Surely, the heavens, even the
highest heaven cannot contain you, much less this house that I have
built. (8:27)

The first is presented as the opening statement of Solomon's
dedicatory prayer and sets forth the logical conundrum of having an
earthly dwelling for a deity who is confessed as anything but earthly.
The second statement begins the petition regarding the place, which
is in fact the historian's explanation of the function of the temple,
and sets forth the contrast with the first statement in bold relief.
There can be no mistaking the fact that the historian understands the
discrepancy between building a physical temple for a deity who is
understood as a nonphysical entity and that the bulk of Solomon's
prayer rejects the notion of YHWH eternally dwelling in the lordly
house.

Verse 28 begins a long series of petitions in which Solomon asks
that YHWH hear the prayers of the people in various situations. In
verse 29 the king requests that YHWH's eyes be continually opened
toward the temple and ever watchful for the prayers of the people.
Verse 30 is the first indication of the significance the historian places
upon the temple.

ושמעת אל־תחנת עבדך ועמך ישראל אשר יתפללו אל־המקום
הזה ואתה תשמע אל־מקום שבתך אל־השמים ושמעת וסלחת:

And listen to the supplication of your servant and your people Israel,
which they pray toward this place, that you yourself may hear in your
dwelling place in heaven, that you may hear and forgive.

This refrain, that YHWH should focus divine attention on the house
that Solomon has built, so that when the people direct their prayers
toward it YHWH can hear them from the divine dwelling place in
heaven and forgive, recurs throughout Solomon's prayer.[110]

---

110 See 8:32, 34, 36, 39, 43, 45, 49. Note 8:48, where the king anticipates the
     people being carried into exile in a foreign land and repenting of their evil
     ways and directing their attentions "toward their land, which you gave to
     their fathers, the city which you chose, and the house which I built for your
     name . . ." The narrowing from land to city to house focuses the attention
     on the house as the center of the other two. Ideologically, the house is the

Previous studies recognize the conundrum of the house in which the deity could not dwell, but fail to understand the iconographic function. Montgomery explains that it is not YHWH who is in the temple, but the divine Presence and further praises the historian's creation,

> These prayers attributed to Solomon compose one of the noblest flights in sacred oratory from the Deuteronomic school. There are notes of the infiniteness of Deity and yet of his readiness to dwell with his faithful, of divine grace and of human responsibility, not only of the people but of the individual conscience . . .[111]

Noth recognizes that the primary function of the temple is as a focal point for prayer, and that the prayerful act is the way one gains entry to the divine presence, but understands this as indicative of the exilic date of the text rather than part of its iconic nature.[112] Gray mentions that the temple is the "effective guarantee of God's accessibility," even though God is understood as transcendent.[113] DeVries describes the temple as a "listening-post or sounding board, continually receptive to any prayer that may be directed toward it."[114]

While the commentaries explain the various ways one might understand the function for a physical dwelling created for a metaphysical deity, the historian identifies it as the focal point of religious attention for the people in the human realm, and the focal point of YHWH's attention in the divine realm. It is precisely the function of an icon to stand as the point toward which religious attention is directed. Moreover, the verbal icon, like the physical icon, is a threshold between the divine and the human realm. The historian identifies the temple as the place where divine and human attentions meet, and therefore as a threshold between the two realms.

The historian's genius is evident in his consistent application of his ideology at two points. First, he transforms a ubiquitous

---

religious center of the city which is the center of the land.

111   Montgomery, Books of Kings, 194-195.
112   Noth, Könige, 193.
113   Gray, I & II Kings, 215.
114   DeVries, 1 Kings, 125.

sanctuary motif into his own textual form. He achieves this when he transfers the ark of the covenant into the central position between the two cherubim. Whether one considers the cherubim of the דביר as guardians or as elements of a divine throne, this places his primary document, the covenant with the people, as the singular symbol for divine presence. Given the importance of the discovery of the Book of the Law to the Dtr reform in the days of Josiah, it is not difficult to understand the prominence of the text of the covenant as a key element in this reform theology.

The second point at which the historian applies his ideology is in the way he explains the iconographic function of his temple description in the dedicatory prayer of Solomon. The Deuteronomistic Historian's ideology does not allow for a physical encounter between the deity and the people, but rather maintains that the relationship is entirely metaphysical. The encounter is effected through prayer: raised hands and spoken words. The relationship of the people with YHWH is embodied in the historian's written words, his verbal icon.

The application of built environment analysis to the building the historian describes allows the reader to move within the verbal icon in a way that would never have been possible in the ancient world. This is one element that makes the ability of the author to describe the temple so incredible, i.e., that he would never have been allowed to tour the temple building in this manner, much less would any of his ancient readers have been allowed such access to the sacred precinct. Yet the form of the text is precisely that of a guided tour through the magnificent temple built by Solomon. It is only through the use of built environment categories of analysis that the modern reader is able to understand the social and cultural cues that are present in the description. Built environment analysis releases the temple description from the stranglehold of reconstruction and sources, and allows the reader to view the icon and to imagine the metaphysical relationship so prevalent in the historian's view of YHWH and the people of Israel.

With all the significance of the verbal icon discernible in the temple description, this is only one element of the historian's ideological presentation. In the following chapter the function of this verbal icon is set forth in the context of the theological debates of the sixth century B.C.E. The reform theology of the Deuteronomistic historian, as embodied in his verbal icon is countered by a counter-reform that modifies his icon in a substantial way.

Chapter 4

Palace and Temple:
Architectural Icons, Verbal Icons, and Religious Reform

I am the victorious one who is stationed in the chariot of Assur; Tiamat together
with the creatures inside her.
                                                              -Sennacherib

Now I have built this house for the Name of YHWH, the god of Israel, and I
have put there a place for the ark, where is the covenant of YHWH that he made
with our ancestors when he brought them out from the land of Egypt.
                                                              -Solomon

The previous two chapters have examined the palace of
Sennacherib and the temple of Solomon as icons created to influence
thought and behavior. The architectural icon and the verbal icon
achieve similar aims, even if they do so in different ways. The
architectural icon influences human social behavior through its
physical presentation of conceptual categories. The verbal icon
influences human social behavior through a conceptual presentation
of a physical space. They were both created to achieve a particular
reform in their respective societies, and they both sparked energetic
responses to the innovative presentations of human and divine
relationships.

Neither of these icons stood alone in the battle over ideology.
There is other evidence from each society of the ideological debates
that raged in response to the reform. In the following discussion, the
palace and the temple will be placed within the context of the other
evidence for the reform and the counter reform movements. It is this
contextualization of the architectural and the verbal icons that
highlights their roles within their individual societies.

Sennacherib's Palace without Rival in Nineveh

The name that Sennacherib gave his palace at Nineveh made a bold claim for high status. The name has dual significance. It refers to those palaces of other kings in the period of Sennacherib's reign as well as to the palaces of his predecessors. With this title Sennacherib places his own dwelling far above any other palace as the unrivaled royal dwelling of his own unrivaled royal person, and thus his claim for his palace is also a claim for his own status. This, in itself, is not an unusual assertion for a Neo-Assyrian king to make. Successive kings typically claim a status that far surpassed all their foreign contemporaries as well as their predecessors on the throne.[1] Sennacherib is an Assyrian king who uses traditional formulas as well as unique expressions to present his reign as distinctive from all who had preceded him on the throne. Sennacherib is an innovator who is able to incorporate new technologies and new forms into his creations, both architectural and textual.[2]

Sennacherib's rhetoric exhibits the language and imagery of creation in his description of his feats of construction and ingenuity. While earlier Assyrian kings might claim to have the special favor of the god of craftsmanship, or to have the understanding of the wise sage Adapa, or even to have founded a city where no previous king had thought to do so, there are no royal records other than Sennacherib's in which an Assyrian king utilizes the image of creation in such a thorough manner to describe his ability to achieve his aims.[3] This literary distinction in the records of Sennacherib is

---

1   See, for example, Luckenbill, ARAB I, §§515, 714; ARAB II, §§83, 104-105.

2   See the discussions of J. M. Russell, Sennacherib's Palace without Rival at Nineveh (Chicago: University of Chicago Press, 1991), 175-190; S. Dalley, Nineveh, Babylon and the Hanging Gardens: Cuneiform and Classical Sources Revisited, Iraq 56 (1994): 45-58, as well as Luckenbill, Annals, 122: 14-26 and 123: 29-36 where Sennacherib describes his own inventive construction processes.

3   The closest parallel to the rhetoric of Sennacherib is that of this own father, Sargon II. In ARAB II, §§ 83, 98-99, 105, 119, Sargon's texts speak extravagantly of his wisdom and understanding and identify him as a unique king in a long line of princes, even using some of the creation language that becomes such a staple of Sennacherib's texts. His son's

indicative of his own sense of the significance of his reign and his status in the world.[4]

Sennacherib's Unique Use of Creation Imagery

The suite of rooms with Room XXXVI (the Lachish Room) at the center is an architectural claim of divine status by Sennacherib. A comparison of Sennacherib's literary rhetoric with his spatial rhetoric within the palace at Nineveh reveals a royal ideology that constitutes a radical reform in the understanding of kingship and divine status during the reign of Sennacherib. Moreover, there is an identifiable chronology of the development of Sennacherib's royal rhetoric from the subtle structuring of a spatial environment, which influenced human social behavior on a subconscious level, to the overt claims of royal inscriptions. The bond that connects this development from the indirect influencing of behavior through the structuring of space to the bold affirmation in royal inscriptions that required conscious agreement is the rhetoric and imagery of creation.

The Palace Texts

The building reports for the Palace without Rival were treated in detail in chapter two. It is necessary, however, to call attention to two texts that highlight Sennacherib's distinctive use of the rhetoric of creation. The first text is his description of palace construction in

---

innovative status is confirmed, however, as will be clear in the following presentation of his thorough reform of Neo-Assyrian society, a feat his father could not achieve.

4   H. Tadmor, Propaganda, Literature, Historiography: Cracking the Code of the Assyrian Royal Inscriptions, in Assyria 1995: Proceedings of the 10th Anniversary Symposium of the Neo-Assyrian Text Corpus Project, ed. S. Parpola and R. M. Whiting (Helsinki: The Neo-Assyrian Text Corpus Project, 1997), 328-330 has commented on the importance of distinctive elements in the inscriptions of Assyrian kings.

which he begins by preparing the site.[5] Although the king did not make direct reference to creation in this text, it is clear that his activities show that he has the ability to manipulate the environment and the topography of the earth to suit his creative needs. He gains control of the raging and destructive Tebiltu, which had undermined the foundation of the former palace. He changes its course and builds up dry ground from the midst of its river bed, and then has the palace constructed upon it. Sennacherib presents himself as a king with divine prerogative by using the imagery of a king who controls the physical topography of his realm.

A second text from the palace inscriptions is important because of the form of Sennacherib's titulary and his identification of his status in the world through the epithets associated with his name. The name of Sennacherib, like other Assyrian kings, is never written with the divine determinative DINGIR. His name is always preceded by the determinative DIŠ, which indicates that the following is one individual name.[6] The standard form of Assyrian royal inscriptions contains passages in which the kings claim particular status because they have been chosen by the great gods to be king of Assyria. They identify themselves as the favorite (king) of the great gods, and with that they designate themselves as holding special status in the society they rule.   They call themselves priest, appointees, and representatives of the deity Assur, and thereby identify their role as king to be the individual upon whom the national deity places the responsibility for the maintenance of the prosperity and well-being of the land of Assur. Sennacherib, however, advances a further claim of status in a text dated circa 694 B.C.E., when work on the palace is nearing completion. The text states:

> É.GAL ᵐᵈ30-PAP.MEŠ-SU MAN GAL MAN *dan-nu* MAN ŠÚ
> MAN KUR *aš+šur* MAN *kib-rat* LIMMU-*ti mi-gir*
> DINGIR.MEŠ GAL.MEŠ *lu-li-mu ir-šú   mal-ku   pit-qu-du*
> *ri-e-um ba-hu-la-ti mut-ta-ru-ú* UN.MEŠ *rap-ša-a-ti a-na-ku*
> ᵈ*be-lit* DINGIR.MEŠ *be-lit nab-ni-ti i-na* ŠÀ.SUR *a-ga-ri-in-ni*

---

5   The discussion above, Chapter 2, pp. 52-58.

6   The standard form of Sennacherib's name in his royal records is DIŠ.DINGIR.30-PAP.MEŠ-SU, which is often transliterated ᵐᵈ30-PAP.MEŠ-SU and normalized as ᵐᵈSin-ahē-eriba.

a-lit-ti-ia ki-niš IGI.BAR-*an-ni-ma ú-ṣab-ba-a nab-ni-ti ú*
^dNIN.IGI.KUG *id-di-na kar-šú rit-pa-šu šun-na-at* ABGAL
A-da-pá iš-ru-ka pal-ka-a ha-sis-su

The Palace of Sennacherib, the great king, the strong king, king
of the universe, king of the land of Assur, king of the four
quarters, favorite of the great gods. Wise stag, prudent prince,
shepherd of humankind, leader of widespread peoples am I.
Bēlit-ilī, the lady of created forms (creatures) steadily looked at
me in the womb of the mother who bore me and properly
executed my features, while Ea provided me wide knowledge
and granted me broad understanding, the equal of the sage
Adapa.[7]

In this text, some ten years into his reign and just a few years before
the completion of his palace, Sennacherib modifies a standard
titulary to exhibit his distinctiveness as an Assyrian king. He claims
that his creation in the womb of his mother was executed by the Lady
of the Gods. The goddess responsible for living creatures had
watched over and carried through the formation of his features
according to the divine plan.[8] Furthermore, Sennacherib claims that
Ea, the deity responsible for skill, craftsmanship, and understanding,
granted him broad knowledge and understanding equal to the
antediluvian sage Adapa. The choice of deities in this titulary was
indeed strategic. Belet-ili and Ea are the two gods who cooperate in
the creation of humanity in Atrahasis, and Ea is involved in the
creation of humanity in Enuma Elish.[9] Sennacherib highlights his
own unique status by identifying his creation in the womb of his
mother as the accomplishment of the deities who created humanity.

The palace was completed in 691 B.C.E. and presented a unique
claim of status. The suite of rooms focused on Room XXXVI stood
as physical evidence of the claim of this inscription while
constituting a spatial rhetoric in support of Sennacherib's assertion.

---

7   Transliteration follows Luckenbill, Annals, 117: 1-4. See Frahm,
     Einleitung, 118 for a discussion of the date of this document.
8   Note the double meaning of *ṣubbu*-- "to look at," "watch over," and "to
     carry out," "execute according to plan."
9   See S. Dalley, Myths from Mesopotamia, World's Classics (Oxford:
     Oxford University Press, 1991), 14-18 and 261-262.

The two texts, one describing the creation of a place for the palace and the other describing the creation of the king himself, demonstrate the development of a royal rhetoric in which the imagery of creation and the motifs associated with creation become a powerful device for this king's attitude toward his own role in the world.   The combination of the textual rhetoric and the architectural rhetoric provide support for the legitimacy of this new royal ideology and present it as though it were part of the very fabric of the created order of the world.

The Battle of Halule

In 689 B.C.E., two years after the completion of his palace in Nineveh, Sennacherib destroys the city of Babylon after putting down another rebellious coalition.   The narration of the battle of Halule, in which he defeats the allied armies, departs significantly from the standard report of military activity and Assyrian victory and employs a remarkable literary style.[10]   The description of the events leading up to the battle, as well as the battle itself, is presented using the language and imagery of the struggle between Marduk and Tiamat.

Sennacherib describes a large coalition of kings from Babylon, Elam, and many other towns, who join forces against Assyria. Shuzubu (Mushezib-Marduk?) is a Chaldean with a career of rebellion against Sennacherib.   Sennacherib describes him with unflattering words like "murderer," "robber," and "runaway."[11]   This man flees to Elam, but later returns to Babylon, where the people of Babylon place him on a throne "for which he was not suited."[12]   The language here is the very same as that in Enuma Elish when Marduk confronts Tiamat.   The text of Tablet IV, lines 81-84 read:

---

10   Luckenbill, Annals, 41-47; see also the comments of H. Tadmor, Propaganda, Literature, Historiography, 326, and the references cited there.

11   Luckenbill, Annals, 42: 22-23.

12   *a-na la si-ma-ti-šu*

^{d}kin-gu a-na ha-'i-ru-ti-ki a-na la si-ma-ti-šu taš-ku-ni-iš a-na pa-ra-
aş ^{d}e-nu-ti a-na AN.ŠÁR LUGAL DINGIR.DINGIR lim-ne-e-ti te-
eš-e-ma ù a-na DINGIR.DINGIR AD.AD-e-a le-mut-ta-ki tuk-tin-ni

You placed Kingu for your consort, for the rights of Anu, for which
he was not suited, you sought evil against Anshar, the king of the
gods and against the gods, my fathers, you confirmed your
wickedness.

Just as Kingu was not suited to be Tiamat's consort or to wear the
Tablets of Destiny, so Sennacherib argues that Shuzubu was not
suited to be king of Babylon. That role is reserved for the unrivaled
king, Sennacherib himself. He further describes the Babylonians as
"wicked demons"[13] who had opened the treasury of the temple
Esagila and used the gold that belonged to Marduk and Sarpanitu to
entice the Elamite king to come to their aid. When Sennacherib
reaches Halule and prepares for battle, he prays to the gods in whom
he trusts for victory, including Bēl and Nabû, two gods with strong
connections to Babylon. Rhetorically, the Assyrian king presents
himself as acting within the will of the Assyrian and Babylonian
deities while the Chaldeans and Elamites were acting outside of the
divine will.

The imagery and language of the description of the battle at Halule
resonate with the imagery and language of the creator conquering the
rebellious minor deities allied with the chaotic powers in order to
restore order and structure. The coalition is so numerous that the
dust raised by their march is described as the dense clouds of a
mighty storm. The actions of Sennacherib as he prepares to go out
for battle bring to mind the preparations of Marduk for his battle with
Tiamat. Though the order is not the same, they include very similar
activities. Sennacherib begins with prayer; he puts on his armor and
the helmet, which is his sign of battle; he hurriedly mounts his battle
chariot; he seizes the bow given to him by Assur as well as the lance,
he raises his voice and thunders like Adad.[14] Marduk's weapons
include the bow and arrow and the net which was a gift of Anu. He

---

13   GAL$_5$.LÁ.MEŠ lim-nu-ti
14   The same language of rumbling like Adad is used of Erra in Erra and
     Ishum, see S. Dalley, Myths from Mesopotamia, 289.

also has the winds, lightning, and the deluge is his great weapon. Then he mounts his chariot wearing a mail shirt, his armor of terror, and his *melammu* aura covering his head.

Sennacherib enters the field of battle and stops the advance of the rebels. Once Sennacherib enters the battle the storm imagery is focused on his activities and the enemy is presented as routed in a dazed flight. The account of the battle is full of blood and gore, as well as the imagery of confusion, as riderless horses gallop back and forth on the field of battle. Sennacherib is victorious over the rebellious kings and reestablishes order in the empire. The imagery of a stormy battle and the ensuing confusion of the fray are integral to the description of the battle between Marduk and Tiamat. Sennacherib's use of this language and imagery from the Creation Epic clearly identifies the Assyrian king with the victorious Marduk and the defeated Chaldean and Elamite kings as the rebellious ones associated with chaos and the lack of proper order. Replacing order in his realm is cast in the language of creation and proper destiny. Shuzubu is identified as a person who was not suited to be the king of Babylon while Sennacherib presents himself as the unrivaled king of Assyria and Babylon, whose destiny is to rule both realms. The use of the imagery and rhetoric of the Creation Epic, as well as elements from Erra and Ishum, which has its own connection to hard times for the city of Babylon, is unprecedented in a victory inscription. Here it is clear that royal ideology is couched in the literary language of his victory. But the claim is still elliptical. There is no direct statement of Sennacherib's status beyond being the proper and unrivaled king. For such boldness one must turn to Sennacherib's religious constructions in Assur and the Temple of the New Year Festival.

Sennacherib's Temple of the New Year Festival Texts

The battle of Halule is the final note of trouble with Babylon in the records of Sennacherib. It came after several military campaigns in which Sennacherib had gone to the south to confirm his control over 'Sumer and Akkad.' The ultimate fate of Babylon is mentioned in a building inscription from Assur dated to "the closing years of his reign."[15] Sennacherib built a temple for the New Year's festival, the *bīt akīti*, at Assur. In the text that recounts his building of the temple, the king tells how he completely destroyed the city of Babylon and brought part of its dirt back to Assur and placed it in the foundation of the *bīt akīti*. His purpose was to quiet or appease the heart of the god Assur and to show all the peoples that Assur was the most powerful of the gods.

> *a-na nu-uh-hi lib-bi* ᵈAN.ŠÁR EN-*ia ta-nit-ti dan-nu-ti-šu*
> UN.MEŠ *a-na da-la-li a-na ta-mar-ti* UN.MEŠ *ah-ra-a-ti*
> SAHAR.MEŠ TIN.TIR.KI *as-su-ha-am-ma* AŠ É *a-ki-ti šu-a-ti*
> *ka-ri-e* DUL *ú-gar-ri-in*

> To quiet the heart of Assur my lord, for the peoples to bow to his laudable might, for presents of distant peoples, I removed dust of Babylon and I piled (it) up in heaps in that temple of the New Year festival.[16]

This fact is made all the more poignant when one realizes that this temple is built for what had been a particularly Babylonian festival. The *akītu* festival was the New Year celebration that culminated with the reading of Enuma Elish, which ritually placed Marduk once again as the high god who maintains order and structure in the universe and who chooses Babylon as the foremost city for his temple. Moreover, near the end of the epic, in the sixth tablet Marduk gives the command for his temple, Esagila, to be built in the city of Babylon. Previous Assyrian kings who controlled Babylon use the fact that they went to Babylon to offer sacrifices to Marduk and to celebrate the *akītu* festival as a sign of their devotion to the religious traditions

---

15   Luckenbill, ARAB II, 183.
16   Luckenbill, Annals, 138: 44-47, translation mine. It is not entirely clear whether the place of storage was a container within the temple or whether the dirt was part of a foundation deposit. The sign DUL= *katmu* "covered," or "secret," can also be read DU₆=*tillu* "hill," or "pile," R. Labat, F. Malbran-Labat, Manuel d'épigraphie akkadienne 6th ed. (Paris: Paul Geuthner, 1995), 205. The verb *gurrunu* as well as the object, *karû* are ambiguous and could also indicate that Sennacherib stored the dust within the temple.

of the Babylonians and their veneration of the Babylonian deities.[17]
Tiglath-pileser III (745-727 B.C.E.) offers sacrifices to the
Babylonian deities, who then accept his priesthood.[18] More
specifically, Sargon II (721-705 B.C.E.), the father of Sennacherib,
enters joyfully into Babylon, grasps the hand of Marduk and makes
the pilgrimage to the Temple of the New Year's Feast.[19] In stark
contrast to his predecessors, Sennacherib destroys Babylon and, after
the *akītu* festival had been neglected for some time, he builds a new
bīt akīti at Assur, the ancient cult city of Assyria. Sennacherib's
texts show that the king incorporates this Babylonian celebration into
Assyrian religious practice after modifying it in order to give it a
distinctly Assyrian form.[20] There is ample evidence that
Sennacherib's construction of the *bīt akīti* at Assur is part of a
theological reform in which Marduk, the god of Babylon, is replaced
by Assur, the god of Assyria and Babylon is replaced by the new city
of Assur as the primary cultic center.[21]

---

17   On this Assyrian tradition, see the comments of H. Frankfort, Kingship and
     the Gods: A Study of Ancient Near Eastern Religion as the Integration of
     Society and Nature (Chicago: University of Chicago Press, 1962 [1948]),
     326-327.

18   Luckenbill, ARAB I, §788.

19   Luckenbill, ARAB II, §70. Note also the comments and the references
     listed by B. N. Porter, What the Assyrians Thought the Babylonians
     Thought about the Relative Status of Nabû and Marduk in the Late
     Assyrian Period, in Assyria 1995, 254. She indicates that Marduk was
     acknowledged as a patron of the Assyrian kings and in Assyrian state
     religion, particularly during the reigns of Sargon II and Esarhaddon, the
     immediate predecessor and successor of Sennacherib. Sennacherib's
     records, however, do not exhibit such devotion.

20   The identification of Assur with Anshar actually began during the reign of
     Sargon II, when the name of Assur began to be written with the signs
     ᵈAN.ŠÁR, but the identification was apparently complete late in the reign
     of Sennacherib. On this see the comments of H. Tadmor in The Sin of
     Sargon and Sennacherib's Last Will, SAAB III (1989): 29-30.

21   See the discussions of A. R. George, Iraq 48 (1986): 133-144; and E.
     Frahm, Einleitung, 220-229. Frahm, 223, asserts that this was not merely
     a case of making Assur look like the Assyrian Marduk, but was rather a
     complete replacement of the Babylonian deity by the Assyrian
     deity, as evidenced by the fact that the Assyrian version of the creation
     story is the same as the Babylonian except for the name of the deity who

At the doorway for this new *bīt akīti* Sennacherib places an engraving in copper that depicts the battle between Assur and Tiamat, the leader of the chaotic powers. In an inscription intended for a foundation stela he describes the scene at the doorway.[22] The text begins with Sennacherib's titulary as the maker of the image of Assur and the great gods, and claims that he is building the *bīt akīti* upon the command of Shamash and Adad after the ceremonies had been forgotten for a long time. The fifth line of the text begins his description of the engraving he places at the doorway:

KÁ.GAL ZABAR HUŠ *ša ma-la a-ga-[sa-lak-ki]*[23] *ši-pir* dSIMUG *ina*[24] *nik-lat ramâni-ia ú-še-piš-ma ṣa-lam* ⌈d AN.ŠÁR *ša ana libbi Tiamat]* ṣal-ti illaku is*qaštu ki-i ša na-šú-ú ina* is*narkabti ša ra-ak-bu a-bu-bu [ša pa-aq]-du* d*Amurru ša a-na mu-kil ap-pa-a-ti it-ti-šu rak-bu a-* ⌈na pi]-i ša dUTU u dIM *ina bi-ri iq-bu-nim-ma ṣi-ir* KÁ.GAL *ša-a-šu e-ṣir*

A gate of copper, burnished as the hatchet (a divine symbol), the work of the God of Metalworking, by (and) my own ingenuity I made and I engraved upon that gate the image of Assur, as the one who is going for battle into the midst of Tiamat, who raises the bow, who rides in the chariot, who appoints the deluge, Amurru, who rides with him as holder of the reins (charioteer), according to the command that Shamash and Adad spoke to me through an oracle.

The text continues the description of the scene, indicating that there were other deities fighting alongside Assur, arrayed all around him in battle formation as they approach Tiamat and all of her creatures. Line fourteen includes an interesting note of the image almost as a snapshot of the battle. It describes Assur as advancing upon Tiamat, but not yet having overpowered her.[25]

---

battles Tiamat and the addition of the names of the allied deities who fought on the side of Assur.

22　I want to thank Jack Sasson for kindly bringing this text and its unique claim to my attention.

23　Following the reading of Frahm, Einleitung, 224. Luckenbill, Annals, 140: 5 reads *ša ma-la a-ga-[le*meš *ša]*, and makes no offering for a translation.

24　Frahm, Einleitung, 224, suggest the conjunction *u*, "and."

25　*a-di la-a* dAN.ŠÁR *Ti-amat i-kam-mu-u*

In this document, and the engraved scene it describes, Sennacherib prominently presented his Assyrian reform theology. The last five lines of the text spell out in clear detail just how profoundly the Assyrian form of the creation story changes its Babylonian predecessor. Line ten reads

ṣa-lam ᵈAN.ŠÁR ša a-na libbi Ti-amat ṣal-ti illaku ṣa-lam
ᵐᵈ30-PAP.MEŠ-SU šar ᵐᵃᵗAššur

The image of Assur who goes into the midst of Tiamat for battle, the image of Sennacherib, the king of Assyria.

Here is a most interesting statement. The asyndetic construction multiplies the possibilities for the meaning of the Akkadian and offers an opportunity to explore Sennacherib's own self image. One may understand the text to be an indication that Sennacherib himself is the model for the image of Assur in his chariot. This in itself would reveal Sennacherib's identification of his own appearance as the most appropriate image for the deity, and therefore show the king's form as divine. Alternatively, one might understand that Sennacherib is claiming that he, in his role as king of Assyria, is the embodiment of Assur as he goes against Tiamat for battle. The former possibility is an identification of Sennacherib as the physical presentation of the god. The latter is the assertion that his royal activity is tantamount to the divine activity of Assur. One might also hold the two possibilities in a tandem relationship; since neither can be excluded grammatically, both meanings are in the king's presentation. The rest of the text clarifies the meaning of this statement, however.

The next five lines list all the deities who are arrayed with Assur in battle. Frahm describes these as well known Assyrian deities, particularly within the territory of the city of Assur.[26] Here Sennacherib changes the unnamed Babylonian pantheon accompanying Marduk in the battle with that surrounding Assur.

26　E. Frahm, Einleitung, 223. S. Dalley, Myths from Mesopotamia, 275n21 refers to this list in order to explain a brief mention of deities accompanying Marduk in the Babylonian Enuma Elish, but offers no further comment.

After the list of deities there are two other interesting lines which clarify the significance of line ten. They read:

[a-na]-ku ka-ši-du ina ^{iš}narkabti ^dAN.ŠÁR šak-nu [Ti]-amat
a-di nab-nit qer-bi-šu

I am the victorious one stationed in the chariot of Assur,
Tiamat together with the creatures inside her.

The loss of the first sign of this line leaves several possibilities for how one should read it.[27] The reading given here is the most bold of the possibilities and follows the structure of the text more closely. The indirect reference to himself as 'victorious prince,' offered by Frankfurt is still a claim by Sennacherib to be in the chariot of Assur, and yet is clearly a circumlocution. Frahm's reading removes Sennacherib from the chariot, returns the reader to understand that Sennacherib is the model for the image of Assur, and introduces a 'conquering weapon' not previously mentioned in the text without giving any further explanation.[28]

The text itself, however, has an internal balance and structure that encourages the reading followed here. Obverse lines 9-10 mention the images of the gods who go before Assur and after him, those who ride on chariots and those who go on foot. Reverse lines 6-7 again mention the great gods who advance into the battle with Assur. Reverse line 10 is the beginning of the list of the gods by name. As indicated above, following the mention of Assur and Sennacherib, in reverse 11-15, all the other deities are listed in the proper groups of those who are in front of Assur and those who are behind him. After

---

27 My translation follows the reading of Luckenbill, Annals, 142. Frankfort's translation, Kingship and the Gods, 327, follows a reading [mal]-ku ka-ši-du, "victorious prince," and indicates that this must be a reference to Sennacherib. Frahm, Einleitung, 224, comments on line 32, reads [GIŠ].TUKUL ka-ši-du, "the conquering weapon." Cf. CAD N/1, 357a

28 Frahm does offer some discussion of the possibility that this reference is related to another text and the listing of ^{d.giš}TUKUL after ^dKa-ši-du-ti in a „Götteradreßbuchs von Aššur," but rejects that understanding of this text. See his discussion, Einleitung, 224, and the references given there. Cf. CAD, K, 289a, kāšidu.

this list is the climactic statement of the king that he is the conqueror who is positioned in the chariot with Assur. Sennacherib indicates that there is actually an image of him within the chariot on the copper doors and that this is one of his attributes as king, i.e., to be Conqueror. He replaces the Babylonian deities with his own native Assyrian pantheon and places himself among the ranks of the gods as the Conqueror who stands in the battle chariot of Assur. His reform is more than an adaptation of the Babylonian creation story. It is a complete reformation of the understanding of the divine realm and an association of his royal person with the creative order of the universe.

In these texts associated with the temple for the New Year festival, Sennacherib marshals his verbal rhetoric to support the destruction of Babylon and the Babylonian cult. He further claims for himself the divine right and power to subdue chaotic elements that would oppose his reign over all areas within his realm. And he does so by identifying the Babylonian forces with the unruly deities who arrayed themselves with Tiamat and himself with the power of Assur to create order out of chaos. The end of the battle of Halule brought the destruction of Babylon, so the use of creation imagery in his account of the battle has special significance.

In the New Year temple texts, the message of Sennacherib's palace is made explicit. In the palace the king structures the approach to his enthroned image in Room XXXVI so that it mirrors the approach to a deity. In the New Year temple Sennacherib states clearly, in word and in relief, that as king of Assyria he has divine status. The recurrence of this theme in the architectural and the verbal rhetoric of this king is ample evidence that Sennacherib's reform theology includes raising himself to the status of divinity. The establishment of the New Year festival in Assur as a replacement for Babylon, and Sennacherib as the victorious one in the chariot of Assur ready to battle Tiamat, is part of the Assyrian king's plan to reform the religious and political ideology of the country so that his position as unrivaled king is secured. It appears, however, that his royal ideology and this theological reform were as treacherous as they were innovative.

Sennacherib's Reform and the Counter-Reformation that Ended His Reign

The palace that Sennacherib built in Nineveh magnifies his role as military conqueror, as well as his role as the creator of Nineveh and Assyria. Later in his reign, Sennacherib advances this same royal ideology using the Babylonian rebellion as the motif with which he presents himself as the unrivaled king able to defeat chaotic powers and establish order within his realm. As yet there are no major relief series from the palace at Nineveh or from other construction projects that present images of the destruction of Babylon. The focus on Lachish in Room XXXVI may be attributable as much to the chronology of the construction as to any other cause.[29] While Babylon may have been the greater victory in maintaining order in the realm of Sennacherib, it may also have proved too volatile an issue for such a focus in relief form.

It is well known that Sennacherib's reign ends with his assassination at the hands of his own sons.[30] This is indeed an ignominious end for a king of such high status; it is an end which has lead to speculation regarding its cause. What events would lead to an act of assassination, which is also regicide and patricide? The answer may lie in his Babylonian policy. Babylon and its royal house were a significant problem for Sennacherib throughout his reign. He ultimately concludes the only way to solve the problem is to destroy the city completely. Having destroyed the city, Sennacherib pursues a policy of assimilation of its religious traditions into those of Assyria by making substantial modifications to those traditions and to how his status as king should be understood. Herein may lie the issues that lead to his terrible end.

There are several reasons for considering Sennacherib's Babylonian policy as one factor that leads to his death at the hands

---

29   One might consider Babylon to have been a city more worthy of such focus, but the palace was completed two years before the destruction of Babylon in 689 B.C.E.

30   Cf. R. Borger, Die Inschriften Asarhaddons Königs von Assyrien (Graz: E. Weidner, 1956); S. Parpola, The Murderer of Sennacherib, in Death in Mesopotamia, Mesopotamia 8 (=CRRAI XXVI) ed. B. Alster (Copenhagen: Akademik Vorlag, 1980), 171-182.

of his own sons. The factors that ultimately lead to the assassination of an Assyrian king must be so emotionally and politically charged that individuals can conceive of regicide as a reasonable redress. First of all, given the ideology of the royal person in the Neo-Assyrian period, the act of murdering the king is tantamount to murdering the ruler who is chosen by the gods to be their representative among the people. It is an act against the deity Assur, as well as all other deities that support the king's reign. One must reason that assassins have substantial support from another deity, in order to conceive and carry out such a plan. It is logical that destroying Babylon and couching its destruction in creation rhetoric could stir opposition among Babylon loyalists and priests and devotees to Marduk.

Since the assassin's blow comes from his own son, Arda-Mullissi, S. Parpola proposes that this son was angered over having been passed over as crown prince.[31] Before Sennacherib destroys Babylon, his eldest son, Assur-nadin-šum, reigns for six years on the Babylonian throne, after which time he is captured and carried away. It is not certain that Arda-Mullissi is the next in line for the Assyrian throne, and he may have had hopes of being king in Babylon after Assur-ahi-iddin (Esarhaddon) is named Sennacherib's crown prince. There are many possibilities for palace intrigue among Babylonian representatives in the Assyrian court and royal sons who become disenchanted with their father's decisions. Esarhaddon's reign is partly characterized by his rebuilding of the city his father had destroyed. This is a clear indication of the influence Babylonian supporters maintain in the Assyrian court.

There are two further reasons for considering the Babylonian policy as contributing to Sennacherib's end. These are reflected in documents from the reigns of his son and grandson. Many of the early documents from the reign of Esarhaddon are apologetic. They offer explanations for why the new king became engaged in the rebuilding of a city considered so vile by his father that it deserves utter annihilation. In fact, much of the reign of Esarhaddon is spent

---

31   See the comments of Parpola, The Murderer of Sennacherib, 175, who concludes that the cause was a power struggle between Arda-Mullissi and Esarhaddon.

refurbishing the city and cult of Babylon and restoring its glory. There is one document in particular which provides an interesting insight into the way Esarhaddon garners support for his rebuilding. The document, which is published under the captivating title, "The Sin of Sargon," presents itself as a posthumous communication of Sennacherib to his son Esarhaddon.[32] In short, it tells of Sennacherib's attempt to determine why his own father, Sargon II, died such a disgraceful death and was abandoned on the battlefield. The result of his elaborate taking of omens by several divination experts (*bārû*) is the answer that Sargon had sinned by having honored the gods of Assyria too much and not having honored the gods of Babylon enough, as well as having broken a treaty in which he had sworn by Assur.[33] Sennacherib is determined not to commit the same mistake and plans to make an image of both Assur and Marduk as a sign of his devotion. Interestingly, he is prevented from completing the image of Marduk by the Assyrian scribes and is punished with an untimely death.[34]

There are numerous inconsistencies in the document with what is known about Sennacherib from his own royal annals and inscriptions.[35] The document is no doubt from the reign of Esarhaddon and is composed as religious and political propaganda in support of Esarhaddon's rebuilding of Babylon and making of a new image of Marduk for the city.[36] What makes this document so interesting, beyond its literary attractiveness as the communication between a father (the former king) and his son (the present king), is the information it provides regarding the political realities of the Neo-Assyrian royal administration. Religious and political concerns are inseparable and this text shows how one king's religious and

---

32   K4730 (+) Sm1816, a translation may be found in Court Poetry and Literary Miscellanea, SAA III, ed. A. Livingstone (Helsinki: Helsinki University Press, 1989), 77-79. A more extensive treatment with accompanying commentary and historical discussion may be found in H. Tadmor, B. Landsberger, S. Parpola, The Sin of Sargon and Sennacherib's Last Will, SAAB III (1989): 3-51.

33   See the comments of Parpola, SAAB III, 48-49.

34   SAA III, 33: rev. 21-23.

35   These have been outlined by Parpola, SAAB III, 45.

36   Ibid., 50.

political activity has to be supported by a document providing divine causation for his actions. Esarhaddon not only invokes the deities, but also invokes the memories of his own father and grandfather, particularly with regard to their interactions with the Babylonian divinities. He embarks on the rebuilding of the city his father had destroyed by claiming that his father had been prevented from his true plans of honoring the Babylonian deity by Assyrian scribes. The irony could not be more acute, nor could the evidence that the issue of Babylon is so volatile that Esarhaddon has to go to great lengths to support his complete contravention of his father's policy.

The second document comes from the reign of Assurbanipal, grandson of Sennacherib. Roughly forty years after his own father rebuilt the city of Babylon, with its mighty temples and images of its deities, Assurbanipal has to subdue a Babylonian threat again. This time it is a rebellion led by his own brother Šamaš-šum-ukin.[37] This account ends with an interesting note in which Assurbanipal tells of his having taken vengeance upon some of the rebellious Babylonians by slaying them between the colossi, "between which they had cut down Sennacherib, the father of the father who begot me, as an offering to his ghost."[38] This note further supports the theory that Sennacherib's untimely end is connected to his Babylonian policy and his Assyrian reform theology.

The claims of Sennacherib to status on par with the gods and his modifications to the political and religious conceptions of Assyria are innovations that could not be achieved merely by the administrative texts that recount his victories and building projects. The palace that he built in Nineveh is an integral element to the legitimation of his ideology. It takes the abstract changes made by his administration and makes them physically perceptible in the environment in which the king performs his royal role. The architectural presentation of the king in this manner supports his claims and attributes legitimacy to them as part of the very fabric and structure of the universe at creation. Ultimately, when Sennacherib incorporates his royal ideology in the texts and in the reliefs of the New Year temple

---

37   See Luckenbill, ARAB II, §§791-798.
38   Luckenbill, ARAB II, §795.

doorway, it may be that the reformation is more than the various members of his administration could tolerate.

Sennacherib's assassination is the beginning of a counter reformation that results in the reconstruction of the city he had destroyed. Moreover, the reconstruction achieved under the guidance of Esarhaddon is not only presented in the imagery of Marduk turning away from his anger against the Babylonians, which is identified as the cause of their destruction, and his consequent decision to shorten their punishment from seventy years to eleven. It also reinterprets the actions of Sennacherib. Presenting Sennacherib as a king who attempts to correct the sin of his own father, Sargon II, but who is prevented from completing his acts of devotion by crafty Assyrian scribes, is an integral part of the counter reformation. This interpretation of the reign of Sennacherib not only stands in direct opposition to the account of his own royal inscriptions, but also places the blame for his dishonorable death on those who prevent him from fulfilling his vow, and thereby bring the vengeance of Marduk down upon him.[39] Clearly, Marduk returns as the separate deity of the Babylonians and Esarhaddon presents himself as the one Marduk chooses to restore the temples and the rites in Babylon in what is nothing less than a counter reformation in response to Sennacherib's reformation.[40]

Babylon outlived Assur and Nineveh and succeeded them as the center of power in the ancient world in the Neo-Babylonian period. This is the ultimate result of the counter reform of Esarhaddon and his supporters who were responsible for the rebuilding of the city. Sennacherib's political and religious reformation was all but lost in the subsequent rise of the empires that, for the most part, inherited the realms over which he had exerted control. The built environment analysis of his palace, particularly the suite of rooms focused on Room XXXVI, brings Sennacherib's royal image and his own

---

39   The improbability of scribes being able to prevent the Assyrian king from completing a religious vow weighs against the explanation, but does provide an indication of the antipathy Assyrian scribes may have felt for Babylonian deities.

40   For a detailed study of Esarhaddon's Babylonian policy, see B. N. Porter, Images, Power, and Politics: Figurative Aspects of Esarhaddon's Babylonian Policy (Philadelphia: American Philosophical Society, 1993).

identification of his status back into focus. By itself, however, it might be dismissed as nothing more than architectural innovation. When combined with his use of creation imagery in his description of the destruction of the Babylonian forces at Halule and the texts describing the construction and decoration of the *bīt akīti*, it is clear that the palace was one part of a radical reform of thinking and behavior in the Neo-Assyrian period.

Solomon's Temple without Rival in Jerusalem

The study of the description of Solomon's temple building in chapter three concurs with the following statement of R. P. Carroll:

> What the great texts of constructing the *miškān* and the temples of Solomon and Ezekiel are about is not the literal building of actual sanctuaries but representations of complex metaphoric and metonymic structures which bear on how the community is to live in the world . . . Those texts describe buildings that never were: grandiose, ideological constructions with no real existence outside of the text.[41]

Carroll explains that the building descriptions are patterned following the ideological concerns of the authors and can no longer be understood to present an actual structure. This shift in perspective is substantial and fundamental to the present study. In the past, biblical scholars constructed the political and religious concerns of tenth century B.C.E. Israel as the historical milieu of the composition of the temple description, but this study proposes that the temple description in I Kings 6-7 is a verbal icon created as part of the ideological presentation of the Dtr reform and therefore is more revealing of the historian's notions of proper worship and religious conceptions in the sixth century B.C.E.

---

41   R. P. Carroll, So What Do We *Know* about the Temple? In Second Temple
       Studies 2: Temple and Community in the Persian Period, JSOTS 175 ed.
       T. C. Eshkenazi and K. H. Richards (Sheffield: JSOT Press, 1994).

If the biblical narrative is a verbal icon that presents the ideology of the author, it has profound implications for understanding the theological development of Israel in the exilic and post-exilic periods. The role of the temple description as a verbal icon is significant in Dtr's presentation of the history of Israel. In the following discussion, the role of the temple and its implements as icons of theological development will be traced to show the impact of this new approach to the biblical narrative.

Theological Debate and the Verbal Icon

There is general assent that Israelite theology was influenced by the international political events culminating in the destruction of Jerusalem by the Babylonians in 587 B.C.E. The recent comprehensive work of T. N. D. Mettinger traces this theological development from confidence in a Zion chosen and ruled by YHWH Sabaoth to the religious reforms and counter reforms of the Deuteronomistic and Priestly groups.[42] The established Zion-Sabaoth theology is based upon the inviolability of Zion as the site chosen by YHWH Sabaoth to dwell, as well as YHWH's choice of the Davidic House to rule over Israel.[43] It expresses the conviction that YHWH Sabaoth is willing to fight on Israel's behalf, incorporating royal imagery for the deity enthroned on the cherubim.[44] The association of YHWH and the cherubim connects the Sabaoth imagery to the ark, particularly in the stories of the ark's early life at Shiloh and its move to Jerusalem. This association has perplexed scholars for more than thirty years because the description of the ark in Dtr has no

---

42   T. N. D. Mettinger, The Dethronement of Sabaoth: Studies in the Shem and Kabod Theologies, Coniectanea Biblica Old Testament Series 18 (Lund: CWK Gleerup, 1982); earlier studies include G. von Rad, Studies in Deuteronomy, trsl. D. Stalker (Chicago: Henry Regnery Co., 1953), 37-44; R. E. Clements, God and Temple (Philadelphia: Fortress Press, 1965), 79-122; J. H. Hayes, The Tradition of Zion's Inviolability, JBL 82 (1963): 419-426.

43   See for example, Isaiah 6; 10:5-11, 27b-34; 14:24-27; 31:4-5; Psalms 24; 89; 132.

44   ישב הכרבים; I Samuel 4:4; II Samuel 6:2; II Kings 19:15.

cherubim. How and when the cherubim and ark came to be associated is the crux of the intractable nature of the traditions surrounding the ark.[45]

Particularly intriguing are the examples of individuals appearing before YHWH Sabaoth with no mention of the ark. In the visionary text of Isaiah 6, the prophet sees YHWH Sabaoth enthroned in the temple (היכל). [46] There is no mention of an inner chamber (דביר) or of the ark.[47] Isaiah describes only the enthroned deity, the attending seraphim, and an altar. This presentation is precisely what one might expect to find in a temple with an image of the deity enthroned on the back wall or in an open cella at the rear of the building, opposite the entrance.

---

45 Regarding the difficulty of the association of the ark and the cherubim, see R. de Vaux, Les chérubins et l'arche d'alliance. Les sphinx gardiens et les trônes divins dan l'ancien Orient, Mélanges de l'université Saint Joseph 37 (1961): 93-124; R. E. Clements, God and Temple, 32-33. For the problems associated with the extent and significance of the ark narratives, see the discussions of F. Schicklberger, Die Ladeerzählung des ersten Samuel-Buches,   Eine   literaturwissenschaftliche   und theologiegeschichtliche Untersuchung, Forschung zur Bibel 7 (Würzburg: Echter Verlag, 1973); A. F. Campbell, The Ark Narrative (1 Sam 4-6; 2 Sam 6): A Form-Critical and Traditio-Historical Study, SBL Dissertation Series 16 (Missoula, MT: SBL and Scholars Press, 1975); as well as the comprehensive assessment of these studies in P. D. Miller, Jr. and J. J. M. Roberts, The Hand of the Lord: A Reassessment of the 'Ark Narrative' of 1 Samuel (Baltimore and London: The Johns Hopkins University Press, 1977).

46 O. Kaiser, Isaiah 1-12 OTL, Second Edition, trsl. J. Bowden (Philadelphia: Westminster Press, 1983), 125, warns against taking this text as an accurate presentation of the appearance of the temple. While his admonitions are an important guard against free reconstructions, the text is, at the least, representative of the type of royal imagery and the arrangement of a sanctuary associated with YHWH Sabaoth.

47 M. A. Sweeney, Isaiah 1-39, with an Introduction to Prophetic Literature FOTL XVI, ed. R. P. Knierim and G. M. Tucker (Grand Rapids, MI: William B. Eerdmans, 1996), 139, indicates that the inner chamber and the ark are there, even though they are not mentioned. This addition of elements not presented in the text does not clarify the significance of the presentation.

In II Kings 19:14ff., King Hezekiah of Judah spreads the letter of Sennacherib before YHWH in the temple and then prays to YHWH, "the God of Israel, who is enthroned on the cherubim." Again, though the details are sparse, it is interesting that this text makes no mention of the ark or of the inner chamber (דביר). The reference to placing the letter and praying "before YHWH" (לפני יהוה), can be an indirect reference to the ark, but could also be a statue of YHWH enthroned in the temple.[48] Most interesting, however, is the fact that neither of these texts, which are so clearly associated with the Zion-Sabaoth theology, mention the ark of the covenant or its special place, the innermost chamber.

The vision of Micaiah ben Imlah recorded in I Kings 22:19ff is the third example of enthronement imagery that lacks reference to an ark. Micaiah proclaims that he saw YHWH upon his throne with the host (צבא) of heaven standing on his left and right. The vision, though not associated with the temple, is revealing. YHWH is presented as a royal figure, and the associated host indicate that the term is less connected to the imagery of armies as it is connected with the heavenly bodies that make up his divine court.[49] The temple of YHWH Sabaoth in Jerusalem may have been a single chambered temple (היכל) with an enthroned image of a deity, before whom was a smoking incense altar.[50]

These references present images of the temple furnishing and layout that stand in stark contrast to the image developed by Dtr. This is all the more reason to understand the temple description in I Kings 6-8 as Dtr's verbal icon because of the discrepancy between the temple that Dtr says Solomon built and the temple descriptions

---

48   J. Montgomery, The Books of Kings, ICC (Edinburgh: T. & T. Clark, 1951), 493; P. K. McCarter, Jr., I Samuel, Anchor Bible (New York: Doubleday, 1980), 106-108, understands II Kings 19 as a reference to the ark as indicative of YHWH's presence. H. Niehr, In Search of Yahweh's Cult Statue in the First Temple, in The Image and the Book: Iconic Cults, Aniconism, and the Rise of Book Religion in Israel and the Ancient Near East, CBET 21, edited by K. van der Toorn (Leuven: Uitgeverij Peeters, 1997), 73-99, takes the opposite view and sees this as an indication of a statue of YHWH enthroned in the temple.

49   In contrast to the opinion of P. McCarter, I Samuel, 106n.

50   H. Niehr, In Search of YHWH's Cult Statue, 89-90.

above. Precisely because of the ark's enigmatic nature, it provides an excellent cipher for the following discussion of the theological reforms and counter reforms in the exilic and post-exilic period.

The Temple and the Ark in the Deuteronomistic Reform

The presentation of the temple in I Kings 6-7 is very different from that of Isaiah 6 and II Kings 19, which present Sabaoth imagery. In contrast to the single chambered temple (היכל). Dtr introduces the inner chamber (דביר) as a place for the ark. The cherubim are present in the דביר, but are not part of the ark and have no described function. The central importance of the ark is evident in the references to it in the description of the temple building and the dedication ceremony. The דביר in the back of the temple is constructed as a place for the ark, and the dedication begins with the journey of the ark from the tent set up for it by David to its place within the דביר.[51] Von Rad recognized the centrality of the ark and called it, "the nucleus around which the whole design of Solomon's temple is built up."[52] Yet, in his own study of the development of the ark, von Rad clearly imagines the ark within the temple to look like the Priestly description in Exodus 25.[53] It must be recalled that the ark in Deuteronomy and the Deuteronomistic literature is a simple wood box that contains the tablets of the covenant, i.e., the

---

51   I Kings 6:19; 8:1-11.
52   G. von Rad, The Tent and The Ark, in The Problem of the Hexateuch and
       Other Essays, trsl. E. W. T. Dicken (London: SCM Press, 1984), 122.
       This essay was first published as Zelt und Lade, Kirchliche Zeitschrift
       42 (1931): 191-204; and subsequently included in Gesammelte Studien
       (Munich: Chr. Kaiser Verlag, 1958).
53   Von Rad, Tent and Ark, 110-113. Von Rad's thinking is clearly influenced
       by the association of the cherubim and the ark and the idea that the ark was
       a (portable) throne, even though he notices the inconsistency of having a
       throne referred to as a "box," (ארון). It is precisely this Moebius strip
       presentation in the biblical text that creates the conundrum that von Rad is
       unable to solve.

decalogue.[54] Therefore, the ark that Dtr places as the central furnishing of Solomon's temple is not the elaborate implement envisioned by the Priestly writer (and consequently, von Rad). Von Rad's tradition historical approach posits a separate development for the ark and the cherubim, but he could never identify the point of association necessary to resolve the relationship between the cherubim and ark.

The fact that biblical scholars often visualize the more elaborate form of the ark is due to the Priestly reworking of the dedication ceremony of the temple and is testimony to the effectiveness of the counter reformation that produced the Priestly supplementation. If one removes the Priestly additions to the Dtr text, the narrative of dedication flows quite smoothly from Solomon's gathering the elders of Israel to the priests carrying the ark into the temple, Solomon's address to the people, and his prayer of dedication.

I Kings 8:1-11

The Dtr version of the story is found in I Kings 8:1, 3, 5, 6, 9, and originally read:

אז יקהל שלמה את־כל־זקני ישראל . . . ירושלים להעלות
את־ארון ברית־יהוה מעיר דוד היא ציון . . . ויבאו כל זקני
ישראל וישאו הכהנים את־הארון . . . והמלך . . . וכל־ . . . ישראל
. . . מזבחים צאן ובקר אשר לא־יספרו ולא ימנו מרב ויבאו
הכהנים את־ארון ברית־יהוה אל־מקומו אל־דביר הבית . . .
אל־תחת כנפי הכרבים . . . אין בארון רק שני לחות האבנים
אשר הנח שם משה בחרב אשר כרת יהוה עם־בני ישראל
בצאתם מארץ מצרים

Then Solomon assembled all the elders of Israel . . . to Jerusalem to bring up the ark of the covenant of YHWH from the city of David, which is Zion . . . Then all the elders of Israel came and the priests carried the ark . . . while the King . . . and all . . . Israel were sacrificing sheep and cattle, which were too numerous to be counted or numbered. And the priests brought the ark of the

---

54   Dt. 10:1-5; there is no mention of gold plating, the cover with the two cherubim, or the poles used to carry the ark.

> covenant of YHWH into its place into the innermost chamber of
> the house . . . under the wings of the cherubim . . . There was
> nothing in the ark except the two stone tablets (of the covenant)
> that Moses placed there at Horeb, which YHWH had made with
> Israel when they came out from the land of Egypt.[55]

This concise description of the ceremony of bringing the ark of the
covenant from Zion to its place in the innermost chamber of the
temple and putting it there under the wings of the cherubim ends with
the Dtr explanation that the ark was nothing more than a container
for the covenant made through Moses at Horeb. Dtr connects the
temple, and thus Solomon's reign, to the seminal event of the Exodus
and the figure of Moses in this introductory description of the
processional of the ark to its resting place.

I Kings 8:14-21

The speech of Solomon in 8:12-13 so strongly contradicts the
historian's view of the temple as a dwelling for the Name, that they
must be a later addition.[56] The king's speech begins in verse fifteen
after he has turned to face the people. This section is intimately
connected to the promise to David in II Samuel 7 and identifies
Solomon as the son YHWH promised would build the house for his
Name. The language of I Kings 8:19 is far too close to that of II
Samuel 7:13 for this to be anything other than literary resumption of
the theme of building a house for the Name.[57] In his dedicatory
speech, in I Kings 8:20, Solomon clearly claims to be the fulfillment
of that promise, but the historian includes a further statement on the
part of Solomon in verse twenty one:

---

55 Cf. the comments and reconstruction of J. Montgomery, Kings, 185-189;
M. Noth, Könige 1, BKAT 9/1 (Neukirchen Vluyn: Neukirchener Verlag,
1968),, 168-175; and J. Gray, I & II Kings, 2nd ed. OTL (Philadelphia:
Westminster Press, 1970), 206-209.

56 Note also the affirmation of I Kings 8:27 that the deity could not possibly
dwell in a house since the highest heavens could not contain him.

57 Both passages include the promise, הוא־יבנה הבית לשמי.

ויקם יהוה את־דברו אשר דבר ואקם תחת דוד אבי ואשב
על כסא ישראל כאשר דבר יהוה ואבנה הבית לשם יהוה
אלהי ישראל ואשם שם מקום לארון אשר־שם ברית יהוה
אשר כרת עם־אבתינו בהוציאו אתם מארץ מצרים

> And YHWH established his word which he spoke and I rose in
> the place of David my father, and I sat on the throne of Israel
> just as YHWH said, and I built this house for the Name of
> YHWH, the god of Israel. Then I put there a place for the ark
> where is the covenant of YHWH that he made with our
> ancestors when he brought them out from the land of Egypt.

Dtr's theology is evident in the double assertion he places in the
mouth of Solomon: Solomon built a house for the Name of YHWH
and he put inside it a place for the ark of the covenant. There is no
way to mistake the historian's point. The covenant that is the central
element in the temple furnishings, the covenant by which the people
are to live and through which they are to approach the deity is the
covenant made between YHWH and their ancestors in the wilderness
at Horeb. By appealing to the Exodus event and the covenant making
at Horeb, the historian offers his religious reform the legitimacy of
the distant past when YHWH first made his requirements known to
the ancestors.

Moreover, as explained above in chapter three, the temple is no
longer to be understood as the place where YHWH Sabaoth is
enthroned forever. Dtr reinterprets the significance of the temple as
a religious icon toward which the people should pray. The people
should no longer think of the temple as the dwelling place of the
deity, since YHWH is a transcendent god whose throne is in heaven
and who cannot be contained in an earthly dwelling.

The ark that stands at the center of this verbal icon is nothing
more than the simple wood box described in Deuteronomy 10:1-5.
There is no gold inlay on the ark, just as there are no cherubim on the
lid. This apparent reduction of the iconography of the temple to the
simple box is in line with the Dtr rejection of the use of images in
accordance with the dictates of Deuteronomy 5:6ff, which are based
on the explanation of 4:9ff. Since the people saw no form when
YHWH appeared to them on Mount Horeb, but only heard the sound
of the divine words, they should not look to anything in the heavens,
on the earth, or in the seas as representative of the deity. There are

only the words of the covenant, which are God's words, and Dtr places those words in the simple box at the center of his verbal icon.

The recent discussion of Israelite aniconism is developing toward an understanding of the programmatic rejection of icons as an exilic development.[58] It appears, however, that Dtr was more anti-image than anti-icon. The historian incorporates a command against the making of images in the worship of YHWH, but he creates a verbal icon as a didactic tool to instruct the people how to remain in proper relationship with the deity. K. van der Toorn contemplates the shift from statues to texts and offers the following explanation of how such a shift is a change of one icon for another:

> Like the icon, the Book is both a medium and an object; as a medium, it refers the reader to a reality beyond itself, whilst as an object, it is sacred in itself. Presented as a divine revelation, the cult symbol, be it an image or a book, tends to be perceived as being consubstantial with God.[59]

A clear innovation of the Dtr school is this shift from image icon to verbal icon. Image icons enhance notions of immanence and identify certain characteristics of the deity by using forms with which those characteristics are associated. The verbal icon, as used by the prophets and Dtr, enhances the notion of transcendence by creating an abstraction that cannot be reduced to image form. The text is more

---

58   Compare S. Schroer, In Israel gab es Bilder. Nachricten von darstellender Kunst im Alten Testament, OBO 74 (Freiburg und Göttingen: Universitätsverlag Freiburg, Vandenhoeck & Ruprecht, 1987); and the conclusions of O. Keel and C. Uehlinger, Göttinnen, Götter und Gottessymbole, Neue Erkenntnisse zur Religionsgeschichte Kanaans und Israels aufgrund bislang unerschlossener ikonographischer Quellen (Freiburg: Herder, 1995), 253-275; and the collection of essays edited by K. van der Toorn, The Image and the Book: Iconic Cults, Aniconism, and the Rise of Book Religion in Israel and the Ancient Near East. In contrast to these studies, see T. N. D. Mettinger, No Graven Image? Israelite Aniconism in Its Ancient Near Eastern Context Coniectanea Biblica Old Testament Series 42 (Stockholm: Almqvist & Wiksell International, 1995).

59   K. van der Toorn, The Iconic Book, Analogies Between the Babylonian Cult of Images and the Veneration of the Torah, in The Image and the Book, 242.

than a communication from the deity. As the above quote indicates, the text is consubstantial with God and makes the deity present through the record of its covenant with the people.

The Dtr reform is ambitious. It removes any notion of an enthroned deity in the temple and develops the idea of YHWH as a transcendent deity who can be approached through prayer and proper obedience to the covenant law. It is only the Name of YHWH that can then be said to have been present in the temple.[60] This leaves very little available as a role for the priestly class in the religious practice of the people. While there are the three annual festivals (Dt. 16:16) at which the people are to bring their offerings to the central sanctuary, there is no deity present in the temple, and therefore no need for daily sacrifices and ministrations in the sanctuary. These are all reason enough for a Priestly counter reformation that would return to the priestly class some measure of control and responsibility in the religious life of the people.

Priestly Counter-Reform

Just as Dtr's theological reform is recognizable in the verbal icon he creates, so the response of the Priestly group is discernible in their icon of counter reformation. As they supplement the Dtr document, the Priestly group incorporate their own notions about proper religious belief and activity. The evidence for the hand of the Priestly writer is in the uneven elements in the temple dedication of I Kings 8:1-13, as well as in other texts. The Priestly supplementation focuses the event toward the concerns of the Priestly group. Verse one, states that the elders were representatives of every tribe of Israel, appointed from the ancestral houses, underscoring the notion that this event was an "all Israel" dedication, during which the whole nation was represented in Jerusalem. Verse two includes a note that every man in Israel came to the King in the month of Etanim, during

---

60   See Mettinger's discussion of the Deuteronomistic Name theology in Dethronement of Sabaoth, 54ff.

the festival which is in the seventh month.[61] The discrepancy here
between 6:38, which indicates that the temple was completed in Bul,
the eighth month, has led to the supposition that there was an eleven
month wait before the temple dedication.[62] The uneven nature of the
relationship between 8:2 and 6:38 is due to the Priestly writer placing
the temple dedication at the annual festival of Sukkoth without clear
regard for the dating of the previous notation. Verses four through
six include several Priestly additions. Verse four includes the tent of
meeting and the sacred items in the tent among the items that the
priests bring up from Zion to the temple. Verse five names the group
that assembled with the Kings as the congregation of Israel,
incorporating a clearly Priestly term. In verse six the Priestly writers
once again make sure that the reader understands that the inner
chamber of the house (דביר הבית) is the Most Holy Place (קדש
הקדשים).

The most telling Priestly additions to the narrative are those found
in verses seven through eight and ten through eleven. The Priestly
writer incorporates his notion of the function of the cherubim using
the distinctive verb סכך. Verse seven reads:

כי הכרובים פרשים כנפים אל־מקום הארון ויסכו הכרבים
על־הארון ועל־בדיו מלמעלה

> For the cherubim spread wings toward the place of the ark
> so that the cherubim covered over the ark and over its
> poles.

Dtr identifies no function for the cherubim when their
manufacture and placement in the דביר is described in 6:23-28. In
6:27 Solomon places the cherubim in the inner chamber and the
wings of the cherubim spread out (פרש) so that they touch the
outside walls of the inner chamber while their inner wings touch each
other in the middle of the chamber.[63] Though Dtr does not indicate

---

61   This is the festival of Sukkoth. Cf. Leviticus: 23:33ff.
62   J. Montgomery, Kings, 187, and the references there.
63   The Chronicler (II Chr. 2:12) describes the inner wings of the cherubim
     as connected using the term דבק, which is possibly a misunderstanding
     of the priestly term סכך[I] which means to "cover," with סכך[II] which

their function as a throne, their positioning is certainly indicative of
this function. This positioning in the דביר, combined with the
references to YHWH Sabaoth enthroned on the cherubim and the
established archaeological evidence that cherubim thrones were a
common royal accoutrement in Iron Age Levant, demonstrates that
the original function of these 10 cubit tall twin cherubim was as the
throne for YHWH Sabaoth. It is the Priestly author who changes
their function to a cover over the ark that conceals it in a protective
manner, and he does so based upon his own description of the
construction of the covering for the ark in Exodus 25:17-21.
Describing the cherubim on the *kappōret*, Exodus 25:20aα reads:

והיו הכרבים פרשי כנפים למעלה סככים בכנפיהם על־הכפרת

And the cherubim should have upward spreading wings
covering over the *kappōret* with their wings.

The priestly writer does not indicate in I Kings 8 that there are now
four cherubim, two on the cover of the ark and two free standing. He
uses the Dtr description of the two standing cherubim, but identifies
their function in concert with his own conception of the ark.

In verse eight, the Priestly writer explains that the poles of the ark
were so long that their ends could be seen from the sanctuary in front
of the inner chamber, though they could not be seen from outside the
temple. This one statement has led to considerable discussion and
confusion among biblical scholars, since on initial reading it appears
that the ark would not fit in the chamber that was made for it.
Though the text never specifies how the ark was placed in the inner
chamber, some scholars are of the opinion that the ark was placed on
the central axis of the building in longitudinal fashion and that it
stood between the cherubim.[64] This placement means that the poles
must have been more than twenty cubits long, since that is the length

---

means to "weave together." Otherwise, in II Chr. 5:8, the Chronicler
indicates that the ark was placed under the wings of the cherubim and that
the wings covered the ark, but he uses the verb כסה.

64   Cf. Mettinger, Dethronement, 23n15. This assumption is no doubt made
because the Hebrew text indicates that only the ends of the poles could be
seen, ויראו ראשי הבדים מן־הקדש על־פני הדביר.

of the דביר, and the doors of the inner chamber would then be
rendered useless. Since the length of the poles is never given in the
biblical text, it is possible that they were this long, though that length
would certainly make the poles more cumbersome than the two and
a half cubit box they were made to carry.

A second concern is the assumption that the ark and its poles did
not fit within the inner chamber constructed for it. This would
certainly be evidence of bad planning. How could Solomon construct
a temple that includes a chamber specifically designed as a place for
the ark, and then have the ark, or at least the poles of the ark, be too
long for the chamber? The only solution to this is the recognition that
the building description is Dtr's while the ark dimensions belong to
the Priestly writer. Again, since P gives no measurement for the
length of the poles, the problem appears insoluble as long as one
imagines the ark sitting along the longitudinal axis of the building.

J. Montgomery and M. Noth both understand the ark as sitting in
a position transverse to the axis of the building, and therefore in front
of the cherubim and not between them.[65] But their explanations are
not entirely satisfactory. Montgomery explains that there must have
been a veil that blocked the view of the ark itself:

> . . . thus we have to assume the presence of 'the veil' . . . as
> concealing the sacred object from vulgar gaze, so making the
> staves themselves of profound interest to the devotee. The veil
> concealed the ark, only the staves might be seen projecting right
> and left by one standing near the narrow door of the sanctuary,
> but not from a greater distance.[66]

In this recreation, a veil must hang somewhere between the doorway
of the inner chamber and the ark, thus blocking the view only of the
ark. But the Dtr description mentions nothing of a veil and
Montgomery obviously has in mind the description of the Chronicler,
or a combination of the tabernacle veil from Exodus 26:31ff. A
second problem is his strange statement that with the veil in place
one could see the end of the poles if one were standing near the
entrance and, presumably, peeping into the inner chamber. The

---

65   J. Montgomery, Kings, 188-189; M. Noth, Könige 1, 179.
66   Montgomery, Kings, 189.

attitude seems very cavalier with reference to what was identified as the Most Holy Place by the Priestly writer.

M. Noth also indicates that the poles were visible and that the notice merely indicates that the poles were longer than the width of the entrance to the inner chamber and could have been seen if one were near the entrance. It is not clear if Noth also assumes the presence of a veil blocking the view of the ark itself, or if he considers the doors to the chamber to block the view of the ark. He must have some sort of veil in mind, since it is unclear how the poles could have been seen with the door to the chamber closed, unless one imagines the wall between the main chamber and the inner chamber as made of latticework. This would make all of the elements of the inner chamber visible if one stood next to the wall.[67]

It must be admitted that the problem of I Kings 8:8 is produced by the fact that the Priestly writer introduces a different form for the ark than is conceived by Dtr, a form that is indicative of the different theological views of the Priestly group. The inner chamber of the temple is the creation of the Dtr writer and is not structured to contain the ark as it is envisioned by the Priestly writer. In fact, the visibility of the ark is not even an issue for Dtr, since there is no theological investment in the ark as a throne or some other symbol of divine presence, as there is for P. The visibility of the poles is mentioned by the Priestly writer out of his hesitancy to change the Dtr text as he receives it, as well as his concern for accuracy and a logical presentation, which forces him to recognize that the Priestly ark would not fit invisibly in the inner chamber created by Dtr. This is clear evidence that the Priestly writer supplements the Dtr text in order to make sure that subsequent readers visualize the Priestly form of the ark when they read the text. The success of this reform is evident in the way that modern scholars reconstruct the ark's development.[68]

Verse ten and eleven describe the cloud of the Glory of YHWH that fills the temple when the ark is placed in the inner chamber. This language is almost identical to the language of Exodus 40:34-

---

67   The possibility of the dividing wall being lattice-work would be a novel
       reading of צלעות in I Kings 6:16.

68   On which see more below.

35, which recounts the placement of the ark in the tabernacle and the tabernacle becoming so full of the cloud of Glory that Moses is unable to enter. The Priestly writer incorporates the theology of the Glory by indicating that the presence of YHWH is visible in the form of the cloud when the ark is put in its place.[69] The appearance of the cloud is in no way related to the Dtr concept of the transcendence of the deity. As explained in chapter three, Dtr removes the deity entirely from the human realm and makes the temple a focal point of religious attention by the deity and the people. Such an appearance of the cloud of Glory is clearly part of the Priestly counter reform and the return of the idea that the deity can be present in the temple where the priests offer sacrifices and perform other services.

Verses twelve and thirteen come from a non-Dtr hand and express notions about the dwelling of the deity which are antithetical to the Dtr reform ideas. As discussed in chapter three, Dtr challenges the claims of verses twelve and thirteen in 8:27 that even the highest heaven could not contain the deity, much less this temple. Dtr asserts that there was no deity dwelling in the temple, only the covenant that exists between the people and the deity. The covenant is there as a symbol of the relationship that continues between them and the requirements the deity places on the people. The Priestly writer counters this claim by reasserting the presence of the deity in the temple. The deity is again enthroned, albeit intermittently, and can again be said to dwell in the midst of the people.

The Priestly reworking of the Dtr text is evidence of the Priestly counter reformation. Dtr's reform made the primary requirements obedience and a relationship through prayer. This type of religious reform goes too far for the priests to agree. It leaves them without any official role on a daily basis since there is no divine presence in the temple before which they can offer the sacrifices and other ministrations. The description of the dedication of the temple is an important text that provides evidence of the Priestly counter reform. They incorporate their own image of the ark, which according to

---

69 See Mettinger, Dethronement, 118-121, for a discussion of the combination of the Kabod theology with the theophanic tradition, and their association with the ark. Mettinger considers this a very early association between the Glory and the ark based on I Sam. 4:21, but this understanding of the ark stories requires further discussion below.

Exodus 25 is much more than a box for the tablets of the law, it is also the portable throne of YHWH. They also incorporate their own presentation of the presence of the Glory of YHWH in the temple, which is in keeping with the Priestly theology of occasional presence of the deity among the people in the form of the cloud of Glory.

The Ark and Religious Reform

The general view regarding Dtr's relationship to the ark is that the historian demotes the throne of YHWH to a simple wooden box that functions merely as a container for the tablets of the law.[70] In contrast to this view, however, is the opinion of R. E. Clements.[71] Clements recognizes that the Hebrew word ארון meant "box" and concludes that this must be its initial function, since otherwise it is difficult to explain how a throne came to be called a box.[72] This confusion among modern scholars, and the apparent intractable nature of the form of the ark is the result of the success of the Priestly writer's counter reform. It is indeed difficult to imagine how Dtr could have taken a symbol as central as the ark, with all of its elaborate decoration, as well as its function as the portable throne of the deity, and have demoted that symbol to a simple wood box that was nothing more than a container for the tablets. This is the crux of the conundrum that surrounds the ark. How could something that functioned as the divine throne and battle palladium for the people have come to be called a box?

---

70   G. von Rad, Studies in Deuteronomy, 41, indicates that Dtr "demythologized" the ark; idem., The Tent and the Ark, 106-107, he states, ". . .he strips away from the ark every trace of magical belief, and it becomes what it had certainly never been before -- a receptacle for the tables of the Law." Cf. also the comments of Mettinger, Dethronement, 23, cited above.

71   Clements, God and Temple, 30-31.

72   Von Rad, Tent and Ark, 112, also recognizes that the ark is never referred to as a throne (כסא), but because he thought of the change to receptacle as the innovation of Dtr, he could not see the term ארון as indicative of its original function.

The analysis of Dtr's verbal icon above and in chapter three points to an entirely different understanding of the development of the ark. It now is clear that the ark is first developed as the ark of the covenant by Dtr. In that role it is the simple acacia wood box that holds the tablets of the covenant. Furthermore, Dtr places this box in the central position in the temple as the focal element in the temple furnishings because of its association with the Decalogue, which is the core of the Deuteronomic covenant between YHWH and the people at Horeb.[73] Dtr makes the association between the ark and the cherubim when he creates the temple description as a verbal icon. This is due in part to the recognition that the primary element in the temple had been a cherubim throne, which functioned as the sign of the presence of the deity.[74] It is this cherubim throne and its association with YHWH Sabaoth that engenders the expression "YHWH Sabaoth enthroned on the cherubim." Dtr retains the cherubim, but gives them no function, other than his connecting their position on either side of the ark with the repeating pattern of cherubim flanking palm trees he describes on the walls, which is a well known Assyrian decorative motif. They can no longer be associated with the enthroned deity because the Dtr reform claims that YHWH is not a deity present in the human realm, but is rather completely transcendent. The Dtr reformers further insure the purity of this conception of the deity by the call for centralized worship.

---

73 Recall that the people saw no form on Horeb, they only heard the sound of the words that were spoken from the fire. (Dt. 4:12)

74 Or there may have been a statue of YHWH seated on the throne in accordance with the theology of YHWH Sabaoth as the divine king. The recognition of Israel as iconic is growing with the work of O. Keel and C. Uehlinger, as evidenced by the essays collected in The Image and the Book. In contrast to this developing position, however, note T. N. D. Mettinger, No Graven Image? Israelite Aniconism in Its Ancient Near Eastern Context Coniectanea Biblica Old Testament Series 42 (Stockholm: Almqvist & Wiksell International, 1995); idem, Israelite Aniconism: Developments and Origins, The Image and the Book, 173-204; and as counter argument to Mettinger's onclusions, see T. J. Lewis, Divine Images and Aniconism in Ancient Israel, JAOS 118,1 (1998): 36-53, whose review article of No Graven Image? provides insightful suggestions regarding future approaches and how modern scholars might study this issue. On this see more below.

There is no better way to control religious practice and iconic presentation than to limit ritualized religious behavior to a central sanctuary where the reformers are able to reinforce their own ideas about the deity.

Priestly writer's concept of the ark is a combination that could only occur after Dtr's association of the ark and the cherubim in his temple description. The Priestly writer goes one better and incorporates the cherubim onto the very lid of the ark itself. This development allows the ark to function as the portable throne of the deity in the wilderness and into the period of the judges. The Priestly counter reform is an attempt to return to the religious conceptions of a deity who is present, and the form and function of the ark are indicative of this change. The Priestly group brought back some of the ideas of the Zion-Sabaoth theology in the way that they return to the notion of YHWH enthroned on the cherubim, but their counter reform places that development at Sinai with the divine instructions to make an ark to hold the tablets of the testimony, which has a cover with cherubim over which the deity would appear.

The Priestly modifications to the ark of the covenant are indicative of the concern of this group to provide an identifiable place where the priest may meet the presence of the deity, and there mediate for the people. The cherubim are also changed in the Priestly description. They face each other and their wings are raised toward each other, forming a covering over the lid of the ark. This is not part of Dtr's idea about the wings of the cherubim; his cherubim form a throne seat with the two middle wings and touch the outer wall of the inner chamber with the others.[75] The inclusion of the description of the poles used to carry the ark is necessary for P since his concept of the ark is as a portable throne or battle palladium. Dtr makes no mention of any special devices for carrying the ark, though he does indicate that it was carried by the priests. Another testimony to the success of the Priestly counter reform is the way in which modern

---

75   All archaeological evidence points to the fact that cherubim were elements associated with thrones. In this, Dtr's description is in agreement with what is independently known about cherubim in the ancient world.

scholars assume the ark is the Priestly version of it even when they are reading a text that is clearly Dtr.[76]

Scholars who maintain the antiquity of the ark invariably point to the Ark Narrative as proof of its importance in an old, pre-Dtr tradition. Even Clements, who maintains the ark is originally a box and not a throne based on it being called ארון, traces the association of the ark with the cherubim, and thus its identification as a throne back to Shiloh.[77] The original connection with Shiloh is based upon I Samuel 4:1b-7:1. This material, known as the Ark Narrative, has long been considered an independent story that is incorporated by Dtr into his history. The extent and reason for its composition have been the subject of most recent scholarly discussion, with the consensus being that the narrative was originally composed during the period after the defeat at the hands of the Philistines at Ebenezer and the rise of David.[78]

The reference to the ark being at Shiloh in these stories need not be separated from the Dtr composition. In their study of the significance and genre of the stories of I Samuel 4:1b-7:1, Miller and Roberts offer comparative Mesopotamian material to show that this narrative fits within the genre of stories about the loss, captivity, and

---

76 G. von Rad, Tent and Ark, 103, explains that he will begin with the latest accounts of the ark (which are the Priestly accounts) and work backwards. But it becomes quite clear in his discussion, 106-109, that von Rad considers this image and function of the ark as a portable throne to be the original and more ancient identity and that the Dtr description is an innovation. Another interesting example of this may be found in P. K. McCarter 1 Samuel, 108-109, in his reference to Joshua 3-4; 6, where the ark is carried through the Jordan and into battle against Jericho. McCarter clearly assumes the presence of poles to carry the ark even though the text makes no mention of them. Poles are clearly connected to the Priestly concept of the ark and entirely superfluous to Dtr's ideas about the ark of the covenant.

77 Clements, God and Temple, 34, identifies Shiloh as the place where the ark and the cherubim become associated with one another and that they move from there to the Jerusalem temple during the time of David and Solomon. See also the more recent studies of Schicklberger, Die Ladeerzählung; A. F. Campbell, The Ark Narrative; and P. D. Miller, Jr., and J. J. M. Roberts, The Hand of the Lord.

78 See Miller and Roberts, Hand of the Lord, 74-75.

return of divine images.[79] They draw a connection between the intent of Mesopotamian stories of the loss of divine images and the story in I Samuel 4:1b-7:1 in order to show that the biblical narrative is a well established literary genre in the ancient world. It is most telling, however, that though they cite a few Old Babylonian examples, by far the most numerous examples of this literary genre come from the Late Assyrian and the Neo-Babylonian rulers. The identification of this story as an example of this genre of literature does not provide evidence of antiquity, but rather points to the later period as the time of composition.

Miller and Roberts also connect the story of the ark in 4:1b-7:1 with the material in 2:12-17, 22-25, which recounts the judgement against the house of Eli. That the notice of the loss of the ark is so intimately combined with the death of Eli's sons, as well as the death of Eli upon his hearing of the loss, makes the connection with these notices in I Samuel 2 unquestionable. As a story of judgement on the house of Eli, Miller and Roberts conclude that the story ends at I Samuel 7:1 and that it does not continue in II Samuel 6.[80]

The implications of the study of Miller and Roberts for the ark traditions have yet to be exploited. Without intending to do so, they show that there is no reason to consider this material as coming from a pre-Dtr independent source. The first narrative is Dtr's story of the judgement on the house of Eli, which results in the temporary loss of the ark. The story of David bringing the ark to Jerusalem is part of Dtr's narrative of David's consolidation of his reign and has several parallels to the story of Solomon and the priests bringing the ark of the covenant into its place within the inner chamber of the house. The processions of II Samuel 6:1-5, 11-13, 15, 17-19, and I Kings 8:1, 3, 5-6, 14, which are led by the kings and the people, include numerous sacrifices along the processional way, concluding with the ark in its proper place and the king blessing the people, and have striking parallels to the scene described by Esarhaddon recounting the return of Marduk to Babylon from Assur.[81]

---

79   Ibid., 9-17.
80   Hand of the Lord, 22-26.
81   R. Borger, Die Inschriften Asarhaddons, Königs von Assyrien, AfO Beiheft 9 (Graz: E. Weidner, 1956), 88-89, lines 18-20.

The historian creates the ark as a container for the tablets of the covenant. The stories about the ark before it came to the Jerusalem temple do not uniformly indicate an association of the ark with the presence of the deity. There is no way to square this type of association with Dtr's Name theology. The ideas of transcendence and the passages that incorporate the ideology of the Name theology with the concepts of the deity as immanent are now ripe for further investigation in light of the conclusions of this study.

Reform and the Verbal Icon

It is now clear that the Dtr reform is innovative in the way that it structures its description of the temple, but more significantly, the question of the ark's association with the cherubim is no longer a problem since the ark is the creation of the Deuteronomistic Historian. The reason it is called a box is because that is precisely what it was in its original form, a simple wood box to contain the tablets. Dtr does not demote, or demythologize, an elaborate portable throne. The development of the ark actually flows in the other direction. It is first conceived by Dtr as a container for the tablets of the law. The inner chamber of the temple is constructed as a place for the container to rest. The cherubim that Dtr includes in his description of the temple are what remains of what must have been an elaborate cherubim throne upon which YHWH Sabaoth had been enthroned. Whether the enthronement was invisible or in the form of a statue is at this point impossible to say.

Dtr's view of the temple is entirely clear in I Kings 8 and is a verbal icon of the Name theology. He presents the temple as the fulfillment of David's desire to build a house for the Name of YHWH, which recalls the promise to David in II Samuel 7. On the other end of the historian's narrative, at the destruction of the temple, there is an interesting silence about the ark, the cherubim, and the innermost chamber. Though the historian goes to some length to connect the temple of the Babylonian destruction with the temple of Solomon by taking time in II Kings 25:16-17 to mention the vessels in the courtyard and to describe the dimensions of the two columns, there is no mention whatsoever of the items within the דביר. In fact, after the placement of the ark in the דביר, there is no further mention of this central element of the temple in the history. Dtr creates the verbal icon of the temple consisting of its spatial arrangement and separate chambers, including the innermost chamber as a special place for the ark of the covenant, narrates the placement of the ark in its special place at the center of his verbal icon, and then drops it. The only reference back to Solomon's temple, as indicated above, is to the implements of the courtyard. This cannot be attributed to the historian's reluctance to narrate something terrible happening to the ark, since there is no such reluctance in I Samuel. The long strange silence regarding the ark in the rest of DtrH confirms the assessment that the historian creates this image of the temple as a verbal icon for his theological conception of the temple as a place for the Name of YHWH, while the deity remains in the true divine dwelling place in the heavens.

The modern tenacity of the image of the ark as an elaborate golden box with cherubim on the lid and the tablets of the testimony within it, as well as the notion that it functioned as a portable throne or battle palladium, are both evidence of the success of the Priestly group in their counter reformation. Dtr's idea of the ark as nothing more than a box for the tablets, in combination with his theology of transcendence, leaves too small a role for the Priestly group, and may have created too much of an abstraction to take hold in the popular consciousness of the day. Whatever the reason for its inability to withstand the counter reformation of the Priestly group, the verbal icon created by the historian stands as witness to his theological innovations and his creative ability to present that ideology in a narrative.

Those who come after the historian certainly follow his lead in the way they present their developing ideologies. The Priestly group does not replace Dtr's verbal icon, they merely modify it so that it includes their concerns. The Chronicler retells the national history using Dtr as his basic material, but incorporates his own perspective. In each case, these later groups use compositional strategies that build upon the foundation laid by the Deuteronomistic Historian. The historian is an innovator of conventional modes of iconic presentation who pushes for an abstract concept of the deity that is also intensely personal. Even though his ideology is pushed aside by the later groups, the fact that they achieve this using his own form of presentation may now be understood not only as evidence of his premier status as a creator of the verbal icon, but also in some way as his own small victory.

Chapter 5

Conclusion

If we wanted and dared an architecture in accordance with our minds . . . then the labyrinth would have to be our model.

Nietzche, *The Dawn*

The image of the labyrinth borrowed from Nietzsche is most appropriate for the conclusion of this study. While it may conjure notions of confusion and frustration for those lost in its intricacies, taken as a whole it is a model of complexity and interconnectivity. The application of one path or approach will not lead to the solution. What is required is an approach that incorporates many paths.

The study of the palace and the temple has shown that these two structures function in similar ways within their respective cultures. The palace of Sennacherib is a physical presentation of the social structure and categories of behavior that he intended to engender within the society of the Neo-Assyrian Empire. The temple of Solomon is the creation of the Deuteronomistic Historian, who intended to influence the religious conceptions and behavior of the members of his own society. The two structures achieve their aims only insofar as they are able to convince the viewers/readers that the behavior and social structures they present were ordained in hoary antiquity and are identifiable with the very fabric of the cosmos. Sennacherib attempted this using the imagery and rhetoric of creation. Dtr gained support for his reform by appealing to the period of the Exodus, the figure of Moses, and the giving of the commandments at Horeb. All of these events come from that period that the Dtr narrative presented as the formative period in the history of the people.

The built environment analysis of the palace of Sennacherib opened the doorway to the king's royal ideology. When combined with the other evidence from his royal documents and building programs, it clarifies the path that leads from the maze of possibilities for meaning within the walls, reliefs, and texts Sennacherib left behind. Interestingly, Sennacherib's own innovations are confirmed in his successor's reactions to them. It is clear that Sennacherib overstepped some authority, either in his claims for divine status or in his destruction of Babylon and Marduk, and his transgression led to his assassination. This is only evident now, however, because Sennacherib's records can be placed within the context of those of his father and son. If one only studies the material left behind by Sennacherib and his administration, it is equivalent to trying the same path of the labyrinth continuously, though it always leads to the same dead end. It is the combination of Sennacherib's palace, and texts with the texts of his successors that allow one to see the complexity that was the Neo-Assyrian Empire. Decisions by one king could affect the reign and choices of a subsequent king, which could then in turn change the effects of the previous king.

The labyrinthine nature of the verbal icon created by Dtr is all the more complex because it exists on many levels at once. Dtr composed a national history that presents the story of the rise of Israel from wandering in the wilderness to possessing the land. Within that national history are multiple themes such as promise and fulfillment, blessing and cursing, obedience and disobedience, but throughout the DtrH the deity is transcendent. There is no image or form to which it can be compared. In this Dtr is like the prophets, his presentation of the deity is deeply influenced by that strain of prophecy that emphasizes the unequaled status of the deity. H. Timm put it this way:

> Der Dtr. ist zwar ein Schüler der Propheten, er trägt aber nicht den Mantel des Propheten sondern den des Historikers und des Gelehrten. In dieser Gestalt ist er unseres Wissens ohne Vorgänger gewesen.[1]

Given the innovative approach to prophetic compositions proposed by M. Dick and the conclusions of this study, it is appropriate to

---

1   H. Timm, Die Ladeerzählung und das Kerygma des deuteronomistischen Geschichtswerks, Evangelische Theologie 26 (1966): 515.

consider the unique nature of the Deuteronomistic compositions. While one might view the prophetic parodies against the use of images, as well as many other prophetic oracles in the biblical material, as the product of a poetic craftsman, the Deuteronomistic History is a prose composition that functions as an icon of identity.

Since M. Noth's first discussion of this work as a unified composition, much of the response of biblical scholars has been in the form of refinements to the theory. The guiding principle in the perception of a new emphasis or concern is evidence of a different redactional layer, which leads to the multiplication of redactors and the loss of unity throughout the material.[2] Rather than further fragmentation of the historiographic material, this study understands the composition as the work of an exilic literary and theological innovator whose goal was the presentation of an account of the history of the people for the purpose of instruction. There is no reason to doubt the reform of Josiah as a beginning point for the influence of the Dtr group in the religious life of Judah. The composition of the national history is the creation of a verbal icon that functions on many levels. It provides legitimacy for the religious reforms by establishing a connection between them and the distant past when the original instructions were supposedly given. It also provides instruction for the people regarding proper behavior and belief in the way the events of the past are structured and presented. The historian provides a lineage of great leaders from distant antiquity right up to the recent past, from Moses to Samuel to David and Solomon and down to Josiah. Along with these are less admirable characters that the historian includes as examples of improper worship and behavior.

This study has focused primarily on the temple description as a verbal icon. The entire DtrH, however, may be understood as a verbal icon. The historian created an icon within an icon. Deciphering the elements of the smaller verbal icon will lead to a better understanding of the larger icon and, perhaps, of the labyrinth

---

2   See the summary of development of the scholarly discussion of the composition of DtrH in G. N. Knoppers, Two Nations Under God: The Deuteronomistic History of Solomon and the Dual Monarchies, vol. 1, The Reign of Solomon and the Rise of Jeroboam, HSM 52 (Atlanta: Scholars Press, 1993), 17-54.

of thoughts and conceptions embedded in the narrative. This approach to the temple description as a verbal icon is the first step in taking a new view of the compositional intent in the biblical material. It is not merely the description of the temple that may be viewed as a verbal icon. In fact, once one begins to view the text as a whole as a verbal icon, then the many different elements within it are facets of the larger image.

The theological debates of the sixth century found their clearest expression in the textual embodiments of the key events in the history of the people. Scholars have long understood the account of those events as having been shaped by the ideologies of those who composed and reworked the narratives. This study proposes another level of reading those narratives. The verbal icon is not merely a novel twist on modern theories of reading, but is rather the function of the text. The narrative does not present the actual chronology and development of events, but rather presents figures and events as icons that instruct the behavior of the reader.

Understanding the temple description as a verbal icon that is related to the architectural icon of Sennacherib's palace is possible because of the application of built environment analysis. Built environment analysis cannot unlock all the secrets of the Neo-Assyrian political and religious innovations, or of the theological debates embedded in the narrative of the biblical material. It is merely a method that is particularly suited to elucidate the conceptual structures that lie behind built forms. This study shows that it is applicable to ancient structures as well as modern, but it also shows that it is applicable to symbolic structures. More significantly, this study draws an equation between the iconic function of images and the iconic function of texts. The human mind is a labyrinth of structure with the ability to interconnect multiple conceptions in a complex array of meaning, and to present that array as though it were part of the fabric of reality and not a construct. The palace of Sennacherib and the Deuteronomistic Historian's Jerusalem temple are human constructs that present the divine-human relationship, icons that embodied the human social behaviors and concepts desired by their creators.

Abbreviations

AB	Anchor Bible
ABD	Anchor Bible Dictionary
ATD	Das Alte Testament Deutsch
BA	Biblical Archaeologist
BASOR	Bulletin of the American Schools of Oriental Research
BDB	Brown, Driver, Briggs Hebrew Lexicon
BKAT	Biblischer Kommentar Altes Testament
BZAW	Beihefte zur Zeitschrift für die Alttestamentliche Wissenschaft
CBET	Contributions to Biblical Exegesis and Theology
CBQ	Catholic Biblical Quarterly
FOTL	Forms of Old Testament Literature
HMS	Harvard Monograph Series
HSS	Harvard Semitic Series
ICC	International Critical Commentary
IEJ	Israel Exploration Journal
JAOS	Journal of the American Oriental Society
JBL	Journal of Biblical Literature
JCS	Journal of Cuneiform Studies
JNES	Journal of Near Eastern Studies

JSOT	Journal for the Study of the Old Testament
JSOTS	Journal for the Study of the Old Testament Supplement Series
OBO	Orbis Biblicus et Orientalis
OTL	Old Testament Library
PEQ	Palestine Exploration Quarterly
RA	Revue d'Assyriologie
SAA	State Archives of Assyria
SAAB	State Archives of Assyria Bulletin
SAAS	State Archives of Assyria Studies
VT	Vetus Testamentum
VTSup	Supplements to Vetus Testamentum
WBC	Word Biblical Commentary
ZA	Zeitschrift für Assyriologie
ZAW	Zeitschrift für die Alttestamentliche Wissenschaft

Bibliography

Ackroyd, P. R. The Chronicler and his Age. JSOTS 101. Sheffield: JSOT Press, 1991.

_____. The Temple Vessels: A Continuity Theme. In Studies in the Religion of Ancient Israel. VTSup 23. Leiden: E. J. Brill, 1972.

Aharoni, Y. The Archaeology of the Land of Israel: From the Prehistoric Beginnings to the End of the First Temple Period. Translated by A. F. Rainey. Philadelphia: Westminster Press, 1982.

Albenda, P. The Palace of Sargon, King of Assyria. Paris: Editions Recherche sur les civilisations, 1986.

_____. Assyrian Sacred Trees in the British Museum. Iraq 56 (1994): 123-134.

Albright, W. F. Two Cressets from Marisa and the Pillars of Jachin and Boaz. BASOR 85 (1942): 18-27.

Andrae, W. Das wiedererstandene Assur. Second edition. Revised by B. Hrouda. Munich: Beck, 1977.

_____. Der Anu-Adad Tempel in Assur. Osnabrück: Otto Zeller, 1984.

Armstrong, R. P. The Affecting Presence: An Essay in Humanistic Anthropology. Urbana: University of Illinois Press, 1971.

_____. The Powers of Presence: Consciousness, Myth, and Affecting Presence. Philadelphia: University of Pennsylvania Press, 1981.

Bachelot, L. La fonction des reliefs néo-assyriens. In Marchands, diplomates et empéreurs. Etudes en honneur de Paul Garelli, edited by D. Charpin and F. Joannès. Paris, 1991: 109-128.

Barkay, G. The Iron Age II-III. In: The Archaeology of Ancient Israel, edited by A. Ben-Tor, translated by R. Greenberg. New Haven and London: Yale University Press, 1992.

Barnett, R. D. and M. Faulkner. The Sculptures of Tiglath Pileser III. London: British Museum, 1962.

_____. and A. Lorenzini. Assyrian Sculpture in the British Museum. Toronto: McClelland and Stewart, 1975.

Baumgartner, W. Herodots babylonische und assyrische Nachrichten. In: Zum Alten Testament und seiner Umwelt. Leiden: E. J. Brill, 1959: 282-331.

Beck, B. E. F. The Symbolic Merger of Body, Space, and Cosmos in Hindu Tamil Nadu. Contributions in Indian Sociology 10 (1976): 213-243.

Berlejung, A. Der Handwerker als Theologe: Zur Mentalitäts- und Traditionsgeschichte eines altorientalischen und alttestamentlichen Berufstands. VT 46 (1996): 145-168.

_____. Die Theologie der Bilder. Das Kultbild in Mesopotamien und die alttestamentliche Bilderpolemik unter besonderer Berücksichtigung der Herstellung und Einweihung der Statuen. Göttingen: Vandenhoeck & Ruprecht, 1998.

Biran, A. and J. Naveh. An Aramaic Stele Fragment from Tel Dan. IEJ 43 (1993): 81-98.

Blanton, R. E. Houses and Households: A Comparative Study. New York and London: Plenum, 1994.

Bloch-Smith, E. "Who is the King of Glory?" Solomon's Temple and its Symbolism. In: Scripture and other Artifacts: Essays on the Bible and Archaeology in Honor of Philip J. King, edited by M. D. Coogan, J. D. Exum and L. E. Stager. Louisville, KY: Westminster John Knox Press, 1994: 18-31.

Borger, R. Einleitung in die Assyrischen Königsinschriften. Leiden: E. J. Brill, 1961.

_____. Babylonisch-Assyrische Lesestücke. Rome: Pontificum Institutum Biblicum, 1963.

Borger, R. Die Inschriften Asarhaddons, Königs von Assyrien. AfO Beiheft 9. Graz: E. Weidner, 1956.

_____. Handbuch der Keilschriftliteratur. Berlin: Walter de Gruyter, 1967.

Börker-Klähn, J. Der bīt hilāni im bīt šahuri des Assur-Tempels. ZA 70 (1980): 258-272.

Burkert, W. Greek Religion. Translated by J. Raffan. Cambridge, MA: Harvard University Press, 1985.

Busink, Thomas A. Der Tempel von Jerusalem, von Salomo bis Herodes: eine archäologisch-historische Studie unter Berücksichtigung des westsemitischen Tempelbaus. 2 Volumes. Leiden: E. J. Brill, 1970 and 1980.

Brinkman, Johan. The Perception of Space in the Old Testament. Kampen, The Netherlands: Kok Pharos Publishing, 1992.

Campbell, A. F. The Ark Narrative (1 Sam 4-6; 2 Sam 6): A Form-Critical and Traditio-Historical Study. SBL Dissertation Series 16. Missoula, MT: SBL and Scholars Press, 1975.

Carroll, R. P. So What Do We Know about the Temple? In: Second Temple Studies 2: Temple and Community in the Persian Period. Edited by T. C. Eshkenazi and K. H. Richards. JSOTS 175. Sheffield: JSOT Press, 1994.

Clements, R. E. God and Temple. Philadelphia: Fortress Press, 1965.

Coogan, M. D. Stories from Ancient Canaan. Philadelphia: Westminster Press, 1978.

Cooke, G. A. Ezekiel. International Critical Commentary. Edinburgh: T. & T. Clark, 1937.

Cross, F. M. Canaanite Myth and Hebrew Epic: Essays in the History of the Religion of Israel. Cambridge, MA: Harvard University Press, 1973.

Crowfoot, J. W., G. M. Crowfoot, and K. M. Kenyon. The Objects from Samaria. London: Palestine Exploration Fund, 1957.

Dalley, S. Myths from Mesopotamia. Oxford: Oxford University Press, 1991.

Dalley, S. Nineveh, Babylon and the Hanging Gardens: Cuneiform and Classical Sources Reconciled. Iraq 56 (1994): 45-58.

_____. Herodotus and Babylon. Orientalistische Literaturzeitung 91 (1996): 526-531.

Damerji, M. S. B. The Development of the Architecture of Doors and Gates in Ancient Mesopotamia. Translated by T. Takaso and Y. Okada. Tokyo, 1987.

Dearman, A., editor. Studies in the Mesha Inscription and Moab. Atlanta: Scholars Press, 1989.

De Odorico, M. The Use of Numbers and Quantifications in the Assyrian Royal Inscriptions. SAAS III. Helsinki: The Neo-Assyrian Text Corpus Project, 1995.

Dever. W. G. Monumental Architecture in Ancient Israel in the Period of the United Monarchy. In: Studies in the Period of David and Solomon and Other Essays, edited by T. Ishida. Winona Lake, IN: Eisenbrauns, 1982: 269-306.

_____. Archaeology and the "Age of Solomon": A Case Study in Archaeology and Historiography." In: The Age of Solomon: Scholarship at the Turn of the Millennium, edited by L. K. Handy. Leiden: Brill, 1997: 217-250.

DeVries, S. J. I Kings. Word Bible Commentary. Waco, TX: Word Books, 1985.

Dick, M. Prophetic *poēsis* and the Verbal Icon. CBQ 46 (1984): 226-246.

Fergusson, James. The Palaces of Nineveh and Persepolis Restored. London: John Murray, 1851.

Finkelstein, I. On Archaeological Methods and Historical Considerations: Iron Age II Gezer and Samaria. BASOR 277/278 (1990): 109-119.

Fowler, H. T. Herodotus and the Early Hebrew Historians. JBL 49 (1930): 207-217.

Fox, Michael V., editor. Temple in Society. Winona Lake: Eisenbrauns, 1988.

Frahm, E. Einleitung in die Sanherib-Inschriften. Archiv für Orientforschung 26. Wien: Institut für Orientalistik der Universität Wien, 1997.

Frankfort, H. Kingship and the Gods: A Study of Ancient Near Eastern Religion as the Integration of Society and Nature. Second Edition. Chicago: University of Chicago Press, 1962 [1948].

_____. The Art and Architecture of the Ancient Orient. Fifth edition. New Haven and London: Yale University Press, 1996. [1951].

Frankl, P. Principles of Architectural History: The Four Phases of Architectural Style, 1420-1900. Translated and edited by James F. O'Gorman. Cambridge, MA: MIT Press, 1968. Originally published as Die Entwicklungsphasen der neueren Baukunst. Stuttgart:Verlag B. G. Teubner, 1914.

Fritz, V. Paläste während der Bronze- und Eisenzeit in Palästina. Zeitschrift des Deutschen Palästina-Vereins 99 (1983): 1-42.

Gates, M.-H. The Palace of Zimri-Lim at Mari. Biblical Archaeologist (June 1984): 70-87.

Giedion, S. Space, Time, and Architecture. Bolingen Series XXXV. Princeton: Princeton University Press, 1964. (Paperback, 1981).

Golzio, K.-H. Der Tempel im alten Mesopotamien und seine Parallelen in Indien: eine religionshistorische Studie. Leiden: E. J. Brill, 1983.

Gray, J. I & II Kings. OTL Philadelphia: Westminster Press, 1970.

Gutman, J., editor. The Temple of Solomon: Archaeological Fact and Medieval Tradition in Christian, Islamic, and Jewish Art. Atlanta: Scholars Press, 1976.

Guy, P. L. O. New Light from Armageddon. Oriental Institute Communications 9. Chicago: University of Chicago Press, 1931.

Haller, A. Die Heiligtümer des Gottes Assur und der Sin-Šamaš-Tempel in Assur. Wissenschaftliche Veröffentlichung der Deutsche Orient-Gesellschaft 67. Berlin: Gebr. Mann, 1955.

Hals, R. M. Ezekiel. FOTL. Grand Rapids, MI: William B. Eerdmans, 1989.

Handy, L. K., editor. The Age of Solomon: Scholarship at the Turn of the Millennium. Leiden: Brill, 1997.

Haran, M. Temples and Temple-Service in Ancient Israel. Winona Lake: Eisenbrauns, 1985.

Hayes, J. H. The Tradition of Zion's Inviolability. JBL 82 (1963): 419-426.

Hegyi, D. Historical Authenticity of Herodotus in the Persian Logoi. Acta Antiqua 21 (1973): 73-87.

Heinrich, E. Die Tempel und Heiligtümer im alten Mesopotamien. Denkmäler antiker Architektur 14. Berlin: W. de Gruyter, 1982.

_____. Die Paläste im alten Mesopotamien. Denkmäler antiker Architektur 15. Berlin: W. de Gruyter, 1984.

Holladay, J. Red Slip, Burnish, and the Solomonic Gateway at Gezer. BASOR 277/278 (1990): 23-70.

Holm, J., Editor. Sacred Place. London and New York: Pinter Publishers, 1994.

Hurowitz, Victor (Avigdor). I Have Built you an Exalted House: Temple Building in the Bible in Light of Mesopotamian and Northwest Semitic Writings. JSOTS 115. Sheffield: Sheffield Academic Press, 1992.

Japhet, S. I & II Chronicles: A Commentary. Old Testament Library. Louisville: Westminster John Knox Press, 1993.

Johnson, N. B. Temple Architecture as Construction of Consciousness: A Japanese Temple and Garden. Architecture and Behavior 4 (1988): 229-249.

_____. Art and the Meaning of Things. Reviews in Anthropology 17 (1991): 221-234.

Kaiser, O. Isaiah 1-12. Second edition. Old Testament Library. Translated by J. Bowden. Philadelphia: Westminster Press, 1983.

Kapelrud, A. S. Temple Building: A Task for Gods and Kings. Orientalia (ns) 32 (1963): 56-62.

Keel, O., and C. Uehlinger. Göttinnen, Götter und Gottessymbole, Neue Erkenntnisse zur Religionsgeschichte Kanaans und Israels aufgrund bislang unerschlossener ikonographischer Quellen. Freiburg: Herder, 1995.

Kempenski, A. and Reich, R., editors. The Architecture of Ancient Israel, from the Prehistoric to the Persian Periods. Jersusalem: Israel Exploration Society, 1992.

Kenyon, K. M. Megiddo, Hazor, Samaria, and Chronology. Bulletin of the Institute of Archaeology, University of London 4 (1964): 143-156.

Knoppers, G. N. Two Nations Under God: The Deuteronomistic History of Solomon and the Dual Monarchies. Volume 1, The Reign of Solomon and the Rise of Jeroboam. Harvard Semitic Monographs 52. Atlanta: Scholars Press, 1993.

_____. The Vanishing Solomon: The Disappearance of the United Monarchy from Recent Histories of Ancient Israel. JBL 116 (1997): 19-44.

Lackenbacher, S. Le roi bâtisseur: Les récits de construction assyriens des origines à Teglatphalasar III. Etudes assyriologique. Paris: Editions Recherche sur les civilisations, 1982.

_____. Le Palais sans Rival: Les récits de construction en Assyrie. Paris, 1990.

Larsen, M. T. The Conquest of Assyria. London and New York: Routledge, 1994.

Lasine, S. Solomon and the Wizard of Oz: Power and Invisibility in a Verbal Palace. In: The Age of Solomon: Scholarship at the Turn of the Millennium, edited by L. K. Handy. Leiden: Brill, 1997: 375-391.

Layard, A. H. Nineveh and Its Remains. 2 volumes. London: John Murray, 1849.

_____. The Monuments of Nineveh. London: John Murray, 1849.

_____. Discoveries in the Ruins of Nineveh and Babylon. London: John Murray, 1853.

Levine, L. D. Cities as Ideology: The Neo-Assyrian Centres of Ashur, Nimrud, and Nineveh. The Society for Mesopotamian Studies Bulletin 12 (1986): 1-7.

Lévy, E., editor. Le Système Palatial en Orient, en Grèce et à Rome. Actes du Colloque de Strasbourg, 19-22 juin 1985. Université des Sciences humaines de Strasbourg, 1987.

Lewis, T. J. Divine Images and Aniconism in Ancient Israel: Review article of Mettinger, No Graven Image. JAOS 118,1 (1998): 36-53.

Liverani, M. The Ideology of the Assyrian Empire. In: Power and Propaganda. Mesopotamia 7. Edited by Mogens Trolle Larsen. Copenhagen: Akademisk Forlag, 1979: 297-317.

_____, editor. Neo-Assyrian Geography. Rome: University of Rome, 1995.

Livingstone, A., editor. Court Poetry and Literary Miscellanea. SAA III. Helsinki: The Neo-Assyrian Text Corpus Project, 1989.

Loyd, S. and H. W. Müller. Ancient Architecture. New York: Electa/Rizzoli, 1986.

Loud, G. Khorsabad I: Excavations in the Palace and at a City Gate. Oriental Institute Publications 28. Chicago: University of Chicago Press, 1936.

_____. An Architectural Formula for Assyrian Planning Based on the Results of Excavations at Khorsabad. RA 33 (1936): 153-160.

_____. and C. B. Altman. Khorsabad II: The Citadel and the Town. Oriental Institute Publications 40. Chicago: University of Chicago Press, 1938.

Lubar, S. and W. David Kingery, editors. History from Things: Essays on Material Culture. Washington, D. C.: The Smithsonian Institution Press, 1993.

Lubicz, R. A. S. de. The Temple in Man: The Secrets of Ancient Egypt. Translated by Robert and Deborah Lawlor. Brookline MA: Autumn Press, 1977.

Luckenbill, D. D. The Annals of Sennacherib. Oriental Institute Publications II. Chicago: University of Chicago Press, 1924.

_____. Ancient Records of Assyria and Babylonia. 2 volumes. Chicago: University of Chicago Press, 1926-1927.

Madhloom, T. Excavations at Nineveh 1965-67. Sumer 23 (1967): 76-79.

_____. Nineveh, the 67-68 Campaign. Sumer 24 (1968): 45-51.

_____. Nineveh, the 68-69 Campaign. Sumer 25 (1969): 44-49.

Madsen, Truman G., editor. The Temple in Antiquity: Ancient Records and Modern Perspectives. Religious Studies Monograph Series 9. Provo, UT: Religious Studies Center, Brigham Young University, 1984.

Mallowan, M. E. L. Nimrud and its Remains. 3 Volumes. New York: Dodd, Mead, 1966.

Marc, O. The Psychology of the House. Translated by Jesse Wood. London: Thames and Hudson, 1977.

Marcus, M. I. Geography as an Organizing Principle in the Imperial Art of Shalmaneser III. Iraq 49 (1987): 77-90.

Margueron, J. Remarques sur l'organisations de l'espace architectural en Mésopotamie." In: L'archéologie de l'Iraq du debut de l'epoque neolithique à 333 avant notre ère. Colloques internationaux du Centre National de la Recherche Scientifique, no. 580. Paris: Editions du CNRS, 1980: 157-169.

_____. Recherches sur les palais mésopotamiens de l'âge du bronze. 2 volumes. Paris: Librairie orientaliste Paul Geuthner, 1982.

_____. Temples et pouvoir politique en Mésopotamie: position du problème et étude de cas fournis par l'archéologie. Ktema 14 (1989): 7-17.

Markus, T. A. Buildings and Power: Freedom and Control in the Origins of Modern Building Types. London and New York: Routledge, 1993.

Mazar, A. Temples in the Middle and Late Bronze Ages and the Iron Age. In: The Architecture of Ancient Israel: From the Prehistoric to the Persian Periods, edited by A. Kempinski, R. Reich, H. Katzenstein, and J. Aviram. Jerusalem: Israel Exploration Society, 1992: 161-187.

McCarter, K. P. I Samuel. Anchor Bible. New York: Doubleday, 1980.

McKenzie, S. L. The Chronicler's Use of the Deuteronomistic History. Harvard Semitic Monographs 33. Atlanta: Scholars Press, 1985.

Meijer, D. W. J. Ground Plans and Archaeologists: On Similarities and Comparisons. In: To the Euphrates and Beyond: Archaeological Studies in Honor of Maurits N. Van Loon, edited by M. C. Haex, H. H. Curvers, and P. M. M. Akkermans. Rotterdam: A. A. Balkema, 1989: 161-187.

Mettinger, T. The Dethronement of Sabaoth: Studies in the Shem and Kabod Theologies. ConBOT 18. Lund: CWK Gleerup, 1982.

_____. YHWH SABAOTH -- The Heavenly King on the Cherubim Throne. In: Studies in the Period of David and Solomon and Other Essays, edited by T. Ishida. Winona Lake, IN: Eisenbrauns, 1982: 109-138.

_____. No Graven Image? Israelite Aniconism in its Ancient Near Eastern Context. ConBOT 42. Stockholm: Almqvist & Wiksell International, 1995.

Meuszynski, Janos. Die Rekonstruktion der Reliefdarstellungen und ihrer Anordnung im Nordwestpalast von Kalhu. Mainz am Rhein: Verlag Philipp von Zabern, 1981.

Meyers, C. The Tabernacle Menorah: A Synthetic Study of a Symbol from the Biblical Cult. ASOR Dissertation Series No. 2. Edited by D. N. Freedman. Missoula, MT: Scholars Press, 1976.

_____. Temple, Jerusalem. Anchor Bible Dictionary VI: 350-369.

Millard, A. King Solomon's Shields. In: Scripture and Other Artifacts: Essays on the Bible and Archaeology in Honor of Philip J. King, edited by M. C. Coogan, J. C. Exum, and L. E. Stager. Louisville, KY: Westminster John Knox, 1994: 286-295.

_____. King Solomon in his Ancient Context. In: The Age of Solomon: Scholarship at the Turn of the Millennium, edited by L. K. Handy. Leiden: Brill, 1997: 30-53.

Miller, J. M. Separating the Solomon of History from the Solomon of Legend. In: The Age of Solomon: Scholarship at the Turn of the Millennium, edited by L. K. Handy. Leiden: Brill, 1997: 1-24.

Miller, P. D. and J. J. M. Roberts. The Hand of the Lord: A Reassessment of the 'Ark Narrative' of 1 Samuel. Baltimore and London: The Johns Hopkins University Press, 1977.

Mitchell, W. J. T. Iconology: Image, Text, and Ideology. Chicago and London: University of Chicago Press, 1986.

Möhlenbrink, K. Studien zum salomonischen Tempel. Stuttgart: Kohlhammer, 1931.

Montgomery, J. A. Archival Data in the Book of Kings. JBL 53 (1934): 46-52.

_____. The Books of Kings. ICC Edinburgh: T. & T. Clark, 1951.

Myers, J. L. King Solomon's Temple and other Buildings and Works of Art. PEQ 81 (1948): 14-41.

Na'aman, N. Sources and Composition in the History of Solomon. In: The Age of Solomon: Scholarship at the Turn of the Millennium, edited by L. K. Handy. Leiden: Brill, 1997: 57-80.

Nagel, W. Die neuassyrischen Reliefstile unter Sanherib und Assurbanaplu. Berlin: Hessling, 1967.

Niehr, H. In Search of Yahweh's Cult Statue in the First Temple. In: The Image and the Book: Iconic Cults, Aniconism, and the Rise of Book Religion in Israel and the Ancient Near East, edited by K. van der Toorn. Leuven: Uitgeverij Peeters, 1997: 73-99.

Noth, M. Könige 1. BKAT 9/1. Neukirchen-Vluyn: Neukirchener Verlag, 1968.

Oates, D. Balawat (Imgur Enlil): The Site and its Buildings. Iraq 36 (1974): 173-178.

Oppenheim, A. L. On Royal Gardens in Mesopotamia. JCS 24 (1965): 328-333.

_____. Ancient Mesopotamia: Portrait of a Dead Civilization. Revised Edition by Erica Reiner. Chicago: University of Chicago Press, 1977 (originally 1964).

Ouelette, J. The Basic Structure of the Solomonic Temple and Archaeological Research. In: The Temple of Solomon, edited by J. Gutman. Missoula, MT: Scholars Press, 1976: 1-20.

Paley, S. M., and R. P. Sobolewski. The Reconstruction of the Relief Representations and their Positions in the Northwest Palace at Kalhu II. Mainz am Rhein: Verlag Philipp von Zabern, 1987.

Parpola, S. The Murderer of Sennacherib. In: Death in Mesopotamia, Mesopotamia 8. Copenhagen: Akademik Vorlag, 1980: 171-182.

Parrot, A. Mission Archéologique de Mari II(1): Le Palais: Architecture. Paris: Institut d'Archéologie de Beyrouth, 1958.

_____. Mission Archéologique de Mari II(2): Le Palais: Peintures et Murales. Paris: Institut d'Archéologie de Beyrouth, 1958.

_____. Nineveh and Babylon. Translated by S. Gilbert and J. Emmons. London: Thames and Hudson, 1961.

Paul, R. A. The Sherpa Temple as a Model of the Psyche. American Ethnologist 3 (1976): 131-146.

Porada, Edith. Battlements in the Military Architecture and in the Symbolism of the Ancient Near East. In: Studies in the History of Architecture Presented to Rudolf Wittkower. New York: Phaidon, 1967: 1-12.

Porter, B. N. Sacred Trees, Date Palms and the Royal Persona of Assurnasirpal II. JNES 52 (1993): 129-139.

_____. What the Assyrians Thought the Babylonians Thought about the Relative Status of Nabû and Marduk in the Late Assyrian Period. In: Assyria 1995, edited by S. Parpola and R. M. Whiting. Helsinki: The Neo-Assyrian Text Corpus Project, 1997: 253-260.

_____. Images, Power, and Politics: Figurative Aspects of Esarhaddon's Babylonian Policy. Philadelphia: American Philosophical Society, 1993.

Proshansky, H. M., W. H. Ittelson, et. al., editors. Environmental Psychology: People and Their Physical Settings. Second Edition. New York: Holt, Rinehart, and Winston, 1976.

Rad, G. von. Studies in Deuteronomy. Translated by D. Stalker. Chicago: Henry Regnery Co., 1953.

Rad, G. von. The Deuteronomic Theology of History in I and II Kings. In: The Problem of the Hexateuch and other Essays. Translated by E. W. T. Dicken. London: SCM Press, 1984: 205-221.

_____. The Tent and the Ark. In: The Problem of the Hexateuch and Other Essays. Translated by E. W. T. Dicken. London: SCM Press, 1984: 103-124.

Raglan, L. The Temple and the House. New York: W. W. Norton, 1964.

Rapoport, A. The Meaning of the Built Environment: A Nonverbal Communication Approach. London: Sage Publications, 1982.

Reade J. E. Sources for Sennacherib: The Prisms. JCS 27 (1975): 189-196.

_____. Assyrian Architectural Decoration: Techniques and Subject Matter. Baghdader Mitteilungen 10 (1979): 17-49.

_____. The Architectural Context for Assyrian Sculpture. Baghdader Mitteilungen 11 (1980): 75-87.

_____. Neo-Assyrian Monuments in their Historical Context. In: Assyrian Royal Inscriptions: New Horizons in Literary, Ideological and Historical Analysis, edited by F. M. Fales. Rome: Istituto per l'Oriente, Centro per le antichità e la storia dell'arte del vicino Oriente, 1981: 143-168.

Renfrew, C. and P. Bahn. Archaeology: Theories, Methods, and Practice. Second Edition. London: Thames and Hudson, 1996.

Rollinger, R. Herodots babylonischer Logos: eine kritische Untersuchung der Glaubwürdigkeitsdiskussion an Hand ausgewählter Beispiele: historische Parallelüberlieferung, Argumentationen, archäologischer Befund, Konsequenzen für eine Geschichte Babylons in persischer Zeit. Innsbruck: Verlag des Instituts für Sprachwissenschaft der Universität Innsbruck, 1993.

Rupprecht, K. Der Tempel von Jerusalem: Gründung Salomos oder jebusitisches Erbe? BZAW 144. Berlin: Walter de Gruyter, 1977.

Russell, J. M. Bulls for the Palace and Order in the Empire: The Sculptural Program of Sennacherib's Court VI at Nineveh. Art Bulletin 69 (1987): 520-539.

_____. Sennacherib's Palace without Rival at Nineveh. Chicago: University of Chicago Press, 1991.

Russell, J. M. Layard's Description of Rooms in the Southwest Palace at Nineveh. Iraq 57 (1995): 71-85.

_____. From Nineveh to New York: The Strange Story of the Assyrian Reliefs in the Metropolitan Museum and the Hidden Masterpiece at Canford School. With contributions by Judith McKenzie and Stephanie Dalley. New Haven and London: Yale University Press, 1997.

_____. Sennacherib's Palace without Rival Revisited: Excavations at Nineveh and in the British Museum Archives. In: Assyria 1995, edited by S. Parpola and R. M. Whiting. Helsinki: The Neo-Assyrian Text Corpus Project, 1997: 295-306.

Sartori, Paul. Über das Bauopfer. Zeitschrift für Ethnologie 30 (1938): 1-54.

Sasson, J. M. Mari Historiography and the Yakhdun-Lim Disc Inscription. In: Lingering over Words: Studies in Ancient Near Eastern Literature in Honor of William H. Moran. HSS 37. Edited by T. Abusch, J. Huehnergard, and P. Steinkeller. Atlanta: Scholars Press, 1990: 439-449.

Schicklberger, F. Die Ladeerzählung des ersten Samuel—Buches, Eine literaturwissenschaftliche und theologiegeschichtliche Untersuchung. Forschung zur Bibel 7. Würzburg: Echter Verlag, 1973.

Schlereth, T. J., editor. Material Culture: A Research Guide. Lawrence KS: University of Kansas Press, 1985.

Schmid, H. Der Tempelbau Salomos in religionsgeschichtlicher Sicht. In: Archäologie und altes Testament: Festschrift für Kurt Galling, edited by A. Kuschke and E. Kutsch. Tübingen: Mohr Siebeck, 1970: 241-250.

Schroeder, Eric. Scientific Description of Art: A Review of Donald Wilber, Architecture of Islamic Iran, JNES 15 (1956): 93-102.

Schroer, S. In Israel gab es Bilder. Nachrichten von darstellender Kunst im Alten Testament. OBO 74. Freiburg und Göttingen: Universitätsverlag Freiburg, Vandenhoeck & Ruprecht, 1987.

Scott, R. B. Y. The Pillars Jachin and Boaz. JBL 58 (1939): 143-149.

Shanks, M. and I. Hodder. Processual, postprocessual and interpretive archaeologies: Interpreting Archaeology, Finding Meaning in the Past. London and New York: Routledge, 1995.

Smith, J. Z. To Take Place: Toward Theory in Ritual. Chicago: University of Chicago Press, 1987.

Smith, M. S. The Ugaritic Baal Cycle. Volume I, Introduction with Text, Translation and Commentary of KTU 1.1-1.2. VTSup 55. Leiden: E. J. Brill, 1994.

Smith, W. R. Lectures on the Religion of the Semites. New York: D. Appleton and Co., 1889.

Sobolewski, R. P. Beitrag zur theoretischen Rekonstruktion der Architektur des Nordwest-Palastes in Nimrud (Kalhu). In: Paläste und Hütte: Beiträge zum Bauen und Wohnen im Altertum. Mainz: von Zabern, 1982: 237-250.

Soden, W. von. Die Schutzgenien Lamassu und Schedu in der babylonisch-assyrischen Literatur. Baghdader Mitteilungen 3 (1964): 148-156.

Stade, B. Der Text des Berichtes über Salomos Bauten, I Kö. 5-7. ZAW 3 (1883): 129-177.

Stronach, D. Notes on the Fall of Nineveh. In: Assyria 1995, edited by S. Parpola and R. M. Whiting. Helsinki: Neo-Assyrian Text Corpus Project, 1997: 307-324.

Sweeney, M. A. Isaiah 1-39, with an Introduction to Prophetic Literature. FOTL 16. Edited by R. P. Knierim and G. M. Tucker. Grand Rapids: William B. Eerdmans, 1996.

Tadmor, H. Observations on Assyrian Historiography. In: Essays on the Ancient Near East in Memory of J. J. Finkelstein, edited by M. D. Ellis. Hamden, CN, 1977: 209-213.

_____., S. Parpola, and B. Landsberger. The Sin of Sargon and Sennacherib's Last Will. SAAB 3 (1989): 3-51.

_____. Propaganda, Literature, Historiography: Cracking the Code of Assyrian Royal Inscriptions. In: Assyria 1995, edited by S. Parpola and R. M. Whiting. Helsinki: Neo-Assyrian Text Corpus Project, 1997: 325-338.

Tappy, R. E. The Archaeology of Israelite Samaria. Vol. I, Early Iron Age through the Ninth Century B. C. E. HSS 44. Atlanta: Scholars Press, 1992.

Thompson, T. The Historicity of the Patriarchal Narratives: The Quest for the Historical Abraham. BZAW 133. Berlin: Walter de Gruyter, 1974.

Thureau-Dangin, F. and M. Dunand. Til Barsib. Paris, 1936.

Tilley, C. Material Culture and Text: the Art of Ambiguity. London and New York: Routledge, 1991.

_____, editor. Interpretive Archaeology. London and New York: Routledge, 1993.

Toorn, K. van der. The Image and the Book: Iconic Cults, Aniconism, and the Rise of Book Religion in Israel and the Ancient Near East. CBET 21. Leuven: Uitgeverij Peeters, 1997.

Tuell, S. The Law of the Temple in Ezekiel 40-48. HSM 49. Atlanta: Scholars Press, 1992

Turner, Geoffrey. The State Apartments of Later Assyrian Palaces. Iraq 32 (1970): 170-213.

Ussishkin, D. The Conquest of Lachish by Sennacherib. Tel Aviv: Institute of Archaeology Tel Aviv University, 1982.

_____. Notes on Megiddo, Gezer, Ashdod, and Tel Batash in the Tenth to Ninth Centuries B.C. BASOR 277/278 (1990): 71-91.

Van Seters, J. Confessional Reformulation in the Exilic Period. VT 22 (1972): 448-459.

_____. Abraham in History and Tradition. New Haven and London: Yale University Press, 1975.

_____. In Search of History: Historiography in the Ancient World and the Origins of Biblical History. New Haven and London: Yale University Press, 1983.

_____. The Life of Moses: The Yahwist as Historian in Exodus-Numbers. Louisville, KY: Westminster John Knox, 1994.

_____. The Chronicler's Account of Solomon's Temple-Building: A Continuity Theme. In: The Chronicler as Historian, edited by M. P. Graham, K. G. Hoglund and S. L. McKenzie. JSOTS 238. Sheffield: Sheffield Academic Press, 1997: 283-300.

Van Seters, J. Solomon's Temple: Fact and Ideology in Biblical and Near Eastern Historiography. CBQ 50 (1997): 45-57.

Vaux, R. de. Les chérubins et l'arche d'alliance. Les sphinx gardiens et les trônes divins dan l'ancien Orient. Mélanges de l'université Saint Joseph 37 (1961): 93-124.

Viviano, P. Glory Lost: The Reign of Solomon in the Deuteronomistic History. In: The Age of Solomon: Scholarship at the Turn of the Millennium, edited by L. K. Handy. Leiden: Brill, 1997: 336-347.

Waterman, L. The Damaged 'Blueprints' of the Temple of Solomon. JNES 2 (1943): 284-294.

Weippert H. Die 'deuternomistischen' Beurteilungen der Könige von Israel und Juda und das Problem der Redaktion der Königsbücher. Biblica 53 (1972): 301-339.

Weiser, A. Die Tempelbaukrise unter David. ZAW 77 (1965): 153-168.

Wheatley, P. The Pivot of the Four Quarters: A Preliminary Inquiry into the Origins and Character of the Ancient Chinese City. Chicago: University of Chicago Press, 1971.

Wiggermann, F. A. M. Mesopotamian Protective Spirits: The Ritual Texts. Cuneiform Monographs 1. Groningen: Styx Publications, 1992.

Wightman, G. J. The Myth of Solomon. BASOR 277-78 (1990): 5-22.

Winter, I. J. Royal Rhetoric and the Development of Historical Narrative in Neo-Assyrian Reliefs. Studies in Visual Communication 7, 2 (1981): 2-38.

_____. Art as Evidence for Interaction: Relations between the Assyrian Empire and North Syria. In: Mesopotamien und seine Nachbarn: politische und kulturelle Wechselbeziehungen im Alten Vorderasien. Berliner Beiträge zum Vorderen Orient, Band I, Teil I, edited by H. Kühne, H.-J. Nissen, and J. Renger. Berlin: D. Reimer, 1982: 355-382.

_____. The Program of the Thoneroom of Assurnasirpal II. In: Essays on Near Eastern Art and Archaeology in Honor of Charles Kyrle Wilkinson, edited by P. O. Harper and H. Pittman. New York: Metropolitan Museum of Art, 1983: 15-31.

Winter, I. J. Reading Concepts of Space from Ancient Mesopotamian
Monuments. In: Concepts of Space Ancient and Modern, edited by
Kapila Vatsyayan. New Delhi: Abhinav Publications, 1991: 57-73.

_____. "Seat of Kingship"/ "A Wonder to Behold": The Palace as Construct
in the Ancient Near East. Ars Orientalis 23 (1993) Special Issue on Pre-
Modern Islamic Palaces, edited by Gülru Necipoğlu. Ann Arbor: Department
of the History of Art, University of Michigan: 27-55.

_____. Art in Empire: The Royal Image and the Visual Dimensions of
Assyrian Ideology. In: Assyria 1995, edited by S. Parpola and R. M.
Whiting. Helsinki: The Neo-Assyrian Text Corpus Project, 1997: 359-381.

Wiseman, D. J. Palace and Temple Gardens in the Ancient Near East. In:
Monarchies and Socio-Religious Traditions in the Ancient Near East, edited
by H. I. H. Prince Takahito Mikasa. Wiesbaden, 1984: 37-43.

Wright, G. E. Biblical Archaeology. Philadelphia: Westminster, 1960.

Würthwein, E. Das Erste Buch der Könige, Kapitel 1-16. ATD 11,1. Göttingen:
Vandenhoeck & Ruprecht, 1977.

Yadin, Y. Solomon's City Wall and Gate at Gezer. IEJ 8 (1958): 80-86.

Yeivin, S. Jachin and Boaz. PEQ 91 (1959): 6-22.

Indices

Authors

Subject

Biblical Texts